Making Use

Making Use
Scenario-Based Design of Human-Computer Interactions

John M. Carroll

The MIT Press
Cambridge, Massachusetts
London, England

This book was set in Sabon by Wellington Graphics.

Printed and bound in the United States of America.

Library of Congress Cataloging-in-Publication Data

Carroll, John M. (John Millar), 1950–
Making use : scenario-based design of human-computer interactions / John M. Carroll.
p. cm.
Includes bibliographical references and index.
ISBN 0-262-03279-1 (hc. : alk. paper)
1. Human-computer interaction. I. Title.

QA76.9.H85 C37 2000
004'.01'9—dc21

For Mary Beth, who is everything to me,
and each day more

Contents

Preface

I am attracted to wide-ranging and somewhat obvious ideas. Scenario-based design is a good example. If you want to design something for people to use, especially an interactive system, it is probably a good idea to explicitly take the nature of that use into account in the design work. Put another way, it is probably a good idea to think about what you are doing as *designing future use,* that is, as designing scenarios. Reading books and articles on design methodology may cause you to think that there are alternatives to scenario-based design, but if you speak with designers or do design work yourself, it becomes clear that there is no way forward in design without some notion of scenario. This is not to say that it is perfectly transparent just what scenario-based design is, how it works, and where it is or should be going as a design practice. In this book, I present a perspective on these questions.

One reviewer pointed out to me that the book itself is not a paradigmatic example of scenario-based design. Touché. Books are of course more rigidly linear than interactive systems, but they need not be read cover to cover. A very busy reader could jump to chapter 3 to decide whether scenario-based design offers the integrated approach to the central challenges of design that I think it does. But one could also read only chapter 4 to see this argument through an example, or only chapter 11 for suggestions about a scenario-based development process, or only chapter 12 for a survey of current scenario-based design work in human-computer interaction and software engineering. A virtue of the wide-ranging and somewhat obvious is its amenability to skipping around. Of course, the further into the book you start, the more backward references you will have missed. Reading the chapters in order will also make some sense.

This book is not a manual, a textbook, or a handbook. It is a technical monograph that simplifies and integrates a series of projects around a set of methodological themes. That said, chapters 10 and 11 do attempt to address concerns of readers with relatively more applied interests. Chapter 10 surveys techniques for generating and analyzing scenarios with pointers back into the preceding chapters. Chapter 11 presents a process model, but as a proposal based on the examples rather than as a tried and proved recipe. I believe the model is a good summary of the book and can be used, but those who try it will have to tell me.

Many colleagues have contributed to the projects and ideas described in this book. I owe a debt to Clayton Lewis and Don Norman, colleagues I met early in my professional life who helped me develop attitudes toward design and development that still appear to be sound. The commitment to taking the nature of design work more seriously in theories and frameworks for human-computer interaction, the critique of popular but inadequate approaches of the mid-1980s, and the basic framework of scenario-based design that underpins this book were developed in 1988 and 1989 with Wendy Kellogg and Mary Beth Rosson. There could have been no book without this collaboration.

The key design and analysis work, the focus of discussion in chapters 5 through 9, was developed with Rachel Bellamy, Jürgen Koenemann, Mary Beth Rosson, and Kevin Singley. This was some of the most enjoyable and personally rewarding technical work I have ever been involved with. The project continues today, and I thank George Chin, Wolfgang Dzida, Louis Erskine, Kentaro Go, Jürgen Koenemann, Stuart Laughton, Mary Beth Rosson, and Alistair Sutcliffe for some of the recent work described in chapters 10 and 11.

I am also grateful to Liam Bannon, Phil Barnard, Susanne Bodker, Robert Campbell, Steve Draper, Susan Chipman, John Long, and Richard Young, colleagues who provided or provoked key ideas along the way. And I am grateful to Hugh Beyer, John Burton, Steve Draper, Rex Hartson, Jürgen Koenemann, Stuart Laughton, Jonas Löwgren, Allan MacLean, Kevin Singley, Alistair Sutcliffe, and several anonymous reviewers for insightful comments on earlier versions of this manuscript; addressing them all will require more than a single book.

Mary Beth Rosson has been my principal collaborator throughout the entire project; she led the software design tool work briefly described in chapter 9, coauthored a 1994 draft that evolved into the pivotal chapter 3, and should have been a coauthor of this book except that she is too busy with new projects, leaving me to sort out where it is we have already been.

Some of the material in this book has appeared before, though in somewhat different form. An earlier version of chapter 3 appeared in the *Proceedings of the 1999 Hawaii International Conference on System Sciences* (Carroll 1999). An earlier version of chapter 4 was incorporated into an article for the second edition of the *Handbook of Human-Computer Interaction* (Carroll 1997). Chapters 6 and 7 draw from an article that appeared in the journal *Human-Computer Interaction* (Carroll and Rosson 1991). Chapter 6 also draws from an article that was published in the journal *Behaviour and Information Technology* (Carroll 1996). And chapter 7 also draws from an article that was published in the *Communications of Association for Computing Machinery* (Carroll 1994) and from a chapter from the book *Design Rationale* (Singley and Carroll 1996). Chapter 8 is drawn from an article published in the *Communications of Association for Computing Machinery* (Carroll and Rosson 1995), from a paper presented at the International Conference on the Learning Sciences (Carroll, Singley, and Rosson 1991), an article published in the journal *Behaviour and Information Technology* (Carroll, Singley, and Rosson 1992), and a paper presented at the British Computing Society's 1993 Human-Computer Interaction Conference (Carroll et al. 1993). Parts of chapter 10 are drawn from an article in the *ACM Transactions on Information Systems* (Carroll and Rosson 1992), and part of chapter 11 is drawn from an article in the *IEEE Transactions on Software Engineering* (Carroll et al. 1998).

I am grateful to several institutions. The IBM Corporation supported my research through 1993, and Virginia Tech has supported my work since 1994. Our current design methodology test bed, the Learning in Network Communities project, briefly described in chapter 11, has been supported by the National Science Foundation, the Hitachi Foundation, Apple Computer, and the Office of Naval Research.

One of the benefits of cultivating interests in the wide-ranging and somewhat obvious is the great potential for communication and interaction. Through the ten years I have been working on this project, I have enjoyed discussions with a great variety of designers, researchers, and students. I hope this book will provoke more opportunities for this, for me and for all others who are interested in design in general and in the design of information technology and human-computer interactions in particular.

1

The Sorcerer's Apprentice

Software developers are today's heroes. They bring to life and try to tame mysterious armies of symbols. They shepherd the creation of new worlds—tools and environments that emerge reluctantly out of a chaos of conflicting, half-articulated, and half-understood goals and needs. When they cast the right spells, we take flight on their visions. Lotus 1-2-3 and the original Macintosh operating system opened new worlds of possibility for many people. When software developers cast the wrong spells, chaos and darkness close around us. The rubbery keyboard of IBM's PC jr., the cloying helpfulness of Microsoft's Bob, and the pointless blinking and dancing of a thousand Java applets are not nightmares; they are real.

Typically, the problem is the process. Software development should not be quite so heroic. Too often the sorcerer will turn out to have been merely a sorcerer's apprentice. As in Disney's *Fantasia,* things will whirl out of control. Too often the result will insult our intelligence, obstruct our goals, and thwart our enjoyment. When we wonder why today's information systems are difficult to learn and awkward to use, why they change our activities in ways we do not need or want to have them changed, the answer lies in the software development process, which is talked about as if it were rocket science but often practiced as if it were black magic.

Computers are badly behaved because they are badly designed. This is not to say there is any shortage of good ideas and technical skills; rather, the good ideas are frequently undone by complementary bad ideas that popped up somewhere in the confusion, or by unfortunate interactions that turn several ideas, each of which by itself is just fine, into an ensemble that is just terrible. There are many good ideas embedded in the designs of most systems, but the whole often turns out to be far less than the sum of the parts.

Example: Designing a Multimedia System

The best examples of the horrors of design are those with the worst design outcomes, but no one wants to talk about them; no one gets credit for participating in or documenting failures, and besides, it feels better just to forget and move on (see Grudin 1996). Ironically, we had the good fortune to study a design project that ultimately failed (Carroll et al. 1994). Like most other investigators, we had intended to analyze a successful example of system design, but it just did not work out that way.

The project we studied was attempting to create a multimedia system for university education in engineering. The vision was of a system that would make it easy for professors to create multimedia case studies, incorporating various kinds of data and background information. The professors would then develop assignments in which students, individually and in groups, worked with the case study materials in an open-ended manner, analyzing them and preparing multimedia reports. All communication regarding the assignments (their initial distribution, questions from students, submission and evaluation of reports) would be carried out over a network.

The project was a collaboration between two large corporations: a computer company interested in developing expertise in new types of systems and applications and a publisher interested in identifying and understanding new markets for its content materials. The project team was diverse. Although most of its members came from the computer company, the team included scientists, programmers, and engineers from a variety of specializations and departments within the company: information retrieval, multimedia systems, human-computer interaction, artificial intelligence—about a dozen people in all. The team also included one member from the publishing company and two university professors who served as educational technology consultants. Notably, the creator of the original project vision did not participate directly in the project, although the university consultants continued to report directly to her. Similarly, the publishing company executive who had formed the initial collaboration with the computing company had no direct involvement.

The objectives of this project and the composition of the project team were entirely appropriate for leading-edge multimedia system development in the early 1990s, when the project was initiated. However, the scope of the technical challenges was considerable. The system had to be accessible to both teachers and students, though the browsing, searching, and authoring activities of these two user groups might be quite distinct. Many of the underlying system services to support such activities had to be developed from scratch: schemes for indexing and searching a multimedia database, algorithms for managing time and space constraints in multimedia presentations, tools for composing and editing multimedia "documents." A set of instructional modules had to be built to demonstrate and test the capabilities of the system. Substantial amounts of data—video, text, sound, image—had to be digitized and converted into standard formats to build these example course modules. And many side issues had to be handled; for example, many of the data appropriate for the course modules were copyrighted, and it was unclear how to get access to this material.

The variety of the technical tasks, the skills and organizations included in the project team, and the fact that the team was distributed across North America made communication and coordination quite difficult. From the start, the team decided to focus on getting a rough prototype up and running, in order to encourage team building and coordination, surface critical issues as early as possible, and provide a concrete demonstration to management in both companies that could ensure continued support. This is a very reasonable and typical approach to design in a novel domain. By definition in such domains, the designers cannot know precisely what they are trying to create. Thus, they could not design to a specification, because no one knew enough to write a specification. Also, many of the team members were already in the midst of developing tools and techniques relevant to the system vision. A demonstration prototype offered a concrete context in which these prior interests and projects could evolve into system components.

The team capitalized on what they perceived to be their unique expertise and technology. Various members had worked on multimedia authoring systems, natural language query systems, computer-supported cooperative work, and object-oriented programming systems. The project was managed to try to take full advantage of these special resources. In some cases, this was clearly a good idea; for example, having in-house expertise and proprietary technology in multimedia authoring was essential to create a novel multimedia information system. However, in other cases the team's blanket commitment to in-house technology caused complications. Two of the team members belonged to a research group that had developed some natural language processing technology. They strongly believed that their approach was original and extensible, so that it could provide the architecture for indexing and searching in the multimedia database. It was clear throughout the project, however, that most of the rest of the team could not see what was significantly unique or how the approach would generalize or become integrated into the overall system. Yet for a very long time, everyone went along with it. Team members not involved in the natural language technology seemed unwilling to criticize or doubt its capabilities, perhaps because they wanted to avoid the uncomfortable group dynamics that would result.

Another problematic commitment to special expertise was the decision to implement the main system in the Smalltalk programming language. Two team members had considerable experience with Smalltalk, and a few others were interested in trying it. Early on, the Smalltalk proponents made an argument for object-oriented software technology as an approach to managing code interfaces, and the rest of the team went along with this judgment. This decision, however, caused a software schism throughout the course of the project. The majority of the team had no working knowledge of Smalltalk or object-oriented programming, and they attained this knowledge only slowly. Thus, the natural language processing services and network infrastructure were implemented in the C programming language, while the user interface and multimedia authoring services were implemented in Smalltalk. Indeed, it was worse in that the two language environments were running under different operating systems and on different hardware; the two parts of the prototype could not directly exchange data.

Progress on the prototype was substantial but hard to see. The core team included two members who had independently developed multimedia authoring systems in the preceding two years. The two approaches to this were fundamentally different from each other, and initially it seemed that a decision would have to be made to adopt one approach and discard the other. In time, a more ambitious solution emerged in which some of the capabilities of one approach were incorporated into the framework of the other. The initial prototype did not include an implementation of this solution, though in a subtle sense, substantial progress had been made on the multimedia authoring strategy.

Another area in which considerable effort led to progress that was difficult to see was data procurement for the example course modules. Initially, the designers, many of them computer scientists, decided to create an example course module on algorithms. They were intrigued by the vision of animated algorithms, but they quickly realized that this idea provided little opportunity for incorporating video, and so they refocused the module design on engineering pathology. Their touchstone example was learning about nuclear power plant design by analyzing the failure of the Three Mile Island reactors. They pursued this idea for several weeks but finally discarded it, in part because the video data that had attracted them were copyrighted (the data belonged to film production companies and to power companies, neither had much interest in making materials available), and in part because the topic was socially controversial. So they moved on to the content domain of bridge design in civil engineering, again envisioning the analysis of interesting failures like the Tacoma Narrows Bridge. Ultimately—months into the project—the publishing company asked them to focus on the design of airport expansions and abandon the engineering pathology approach. The rationale that finally won out was that the publishing company had lots of material on airports.

A month after the unmet deadline for the initial rough prototype, the team held its first all-hands meeting. A prototype was in fact demonstrated, and much of the team felt that they were now on track, and only a month late. A serious complication was that the university consultants brought *their own* prototype to this meeting. The two prototypes were almost disjoint with respect to their objectives: the core of the team had sought to implement rapidly in Smalltalk the basic user interface for the ultimate system, leaving "hooks" for the underlying system functionality that would be developed later. The consultants' prototype was written in an interface scripting language purely to show what user scenarios might *look like* in the ultimate system. Thus, the core team prototype looked less finished but constituted a concrete beginning on the actual system implementation, whereas the consultants' prototype looked very finished but was intended only to focus goals and issues. However, the team could not escape the obvious, though superficial, competition between the prototypes. The team member from the publishing company (perhaps the least technically sophisticated member of the entire team) was obviously captured by the consultants' prototype. The core team reacted somewhat defensively.

The upshot of this meeting was that the core team pulled together and began working frantically. The university consultants were effectively peripheralized after this meeting, though it was they who were given the opportunity to summarize the meeting for the project visionary (recall that the consultants reported to the visionary, who herself had no active role in the project). A few months later, the publishing company withdrew from the collaboration, and the project was terminated. Ironically, this happened just as the basic functionality of the prototype was finally designed and implemented.

Guiding and Coordinating Discovery

There are always too many plausible accounts of why things did not work out. In this example, it is natural to ask why the project management did not adopt a more structured style. Part of the reason is that they correctly recognized that no one on the team was in a position to specify the project's ultimate objective and approach a priori. They realized that to a considerable extent, these would have to be discovered, not specified. Another part of the reason is that they recognized that a key to their success would be effective leveraging of the special expertise distributed among team members and that a structuring of the project by management might be seen as arbitrary redirection by some team members. Figure 1.1 summarizes some of the complex factors that were interacting within this design project and contributed to the open-ended discovery process followed by this design team.

The project was indeed managed to exploit discovery. People were allowed to develop their special expertise and technology within the prototype context—to explore what the system might be, and not merely

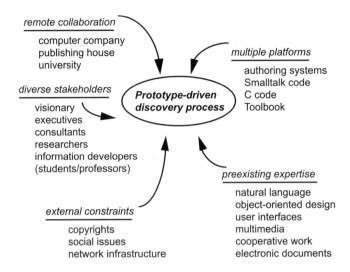

Figure 1.1
Many dynamic and interdependent factors operating in the multimedia education project led to a management approach that relied on concrete work with the prototype to discover successively more about the design problem and possible solutions.

to implement it. In some cases, this worked well; for example, the two approaches to multimedia authoring were ultimately converged. However, even when it did work well, it worked slowly. And in other cases, it took a long time to *not* work well. The natural language processing work was never integrated into the prototype; indeed, the natural language people ended up prototyping their own browser interface since they could not coordinate their C-based development efforts with the "main" Smalltalk prototype. In the final phase of the project (the phase carried out *after* the decision to terminate the project had been taken but before it was effective), the natural language processing subgroup dropped out of the project, and the system was built completely in Smalltalk.

The discovery-oriented management style allowed key constraints to emerge as the project went forward. Consider the course module topic. The several candidate topics that were developed and abandoned might suggest aimless thrashing, but in adopting and pursuing these various possibilities, the team discovered critical attributes of what they needed in a course topic (for example, lots of video without copyright complications). No one could have guessed how big the problem of procuring access to copyrighted materials would turn out to be. This is the type of knowledge that emerges from experience.

A specific question is why the project management seemed unable to coordinate with the university consultants. One reason is that the designers did not perceive that they *needed* the consultants. Another is that both consultants were three thousand miles away, working with different hardware and software, and with different concerns and perspectives and very different expertise. The project team was told to work with the consultants by the original visionary, and dutifully included them on e-mail distributions and in the all-hands meeting. This seems clearly to have been a management failure but an understandable one. The team, including its leaders, was focused on the prototype and the many issues pertaining to it. From that workaday perspective, worrying about consultants, who were not in fact providing any consulting to the team, would have seemed a very low priority concern.

The kind of phenomena that typify breakdowns in design are quite evident in this example, even though in many ways the team worked well together and accomplished a great deal. The novelty and complexity of the technical issues, the interactions among these issues, and the special skills and commitments of various team members demanded a discovery-oriented design process. The team needed management support, compatible with its discovery-oriented approach, but also capable of providing coordination and integration of subgroups and subactivities. They needed a way to share concretely and develop the vision of the multimedia system among all team members, to help the consultants, the natural language experts, and the Smalltalk programmers pull in the same direction. They needed a way to recognize and confront specific strengths and weakness in their technical vision when it was still early enough to do something.

Example: Designing a Library System

The problems of managing novelty and complexity in design are no doubt exacerbated in cases like the multimedia system in which the technological issues were quite novel and tangled and the team large, diverse, and distributed. However, similar problems can be observed in milder forms even in design interactions among much smaller teams, working on relatively routine design problems of far more limited scope. One of the first empirical studies we made of information system design involved videotaping a working meeting between the head librarian at a large research center and a systems engineer (Carroll, Thomas, and Malhotra 1979; Malhotra et al. 1980). This was a very positive interaction, one that was both efficient and revelatory. Even so, it too illustrates some of what makes design so difficult to systematize and control.

The librarian came to this design meeting with several fairly specific concerns pertaining to the increased frequency of on-line reference searches. The library had installed four terminals, with a control unit and a local printer, near the reference-circulation desk to support these searches. The terminals were connected to one of the research center's mainframe computers and to the remote mainframe that housed the reference database. Providing the on-line search facility had clearly been a good idea, because the four terminals were heavily used. But it also caused congestion around the reference-circulation desk. Moreover, after a reference set was identified, it was printed locally, a noisy and slow process.

A recent complication in the situation was that a new reference system was about to become available. It would not supersede the current system but would augment it. And it required a different type of terminal connection. Thus, in addition to his standing concerns about congestion and noise with the current system, the librarian was worried about where the additional terminal equipment for the new reference system could be located.

The design meeting took an interesting course. At the start, the librarian focused on the congestion of the current spatial arrangement, sketching ideas about alternative placements for the four terminals and the control unit. He was particularly concerned with moving the control unit. However, after describing this problem and his sketch of a solution to it, he seemed to change perspective, saying, "This part of the problem, I realize, is not particularly difficult. Now what I see as being a problem is that we are bringing in a new library system." The new reference system raised the problem of locating still more terminals in the congested space.

Again, the librarian made an abrupt switch in his problem analysis, returning to the space and congestion problems regarding the printer and the control unit in the current arrangement: "I'd love to get the control unit buried in the floor somewhere." In fact, the problem of locating the control unit turned out to be quite minor. The systems engineer immediately responded that the control unit could be up to two thousand feet from the terminals, and hence could be removed completely from the reference-circulation area.

The librarian resumed his consideration of the need for an additional terminal to access the new reference system. He posed the question of whether his current control unit and modems could handle a system configuration in which one terminal is accessing the current on-line reference system and another is accessing the new reference system. He was specifically concerned that he might have to add control units for such a heterogeneous system environment. The systems engineer determined that this would not be a problem.

Having reached some satisfaction with respect to the question of control units, the librarian returned to the problems regarding the printer, specifically the problem of locally printing large reference sets. He apparently had a candidate solution in mind and asked directly if large files could be spooled to the remote, high-speed printers in the computing center. The systems engineer first raised the possibility of replacing the current noisy printer with a less noisy local printer. However, he also acknowledged that spooling to the remote printers was feasible: "I'd have to consult with our software people and that may be a project of a month to have the software written."

At that point, the librarian introduced a quite dramatic shift in focus. He suggested that access to the on-line reference systems could be managed through the research center's mainframe computers and that every staff member could get access to these facilities from his or her desk. This suggestion changed everything, virtually obviating the design work up to that point. The library terminals would not need modems or control units; they were already hardwired to the research center's mainframes. The librarian's attitude toward his "noisy" local printer was immediately transformed: "Leave it alone. That's fine. If the guy's in the library and he wants a little thing and he wants it here and now . . ." He quickly realized that the library would need fewer terminals, since those terminals would only be locally supplementing the many terminals throughout the research center. He concluded that in fact one would be enough—which incidentally solved the congestion problem that had started off the design meeting.

This meeting wound up with the librarian's acknowledging that the current arrangement implicitly discouraged use of the on-line reference system, since people had to come to the library to use it, and even then could get onto the system only if a terminal was free. He also speculated with the systems engineer about the kind of training approach he thought might be adequate if the more distributed access to the on-line reference systems were implemented. Finally, they discussed how long it might take to implement this new approach, though the librarian stated that even six months would be fast, given the problems and delays he already faced in trying to accommodate the new reference system.

Identifying the Real Problem

The participants in this design meeting were both highly experienced in designing information systems and clearly took this interaction as routine and successful. However, from a critical perspective, the flow of events in this meeting also suggests why design is so fascinating to those who would analyze it and why it is both engaging and maddening to those who practice it. One fascinating element of the design process, quite vivid in this meeting, is that a set of partial problems and partial solutions are sometimes pursued rather opportunistically and then integrated and cumulated, often by being reformulated. We focused on this element in our early theorizing (Carroll et al. 1979; Carroll and Rosson 1985; Malhotra et al. 1980; see also Guindon 1990).

But this same structure in the design process—or perhaps one should say *lack* of structure—is also problematic. Notice that the issue of the congestion problem that the librarian initially focused on ultimately becomes a nonissue. The problem of where to place the printer, the control unit, the terminals, and modems dissolves when the functions of the control unit and the modems are delegated to a computing center and most of the printing and terminal functions are distributed to individual users of the system. This raises an obvious question about the design process: Was it necessary at all to have worked through the problem of locating the various system components, only to have discarded both the solution and the problem?

Another way to put this question is to ask about the risks that the design process exposes us to if it is organized in the rambling, opportunistic manner of the library design. For example, the formulation process may stop too early, and the solution that is eventually implemented may address an intermediate stage of design analysis. Suppose that the librarian and the systems engineer had stopped just at the point when the systems engineer determined that the control unit could be hidden in a closet two thousand feet from the reference-circulation desk and that a single control unit could support switching between the two on-line reference systems. They would have ended up moving the control unit and avoiding the addition of terminals for accessing the new reference system. The congestion problem would have been addressed to some extent.

Now suppose that they had gone on to consider printing the references remotely, in the computing center. In this case, they would have mitigated the congestion and the local printer noise. Indeed, hiding the control unit and providing the option to print the search results remotely addresses all of the issues that the librarian articulated in the design meeting. What is important about these two counterfactual variations on the design outcome is that they are so different from the solution that emerged and was implemented. The actual solution is not only much different; it is much better. But how do you manage a design process so that you reliably get to the better solution?

In this regard, it is particularly curious that the librarian's reflections on the dysfunctionality of the current arrangement are voiced only *after* an alternative design approach has been developed. Why did he not acknowledge at the very outset that the current arrangement of dedicated terminals in the reference-circulation area discouraged use of the on-line reference system? He would surely have directed the design effort toward more radical issues than merely the location of a control unit and the noisiness of the local printer. Curiously, it seemed that this problematic consequence of the dedicated terminals in the reference-circulation area became salient to him only when he had a solution to it in hand.

The focus on layout design allowed the designers to work very concretely. Both the librarian and the engineer understand the language of freehand sketches. The multimedia design team needed, but did not have, such an integrative and flexible representation. However, the focus on physical layout design pushed the concerns of the people who use the library into the background. It is interesting to imagine how the design session might have gone if the designers had had a concrete and flexible representation for the concerns of the library's clientele instead of for equipment layout. Congestion and noise would still have been prominent, but convenient access to on-line resources from outside the reference-circulation area might have been more of a driving requirement than a reflection after the fact.

The multimedia system and the library system both illustrate the use of scenarios in design. The multimedia project created a day-in-the-life video illustrating the envisioned system and its use; the librarian often restated design proposals in terms of scenarios of use. However, in retrospect, both projects could have benefited from employing scenarios earlier and more systematically. The librarian couched design proposals in terms of impacts and opportunities for users, but he did not present the original problem in this way. Had he done so, he could have made it easier to contrast the problems in the current situation that motivated the design project and the solutions proposed to address those problems. The multimedia team created a scenario envisionment early, but they did not actively use the scenario to coordinate the activities of various subgroups. Taking their own scenario more seriously could have made obvious the need to integrate these efforts better, particularly the need to integrate the educational consultants' activity.

Thriving on Design

This book is not about heroic designers, nor is it about step-by-step methods that crank out better designs. It is about making more of a modest but pervasive element of design practice: the use of scenarios. The multimedia and library projects both employed scenarios, but in somewhat limited and ad hoc ways. I ask here how such projects might benefit from taking scenarios more seriously—in understanding people's current needs and preferences, envisioning new activities and technology, designing systems and software, and evaluating and drawing general lessons from systems as they are developed and used.

Chapter 2 examines the general nature of design problem solving. Designing software, like designing anything else, is a poorly structured activity. Design problems are incompletely specified; identifying the problem is the biggest part of a design problem. The problem space of allowable and possible "moves" is also not determined a priori. Indeed, the goal or final state is not known; identifying the goal and solving the problem are typically one and same thing. Design problems characteristically involve many trade-offs; any move creates side effects. Many of the most significant and most interdependent consequences of design moves and of designs are impacts on human activities. Design requires many kinds of knowledge and skill; it typically requires teamwork, problem decomposition, and a lot of management.

Textbook approaches to design typically manage these properties by *abstraction*. Thus, one can address design problems by treating them "as if" they were compositions of puzzles, or other "toy" problems (Simon 1973), or by assuming that deductions from a science base will bound the design space significantly (Newell and Card 1985). Scenario-based design tries to manage the complexity of design problem solving by *concretization*. A scenario is a concrete story about use: "A person turned on a computer; the screen displayed a button labeled Start; the person used the mouse to select the button." Instead of designing software by enumerating lists of requirements, functions, and code modules, one can design the software by observing, describing, inventing, and developing scenarios that are or will be enabled by that software.

Chapter 3 sketches how scenarios address the challenges of design. Scenarios concretely anchor design thinking and design action, but ineluctably evoke reflection, and focus that reflection on situations of use, both as they occur in the world as it is and as they might occur in the world as transformed by design. Scenarios are paradoxically concrete but rough, tangible but flexible. They are accessible and manipulable by all stakeholders in a design; they implicitly encourage "what-if?" thinking among all parties. They permit the articulation of design possibilities and consequences without undermining innovation. These characteristics address the lack of specification for design problems and moves, and the indeterminacy of design goals.

Scenarios compel attention to the use that will be made of the design product. They can describe these situations at many levels of detail, for many different purposes, and from many different perspectives, helping to coordinate various aspects of design projects and opening up the design process to all of its stakeholders. These characteristics address the myriad human impacts and inherent trade-offs in design and the need to integrate many kinds of knowledge and skill.

The balance of the book develops a particular approach to scenario-based design that has been applied to a variety of software development projects. Chapter 4 discusses a video information system; chapters 5 and 6 discuss an ensemble of tutorial and tools for Smalltalk programming. A key idea in these examples is that scenarios can become more powerful design objects if they are analyzed as more than merely narrative descriptions. The events in a scenario can be analyzed in terms of underlying cause-and-effect relationships—for example, the person might have selected the Start button because it was the only selectable object displayed on the screen, or because Start seemed like the appropriate first thing to do. Causally explaining the events in scenarios puts those events in a larger context. Some are significant and some are unimportant; some reveal confusions on the part of a human participant; some reveal user interface design errors.

Chapters 7 and 8 further develop the possibility that scenarios, and the causal relationships they describe, can be a means for knowledge building in design. Chapter 7 explores how scenario-based design can make design cumulative in the traditional sense that science is cumulative. The cause-and-effect relations in one design can be saved to guide the development of subsequent designs. This gives technical content to traditional but informal notions like design genre or design pattern and illustrates how we can see design as a scientific method. Chapter 8 argues that the approach allows design evaluation and design theory to be systematically converged. Identifying underlying causal relations supports more incisive interpretations of evaluation data; mapping these causal relations to particular design genres supports attributions from specific data to design abstractions.

Chapter 9 suggests that the causal description of interaction scenarios can also directly guide software design—the planning and creation of code itself. This converges scenarios with the notion of use case that has become popular in object-oriented software engineering. Our proposal is that scenarios can provide the benefits of use cases for developing object models. The "lots of uses" theme of chapters 7 through 9 is critical. The hope that scenario-based design can support the reuse of technical knowledge hinges on demonstrating that there are immediate-term reasons for designers to take scenarios more seriously. Visions of reuse often fail because of the extra work required to make one's own work reusable. Effective reusability has to be almost a side effect.

Chapters 10 and 11 present and illustrate methods and techniques for identifying and analyzing design scenarios. Chapter 10 enumerates techniques for identifying and developing scenarios and for analyzing them by identifying the central causal relationships implicit in scenarios. Chapter 11 presents an overall information flow for scenario-based system development. These two chapters are far less than a step-by-step manual for scenario-based design. They try to show that scenario-based design can be less a matter of opportunistic discovery and more a matter of systematic reasoning from and about concrete situations of use. Chapter 12 briefly surveys current directions in scenario-based design for human-computer interaction and software engineering, including open issues that need to be addressed.

I believe that scenario-based design is a simple, general, and powerful approach for all design. I am not in a position to demonstrate this directly, of course. There is a conundrum for making the general argument that concrete details of use are a key to design; no one can investigate every design problem or even a representative of every kind. Practically speaking, the problem is even worse. Personally, I have worked on only a small number of relatively self-similar design problems, all pertaining to work and technology in the development of modest interactive software systems. Accordingly, I must leave generalization to others. In the past two years, however, I have given several seminars for the U.S. National Aeronautics and Space Administration (NASA). The attendees are engineers; very few are software developers. After one of these seminars, a senior engineer told me that scenario-based design would be the key to developing the commercial aircraft concept for the next-generation space shuttle. His team needed a flexible approach to explore envisioned situations systematically, though in their case, human-computer interaction per se was a side issue.

Scenario-based design is not intended to make sorcerers of sorcerers' apprentices. It is, rather, intended to help remove the need for sorcerers at all. Good software cannot reliably be designed by magic; we ought to know that by now. Scenario-based design may seem like magic to someone who has only seen a computer system described by formal gibberish. But scenario-based design is mundane. We identify the activities we want to support, or support better, and then allow descriptions of those activities to drive everything else. Computers most essentially are not formal gibberish; they are the tasks that people can do with them and the consequences entrained for people and their tasks.

In the 1950s, C. Wright Mills (1959) complained that science had failed in its obligation to provide effective guidance for the development of social policies, practices, and institutions. His book, *The Sociological Imagination,* criticized the penchant for "grand theory": precise, formal, intellectually awesome, but also low level, limited in scope, and impossible to apply. Mills was understandably concerned that a grand science that failed nonetheless to guide practical decision making might on balance be worse than no science at all. He called for a new perspective, for the development of "middle-level abstractions" that would be better grounded in social reality and better suited to application in actual social contexts.

System development is now in need of a guiding middle-level abstraction, a concept less formal and less grand than specification but that can be broadly and effectively applied. Scenarios are not formal; they are not technical in any fancy sense. We know that they can be used because they already do play many roles in the system development life cycle. Perhaps the time has come to consider how a more integrative scenario perspective for system development can be constructed. Design methods live on a razor's edge between creative intuition and grounded analysis. Perhaps scenarios can help balance the need for flexibility and informality with the need to progress systematically toward creative, effective, and usable computer systems and applications.

2

What Is Design?

Design is a particularly interesting category of human activity. If it is not in fact *the* quintessentially human activity, it is at least the kind of activity humans like to regard as defining of human intelligence. In design, we respond to situations in the world by creating novel artifacts to facilitate our activities and enrich our experience. Not every design effort succeeds in facilitating and enriching human existence, but each alters the world to some extent. The so-altered world presents us with new situations to which we eventually respond with new designs.

Design is not an easy or routine kind of problem solving. First, design problems never completely specify their starting conditions. Typically a critical first step in design is identifying the relevant description of the current situation in the world that is to be altered by the design work. For example, in the library project, the implicit assumption at the start was that the current situation was a particular physical arrangement of four terminals, a controller, and a printer. A turning point in this design work occurred when the librarian recast the current situation in terms of information access: this description enabled the ultimate design solution. A common problem in design work is that the description of the current situation in the world that drives the design reasoning is incomplete, inaccurate, or irrelevant. The design of the multimedia educational system, for example, included virtually no effort directed toward determining the actual problems and needs of undergraduate engineering education.

A second difficult characteristic of design problems is that the possible moves that designers may take in reasoning from a description of the current situation in the world toward an improved version of that situation are not specified. Thus, having decided, on whatever basis, that engineering education could benefit from the use of multimedia case studies, how does one get from here to there? What steps are possible? relevant? productive? None of this is given in a design problem. The library design is a good example of a client and designer considering possible moves (putting the controller in a closet) and then, on the basis of a new description of the problem, jumping to an entirely different space of moves (printing the search results in the computer center).

A third difficulty is that design problems do not specify the goal or solution state. We may know that there are layout and access problems with the on-line reference systems in the library, or suspect that under-graduate engineering education could be enriched through the pervasive use of multimedia, but to the extent that these are design problems, our initial understanding of the problem does not specify precisely *how* to provide better access to the reference facilities or to create effective educational multimedia systems. In this view, when the solution state is specified, the design work per se is complete.

Walter Reitman (1965) discussed these three properties of design problems in his monograph *Cognition and Thought*. His concern was to contrast design problems with the puzzle problems characteristically studied in academic psychology. This contrast is just as sharp today. A classic example is the Tower of Hanoi problem in which the problem solver moves disks among a set of pegs. The problem is absolutely clear at the start, the goal can be specified with precision, and the possible moves can easily be listed (there are only a few moves from any possible problem state, and there are only a few possible problem states). Surprisingly, there have been dozens, if not hundreds, of psychological studies of such puzzles, but very few studies of problem solving in design. Reitman called design problems "ill structured" to distinguish them from routine puzzles.

Reitman's consideration of design viewed it from the perspective of individual cognition; his paradigmatic example of design was writing a fugue. This was a good choice for heightening the contrast between design problem solving and puzzle solving, but it masks several further properties of design—properties that are particularly important in the design of new technology. Thus, a fourth characteristic of design problems is that they involve trade-offs among many interdependent elements. For example, designing multimedia education for engineering students might involve the creation of both an authoring tool and a database query facility. These two components may compete for resources in the project; moreover, either one may constrain the design of the other. Which will have priority when such conflicts arise? Nuclear power plant failures were an attractive course topic because students were expected to be intrinsically interested in them, but it was also a problematic choice because power companies were reluctant to cooperate. The librarian complained about the noise and the clutter of having a printer in the circulation-reference area, but this traded off with the convenience of the printer for the library's clientele. In the final design, the printer was still there. Decisions about trade-offs like these are typical in design work.

A fifth property of design problems is that they require a diversity of skills and knowledge. The librarian knew about the layout problems and reference tasks of the library; the systems engineer knew about possible locations of controllers and modems and about how to access systems remotely. *Together* they knew enough to clarify the problem and design a solution. Similarly, no single member of the multimedia project knew enough or could do enough to create both the multimedia authoring tool and the natural language query capability. In this case, the *failure* of the team to manage and integrate these skills and knowledge caused them never to complete their design. Trade-offs among design elements and the need to marshal diverse knowledge and skills could surely be important factors in the design of a fugue, but because they would arise and be resolved within the composer's own thought processes, they might be less salient than in team design projects.

Finally, design has broad impacts on people. Design problems lead to transformations in the world that alter possibilities for human activity and experience, often in ways that transcend the boundaries of the original design reasoning. The librarian and the systems engineer were addressing problems of access and equipment clutter in the vicinity of the circulation-reference desk, and they developed an insightful and radical solution to these problems. Nevertheless, their proposal to distribute access using the mainframe raised other access problems. For example, after this solution was implemented, every staff member who wished to

Box 2.1
Six characteristic and difficult properties of design

- Incomplete description of the *problem* to be addressed
- Lack of guidance on possible design *moves*
- The design *goal* or solution state cannot be known in advance
- *Trade-offs* among many interdependent elements
- Reliance on a *diversity* of knowledge and skills
- Wide-ranging and ongoing impacts on human *activity*

---

use the library had to have—and pay for—a personal account on the library reference system. Moreover, the terminals and the printer in the circulation-reference area could not in the end be eliminated, since people who encountered a reference need while visiting the library would want to pursue it there and then, rather than having to return to their offices in order to access the on-line reference system through the mainframe.

Box 2.1 summarizes the six properties of design problems; the balance of this chapter examines each property in more detail. Seeing design as a particularly indeterminate and complex kind of problem solving begins to explain why design is difficult and why managing the design process is difficult. In general, standard design methods do not effectively address these six issues.

Clarifying the Problem

The first big step in design is to identify the problem: What is wrong with the current state of affairs? What is needed? What could be improved? Is the problem a matter of relocating a controller? Is the problem congestion in the library's reference-circulation area? Is there a need to improve access to on-line reference databases?

The standard approach in software development is to carry out some sort of "requirements analysis." This analysis may initially be couched as a fairly high-level statement—for example, "Undergraduate engineering students need access to a variety of rich case study materials." Such a statement may be provided by the client (the person or organization that commissioned the design work); it may be developed by, in collaboration

Box 2.2
Partial requirements for the multimedia education project

- Integrated television and film footage, textbook descriptions, and images
- Authoring facilities suitable for both professors and students
- Familiar card catalog metaphor for hierarchical browsing
- Flexible information retrieval through lexical co-occurrence networks
- Rapid transmission of video/text/image data over gigabit network
- Transparent distributed access over heterogeneous networks

with, or from observation of prospective users of the system to be developed; or it may be based on the hunches and dreams of the designers. This initial requirements statement is successively elaborated and refined to obtain a precise description of the situation that highlights the specific needs that the design work will address.

Box 2.2 presents a partial requirements statement for the multimedia education project. In this case, the elaboration of the requirements reinforces the diversity among the various stakeholders in the project, with some of the team members focused on the content and format of the information itself, others on the presentation of the materials to students and professors, others with novel information retrieval technologies, and still others on applications of high-speed network facilities. As in many other design situations, the requirements for this system were strongly influenced by the skills and resources that team members were able to contribute to the project.

Developing precise and accurate design requirements is not easy. Requirements that reflect the hunches and dreams of designers will be accurate just to the extent that the designers themselves possess rich prior experience in the target domain. But no designer can be an expert in all domains; the designer who is an expert programmer may be able to generate appropriate requirements for a debugger but not necessarily for a payroll system. Moreover, designers pursuing their own hunches may overestimate the pertinence of their design ideas; investing time and effort in developing an idea tends to increase one's confidence that it is a good idea (Festinger 1957). The requirements paradigm of designers working from their own tacit hunches is fairly typical in small, commercial software companies—but the rate of success within this paradigm is quite low. The multimedia education project is an example of requirements derived largely from designer hunches.

It is desirable to involve clients and prospective users directly in identifying and developing design requirements. Accurate requirements, after all, must satisfy the client and must reflect the characteristics and practices of the people who will use the system. This is less straightforward than it may at first appear. To begin with, "clients" and "prospective users" are frequently not the same people; clients are often managers and administrators in the target domain, corporate management information system (MIS) specialists, or the employers of the people who will use the system. In the library design, the librarian was the source for requirements, but his role was to manage the library, not to use it. A client who is not a user may, of course, have an accurate understanding of the user requirements, but in many cases such a client may have only a prescriptive notion of what the user requirements *should be*. As Churchman (1970) observed, hospitals are designed to serve doctors but not patients.

Until recently, it was typical for large software companies deliberately to *limit* their designers' contact with customers. There was a standard division of responsibility in which marketing representatives met with customers to gather requirements and then conveyed what they learned to the designers and developers. Much information is lost in such arrangements. However, even when the requirements are obtained directly from prospective users, the process of problem analysis is not straightforward. Long ago, Dreyfuss (1955) discovered that people often provide answers that they think will please the interviewer or that project a view of themselves they find attractive. While gathering requirements for a clock, Dreyfuss once posed as a store clerk to get direct access to what people were actually thinking and doing at the point of sale.

Expert workers by definition know what to do, but they do not necessarily know how to *talk* about what they do; indeed what they say about what they do may be egregiously inaccurate (Blomberg 1995). There are strong incentives for people to remain blind to the problematic aspects of their own work situations. Allowing these aspects to come into consciousness could obstruct work performance and even jeopardize their employment. People try to make problems and unmet needs invisible by working around them, but this undermines their ability to present designers with comprehensive requirements. There are also differences in worldviews and language that prevent effective communication. Designers are looking for problems that match categories and techniques they already have mastered and can apply. Even when a prospective user is clearly expressing a need, the designer may fail to recognize it as a requirement.

These problems have motivated approaches to design that have high ambitions with respect to identifying design requirements. In *empirical design*, existing situations of use are studied carefully. Current practices and evident needs are documented with videotapes. People are asked to think aloud as they work in order to shed light on why they do the things they do, and on the consequences of their actions (Carroll and Rosson 1985; Dreyfuss 1955; Hughes et al. 1994). This approach reduces the reliance on the sometimes-dubious introspections obtained through interview techniques. However, it places a difficult analytical burden on the designer, who must now serve as a sort of anthropologist-psychologist. It is no easy matter to "see" another person's reality accurately.

In *cooperative* or *participatory* design, prospective users literally join the design team, or at least maintain a close and continuing involvement in the team's work (Kyng 1995; Schuler and Namioka 1993). People with a real stake in the usefulness and usability of the technology being developed are not merely interviewed or observed; they participate in workshops and exercises along with designers, working collaboratively to generate and refine requirements. This approach addresses many of the problems enumerated: the users on the team learn how to characterize their current situation in a way that designers can recognize as requirements, the designers learn how to convey design concepts in ways that relate meaningfully to work practices and experiences, and both groups learn to work together to test the accuracy of the requirements as they emerge and improve the precision of the requirements statements. The major downside in this approach is cost: not every design team has the time, money, or level of commitment to work this hard on getting the requirements right.

Empirical design and cooperative or participatory design are very compatible and can be used in combination to produce even richer and more accurate requirements analyses. But such an approach is extremely demanding and costly, exacerbating the fundamental contention between preparation for action and action itself. Designers are professional problem solvers and know very well that effective problem solving requires adequate planning and preparation. But it is very difficult to hold off on one's creative instincts, to deliberately suspend generation of possible solutions, and to instead gather and clarify requirements information. Design problems, because they are at an extreme of being under-specified, over-constrained and open-ended, are particularly rich opportunities for creative thinking. And though part of the discipline of design is the ability to pull back from action and reflect, designers are always susceptible to being "captured" by a problem and swept into premature solutions.

The worst misstep one can make in design is to address the wrong problem, to address requirements that do not accurately or completely describe the relevant aspects of the domain. Empirical and cooperative methods are keys to avoiding this, but they too are not unproblematic. Shared understandings between developers and users can be ephemeral and illusory; the phrases agreed to once may mean different things to different people at a subsequent meeting, and so forth.

Identifying Design Moves

To the extent that a design problem can be clarified, how does one then move toward a solution? Unlike solving puzzles, design takes place in the "open system" (Bhaskar 1979) of the real world. We cannot know what specific moves are possible or useful a priori; part of the creativity of design is discovering the relevance and effectiveness of a move that has not been tried before. But this is obviously hard. Much work on design methods has focused on describing what are sometimes called "weak methods": general techniques for problem structuring and decomposition. The basic strategy of these methods is to organize an overall design problem into a set of component subproblems, each simpler than the original problem. This process can be reiterated until the subproblems are easily solvable, perhaps even recognized as examples of known problems with known solutions.

Simon's (1973) discussion of ill-structured problems makes a typical and general argument of this sort. Indeed, he claims that the key property of ill-structured problems is that the solver has not yet made a satisfactory decomposition. In this view, the critical move in solving a design problem is to decompose it such that it is, in essence, no longer a design problem. Simon considered the example of designing a house, and suggested the following decomposition:

"HOUSE might transform to GENERAL FLOOR PLAN plus STRUCTURE, STRUCTURE to SUPPORT plus ROOFING plus SHEATHING plus UTILITIES, UTILITIES to PLUMBING plus HEATING SYSTEM plus ELECTRICAL SYSTEM, and so on. (p. 190)

This example illustrates the kind of simplification that can occur as an overall problem is hierarchically decomposed, but it also exemplifies some of the downsides of decomposition as a central design method. Decomposition tends to simplify problems in ways that implicitly discourage creative solutions. Simon's decomposition is based exclusively on a priori categories—the standard functional components of a house. Starting design work with such a decomposition makes it unlikely that a radically creative functional subsystem could emerge; Simon's approach to design is likely to produce reshufflings of known components.

Weak decompositions can also be pernicious with respect to critical domain-determined constraints. The house decomposition makes it difficult to conceive of interactions among components, or to investigate questions about relationships among them. Consider a roof-mounted solar collector, which merges the ROOFING and HEATING SYSTEM components, or an exposed column in the living room, which mixes GENERAL FLOOR PLAN and SUPPORT. How will this decomposition help ensure that groceries do not have to be carried from one end of the house to the other? Will family members staying up late to watch a movie disturb those who are trying to sleep? There is a question of whether Simon's house will stand up at all: the floor plan and structure are divided into independent subproblems with no means of constraining one another.

Of course, designers do try to decompose problems, often in just the way that Simon suggests. The multimedia education project structured the effort into subproblems such as natural language query, multimedia authoring, and courseware content. However, the coupling among these subproblems rarely turns out to be as simple as in Simon's hypothetical house. In the multimedia project, the coupling of the natural language query effort was never successfully specified; the effort drifted off on its own and never became integrated with the rest of the project. Design moves often have side effects; thus, adapting preexisting expertise, project activity, and software is often a good move, but it makes project integration more difficult.

Another difficulty with comprehensive weak decompositions is that requirements typically change through the course of design work. Of course, manifest needs and the felt needs of customers, clients, and prospective users change through time. Situations in the world are constantly changing, and even when they do not, people can change their minds as to how they think about a situation. Design work itself is a potent trigger for such changes in both designers and users. A given design move or domain experience can change the requirements. For example, a person who has used a spreadsheet program may have different needs and priorities from a person who has used only a paper ledger. In the library project, after their analysis of physical clutter around the circulation-reference desk, the librarian and the systems engineer were able to redescribe the problem as one of access to the remote reference system, significantly changing their understanding of the requirements.

The designers may find that they cannot produce a solution that meets all the requirements identified and agreed to at the outset. They may decide that some requirements have to be altered or even abandoned in order to get a solution at all. Sharrock and Anderson (1996) studied a design team charged with developing a high-capacity feeder for a photocopier. This project was carried out under enormous pressures: recent staff downsizing caused the design team to be composed mainly of former managers and to lack critical skills, the business case for the feeder forced an impossibly tight schedule that did not allow for any experimentation or refinement, and a formal corporate structure of design reviews loomed as a constant threat to the project. Well into the process, the design team faced a set of serious and unsolved problems, and a review was imminent.

At this point, the team came up with what was probably the only move that could save their project: they rewrote the requirements. At the outset, it had been determined that the feeder should not connect directly to the copier's CPU, since the feeder was an add-on and such a connection would complicate installation. However, direct communication with the copier's central processor allowed the feeder to monitor the state of paper and trays, and allowed the team to solve enough of its critical problems to pass the design review. A rigid problem decomposition method would have prevented them from even seeing this solution.

These examples illustrate an actively synthetic design method of planning by doing that is complementary to the relatively analytic techniques of problem structuring and decomposition. The design moves that were taken arose from the dynamic context of the solution process itself. The librarian and the systems engineer did not invest time in explicit analysis and planning to develop a well-structured problem decomposition; rather they immediately began working on concrete subproblems. Working on the various library subproblems helped them to recognize the problem of information access that drove their final solution. The copier design team did not derive the need for a direct connection between feeder and CPU by problem structuring and analysis; they were in the midst of actually specifying their design solution and realized that they were up against insoluble constraints: something had to be thrown overboard.

Ideally, designers might want to be able to make provisional design moves within a concrete design space, explore and develop requirements, and test the consequences of moves before committing to them. The examples from the photocopier and the library projects are imperfect approximations of this. In the photocopier project, the designers were compelled to open up their process or declare failure; they made irreversible commitments without having explored the consequences. In the library project, the requirements successfully evolved through the course of exploring a series of provisional design moves, but the trajectory of the design process seemed to be driven largely by luck.

Envisioning the Solution

The objective in design is to produce or specify an artifact that satisfies needs identified in the current situation. The solution is typically described by technical drawings and diagrams and written specifications. Describing a design in such vocabularies is in many respects a tedious bookkeeping task; its virtue is that it *precisely* documents the design solution. It provides detailed guidance for those who will implement the design and for those who subsequently may debug, enhance, or otherwise maintain the designed artifact. However, these vocabularies also tend to filter out the richness of tool use in real situations; they render vivid and open-ended designs as stilted enumerations of features and functions. Such specifications can be obstacles to the full participation in the design process of clients and prospective users. Such domain experts speak the language of the use situation, but not the language of software specification.

Specifications can also be problematic for designers. Even if designers achieve a good understanding of the problem domain and thoroughly explore and consider the space of possible moves in developing their solution, the switch to enumerating features and functions can cause them to lose the big picture. Listing isolated design elements can capture attention; it can become a task unto itself, diminishing attention to how those elements might work together to address the user needs that were originally identified. Yet the essence of an interactive computing system is that it is dynamic and responsive: how can this be captured in an static list of features and functions? Nevertheless, the apparent precision and completeness of a specification can engender a false confidence that the design problem has been "solved."

Box 2.3 displays a specification for the Inspector tool in Smalltalk/V (based on Digitalk 1990). This sort of description is often called a functional specification because it emphasizes a function-by-function view of the specified design. From this standpoint, it is a good characterization of this particular Smalltalk/V tool. It reflects a systematic structuring and decomposition of the inspection problem: each object, property, and function can be seen as a specific design response to some portion of a requirements analysis. It supports further systematic decomposition and design development—for example, specifying the Smalltalk code used to initiate an inspection. However, this description only implicitly indicates how the Inspector tool might be *used* by a programmer. To a great extent such details can only be guessed at from this description (see Carroll and Rosson 1990).

It is difficult, perhaps impossible, to depict a design solution fully without implementing it. Many have argued that the only adequate specification for a computer system is the system itself (Carroll and

Box 2.3
Illustrative functional specification for a Smalltalk/V Inspector

---

The Inspector is a low-level debugging aid used to examine and edit objects

Inspector Components

The *instance variable list* appears in a list pane positioned as the left pane of the tool. The first instance variable in the list is `self`, the object being inspected.
The *instance variable contents* appear in a text pane on the right of the tool. This pane displays the contents of the variable currently selected in the list pane.
There is a special Inspector for Dictionary objects: the instance variable list contains Dictionary keys rather than named or indexed instance variables. The special variable self is not included in the Dictionary Inspector variable list. There is also a special "method context" Inspector used by the system debugger (see below).

Inspector Properties

Browsing the instance variable list: Instance variables (including `self`) can be selected (clicked on) in the list pane; this causes the selected name to highlight the contents of the variable to be displayed in the instance variable contents pane.
Evaluation in the instance variable contents pane: Message expressions typed in the instance variable contents pane can be evaluated.
Evaluation under the scope of self: Any of an inspected object's instance variables can be referenced in the message expressions evaluated in the instance variable contents pane.
Save and update: Expressions evaluated in the instance variable contents pane can be used to modify an object's instance variables; if an expression is "saved," the value of the selected instance variable will be set to the result of evaluating the expression.

Interface with Other System Tools

A "method context" Inspector is incorporated into the system debugger. The object inspected in this case is the receiver of the currently selected method in the process walk-back list. However, the instance variable list pane of this specialized Inspector displays on the receiver (`self`), the arguments to the method, and the temporary variables defined in the method.

Box 2.3
(continued)

Inspector Functions

Inspection: Inspection is initiated by sending the inspect message to an object (e.g., via an expression typed and evaluated in a Workspace). Inspection can also be initiated by selecting an object and choosing Inspect from the Smalltalk menu. Within the Inspector tool, the menu for the instance variable list pane offers a single function Inspect, which opens a new Inspector on the currently selected instance variable.

Text-editing: The instance variable contents pane provides the standard text-editing menu, supporting the Restore, Copy, Cut, Paste, Show It, Do It, Save, and Next Menu functions.

Windowing: The window menu for the Inspector contains seven standard window functions: Color, Label, Collapse, Cycle, Frame, Move, and Close.

Campbell 1989; Newman 1988; Wasserman and Shewmake 1982). Newman, for example, provides nice examples of basic user interface questions that would be routine and important to a person using a system, and yet indeterminate from a written specification:

The user selects part of the text of a displayed document and changes the font size to 7.4 points. How will the characters be displayed? Will they be legible? Will the user be able to distinguish between similar characters, e.g., 'l' (lower case L) and the numeral '1'?" (p. 124)

In an interactive system, thousands of such questions can be posed. Elaborating the specification document to address each of them thoroughly would make design intractable.

Henry Dreyfuss, in his 1955 book *Designing for People,* energetically confronts these points. Dreyfuss is perhaps best known for the telephone handset he designed in the 1940s, which remained a standard for thirty years. He learned to draw upside down so that the client could have the best view of what was what sketching. Even so, he realized that drawings could be too abstract, even misleading, not only to clients and users but to designers as well: "We get a form into clay and actually do our designing in this pliable material" (p. 47).

Dreyfuss recognized that the concrete details of a design are part of the designer's natural language. The grids of an electronic spreadsheet, for example, evoke the well-entrenched concept of an accounting ledger. He called these reused elements "survival forms" (p. 59). The goals of both the designer and the person who will ultimately use a designed artifact are facilitated by the use of survival forms: "Our senses quickly recognize and receive pleasure when a long-forgotten detail is brought back. . . . Somehow these recollections of the past give us comfort, security, and silent courage. By embodying a familiar pattern in an otherwise radical form, we can make the unusual acceptable to many people who would otherwise reject it" (pp. 59–60).

Dreyfuss pioneered many empirically based design methods, but perhaps his greatest contribution was his inspired use of mock-ups. For example, in designing an airplane interior for Lockheed, Dreyfuss sent two associates back and forth across North America on commercial flights. They found that passengers were often baffled by design details like water taps that were unnecessarily novel; they were impressed that people wanted to think of airplane seats as armchairs, not as "devices" (although increasingly they are and will be devices). Initial designs were prototyped in a Manhattan warehouse and a full flight of "passengers" were hired to occupy the mock-up for ten hours: to store carry-on luggage, eat meals, use lavatories. This served as a concrete specification for seating, storage space, lavatory door latches, and so forth—and permitted low-cost, iterative reworking of the original designs.

Dreyfuss emphasized getting the "feel" of the design situation. When he designed his first typewriter, he interviewed secretaries and spent days observing their use of typewriters. He discovered that the glossy black lacquer finish reflected overhead lighting and caused headaches; he substituted a dull, wrinkle-finish lacquer, which became standard. When he worked for the Veterans Administration designing artificial limbs, he and his staff strapped them on. They worked closely with amputees to understand how the limbs were controlled in practice; they discovered how the amputees managed to achieve a sense of touch: "Through design, the weight of the device was better distributed and it was thus made easier for the wearer further to develop this remarkable ability" (p. 29).

Dreyfuss wanted to present a design as something tangible, sharable with clients and prospective users. He saw that designers and their clients and users need to feel the situations for which they are designing and the materials in which these designs will be embodied. He created a design paradigm of active, mutual engagement in which designers and their clients and users work in close coordination, noticing the world as it is and responding with mock-ups of the world as it might be.

Recognizing Trade-offs and Dependencies

The fourth characteristic of design problems is subtle trade-offs and dependencies regarding functionality and usability. The sheer number of important details and their many interactions is an intriguing yet exasperating property of design. The systems engineer and the librarian were able to develop a solution when they recognized the relationships among layout and information access requirements. The multimedia education group failed in part because they did not weigh the downsides in their decision to develop system components on different hardware and software platforms. Structured design methods seek to manage interactions by grouping requirements and constraints to specify subsolutions to subproblems, and thereby to build up a comprehensive design solution. Of course, the problem decomposition imposed through such methods powerfully shapes the ultimate solution, and may in fact obscure or conceal important trade-offs and dependencies.

Specifications that are developed strictly subproblem by subproblem cannot ensure an overall coherence in the design. Consider again Simon's house. Developing a house's general floor plan and its structure as independent subproblems may lead to a house that collapses immediately, but in a sense the design outcome might be worse if the house continues to stand. The central hallway of a colonial floor plan would fit poorly within the space created by an A-frame structure: Where would it lead? Sliding glass doors and exposed beams would produce a jarring effect as part of a colonial dining room.

Christopher Alexander, in his book *Notes on the Synthesis of Form* (1964), was particularly concerned about decompositions that were incoherent in this sense. Alexander differentiated between "selfconscious" and "unselfconscious" decomposition of design problems. Selfconscious decomposition, in his view, is forced or imposed on the design. It tends to refer to a priori categories of design subproblems and tends to under-estimate the interdependencies among the subproblems. Simon's decomposition of the house is a perfect example. Unselfconscious design, in contrast, seeks to *discover* the decomposition implicit in the functional organization of the design problem.

As a leader in the 1960s design methods movement (Jones 1970), Alexander (1964) sought formal methods to guide unselfconscious decomposition. His approach was to represent a design as a space of interconnected points: each point was a requirement, and its connections to other points reflected its dependencies on other requirements. Clusters of densely interconnected points in this representation correspond to highly interrelated requirements. Alexander imagined using this bottom-up method to partition a complex space of design requirements, and thereby discover an unselfconscious decomposition of the design problem.

Dreyfuss represents a more concrete perspective on the issue of managing trade-offs and dependencies. He stresses the importance of empirical methods (i.e., the development of design mock-ups and observations of them in use) for instantiating and evaluating trade-offs and dependencies in a design. The understanding gained through these empirical means could then be used to refine the design solution. It is also hard to ignore the fact that Dreyfuss actually *designed* things and drew on real case studies; Simon and Alexander wrote as design theorists and referred exclusively to contrived and highly schematic examples.

Interestingly, both Alexander and Dreyfuss discussed the vacuum cleaner as a design problem. The requirements these two methodologists discussed are strikingly different with respect to consideration of human impacts. Alexander listed simplicity (the number and variety of components), performance (cleaning power), jointing (ease of assembly), and economy (cost). He observed, for example, that simplicity and jointing are codependent; simpler componentry entails simpler assembly.

Dreyfuss (see box 2.4) had a different list and a different level of analysis. He required anthropometrically appropriate handle length, handle grip, and positioning of foot controls, noting that these would make it easier to push and pull. He required that a headlight be positioned so as to facilitate seeing into dark recesses. He wanted a low profile to help the

Box 2.4
Comparison of Alexander's and Dreyfuss's design requirements for a vacuum cleaner

Alexander	Dreyfuss
Simple set of components	Ergonomic handles and controls
Easy assembly of components	Headlight for recess illumination
High cleaning power	Low profile for occluded access
Low cost	Protective rubber bumper
	Carry handgrips
	Kink-resistant cord
	Multipurpose packing materials
	Accessory rack
	Easy-to-use disposable dust bag
	Easy-to-clean surface
	One-piece construction
	Pleasing and elegant lines

vacuum slide under furniture more easily. He specified a rubber bumper to protect walls and furnishings. There would have to be handgrips for convenient carrying. The electrical cord would have to be constructed so that it would not kink, even when coiled. The carton would have to serve both shipping and storage purposes. There would be a rack to hold the cleaning accessories, and it would have to make them accessible and orderly for the operator of the vacuum cleaner.

Dreyfuss required a disposable paper dust bag to relieve the operator of the need to empty bags; the dust bag would have to be easily removable and installable. The outside surface of the machine would have to be easy to clean. Dreyfuss required that the motor housing and main casting be incorporated into one piece, with the name plate attached afterward, and that a one-coat enamel be used—all to reduce manufacturing costs. He felt that it would be important to convey ease of use, lightness, and balance in the physical design and to integrate line, proportion, form, color, and texture. The dependencies and trade-offs in Dreyfuss's analysis are quite concrete. For example, the positioning and angle of the head-light and the nature of the accessory rack depend on the height the main housing (required to be "low profile").

Integrating Diverse Knowledge and Skill

Organizing a group of individuals to work together is a difficult problem in any type of undertaking. There are well-known group effects that can distort collaborative working arrangements and distract attention from substantive matters. For example, people tend to conform to the views of powerful group members and accede to perceived group consensus (Latane 1981). In the copier feeder project, Sharrock and Anderson (1996) noted that the team went along with a critical bad decision of the team leader, even though most of the individuals on the team were certain that it was the wrong decision. They went along because they believed that the team leader's authority would be undermined if this decision was questioned, and they did not want to undermine the group's ability to function as a group.

Design projects often require the collaboration of team members possessing a variety of knowledge and skill. It can be quite stimulating to participate in such teams. Besides achieving a result richer than might be possible with a smaller or more homogeneous team, such interdisciplinary collaboration provides many opportunities for learning from team members. Nevertheless, as Fred Brooks stressed in his book *The Mythical Man-Month* (1995), individual contributions may not add linearly. A talented and diverse team may produce a poorer design result than a single designer could have done, and take more time doing it. Adding people to a design team brings overheads of communication and coordination. It takes time for team members to pool their knowledge in discussions, negotiate decisions, coordinate their efforts, and incorporate the work of others in their own efforts.

Brooks (1995) reflected on the trade-off between nurturing vision and coherence in a design, and managing complexity by dividing the work among many designers, based on his experiences managing the design of the IBM System/360 and its operating system OS/360. These projects were extremely large and complex. Nevertheless, Brooks stresses that creating and maintaining conceptual integrity in the designs was more of a challenge than managing the details. In the design of System/360, conceptual integrity was attained by restricting the initial design work to a small group of system architects. Ironically, it was further *enhanced* by budgetary constraints that encouraged reuse among the designs of the nine variant models of System/360. In the design of OS/360, Brooks says he made a "multimillion dollar mistake" by putting a much *larger* team of designers to work on the system architecture: "The lack of conceptual integrity made the system far more costly to build and change, and I would estimate that it added a year to debugging time" (p. 48).

The point is not one of talent, but one of collaboration. The larger team will likely consider and develop more good ideas, but each idea will be developed in the context of those many other ideas, each will be integrated with other ideas, and each will be compromised, if only a tiny bit, as it is combined with others. Brooks concluded that fewer good ideas developed with greater conceptual integrity lead to a better final design that can be implemented at a lower final cost. In Brooks's OS/360 story the "multimillion dollar mistake" was combining a relatively small group of system "architects" with a much larger group of system "programmers." Brooks was convinced to do this by the argument that the programmers would otherwise have had to wait until the architects finished specifying the initial design.

Brooks's example is important, but it is in many ways a simple case. System/360 and its operating system are from the bygone era of data processing. The team was designing a general purpose computer for professional system administrators. Brooks's story pits the core design concept against the detailing and implementation of function, concluding that the architects should have worked in isolation from the programmers, handing off their results. Such a linear "waterfall" design process is possible in this case because, for the most part, dependencies flow from the architecture to the detailed design (Brooks 1995).

In the design of contemporary interactive systems, dependencies among components are more complex. For example, the user interface constrains the functions required, but the functions also constrain the user interface. It is not effective to develop one in isolation from and prior to the other and then merely hand off a final specification. And it is difficult to maintain coordination among various subgroups. Just as designers and their users may speak different languages and take for granted different worldviews, so may different kinds of designers. User interface specialists may see everything in terms of keyboard and display events; software designers may see everything in terms of the interactions among code modules. Poltrock and Grudin (1994) studied several large design projects whose collaborations were organized decompositionally and found that the information that was conveyed among groups was not adequate to guide subsequent efforts.

The integrated team-oriented approach is a recent alternative to decomposition into homogeneous subgroups. In the team approach, there is a deliberate mixing of diverse knowledge and skills and a dynamic notion of individual roles. It is intended that members will spend considerable time learning, widening the scope of their personal expertise, even learning each other's jobs. Team members are given greater autonomy and responsibility; management functions such as authorization and review are curtailed. Leadership rotates among group members as they feel they have specific leadership to offer. The technical focus is on partial solutions, continually produced (Takeuchi and Nonaka 1986). The success of this approach clearly depends on a selfless commitment of team members and the ability of project managers to relinquish control.

The multimedia education project sought to establish a team organization; however, the project's management structure remained conventionally static and as such was ineffective. In many cases, the team members made very narrow commitments to the project. Thus, the natural language group continued to see everything as parsing; as one designer put it, "I'm just parsing text." The gulf between this language processing view of the system and the multimedia browsing and authoring view was never coordinated. The challenge to coordinate diverse expertise implies a generalization of participatory design. Beyond the possibility of active and meaningful roles for clients and prospective users, there are many kinds of designers and developers who also must work together.

Anticipating Impacts on Human Activity

Design is about altering the world to facilitate human activities and enrich human experience. There is a great deal of uncertainty in pursuing such objectives; it is not always clear what "to facilitate activity or enrich experience" means. To take a textbook example, if a technological artifact helps a person carry out a task more rapidly, does it by that fact alone facilitate human activity? In a sort of obvious and commonsense way, the answer has to be yes. But faster is not always better. Workers may feel that the machine has taken control of the task, setting the pace and specifying the criteria for competent performance. Doing things faster can increase stress and diminish the personal satisfaction of mastering a task. Workers may feel deskilled. The sixth characteristic of design problems is the broad range of impacts the results can have on people and their organizations.

Designed artifacts have a myriad of consequences for people—some intended, some unintended, some that empower people and enrich their lives, and some that frustrate and punish people. Even if we can identify the consequences, we cannot always choose among them. Mesthene (1970) observed that new technology "has both positive effects and negative effects, and it usually has the two *at the same time and in virtue of one another*" (p. 26). Artifacts in use are complex agents of change; they alter our tasks and our social structures. Historically, these complications work themselves out through trial and error. Doing better than this requires sophisticated analysis of use situations coupled with flexible strategies for refinement and redesign.

Designed artifacts reflect substantial and complex theories of human activity and experience (Carroll and Campbell 1989; Winner 1986). From the standpoint of social science, these theories are not the single-factor variety that often form the core of academic discussion. Rather, they are comprehensive theories of everything that occurs within a situation of use and every causal implication for what happens subsequent to that situation. Of course, when designers envision and implement new ideas, they rarely articulate these theories in any detail. Often just a few words identify a key concept or a few reasons are offered as design rationale. If everything works out, this may be fine. But if complications develop, if there are trade-offs, if correlated positive and negative consequences cannot be disentangled, then this sketchy level of theory may not suffice.

But even making explicit the latent theory in a design may not be enough. The potential consequences for people and their organizations must be verifiable and effectively coupled to further design work. For example, if a machine is designed to help people carry out a task more rapidly, then that property should be verified by measuring performance time. If it is suspected that the design might also cause workers to feel stress, then that too can be measured, perhaps by observing or interviewing the workers. Of course, many properties of the use of systems are not explicitly stated in the design concept or rationale; thus theory-based evaluation needs to be complemented by discovery-oriented evaluation. The machine might have been designed to decrease task performance time, but there may be some subset of tasks (for example, recovering from certain errors) for which performance time increases. It is fairly typical that the performance of errors is not explicitly designed; designers often hope that their users will not make errors, or at least that they will not make errors frequently or routinely.

This process of broad analysis followed by even broader evaluation must be used to guide an iterative process of refinement and redesign. Such an approach to design is often called prototyping or rapid prototyping (Wasserman and Shewmake 1982). This approach can include the use of mock-ups, in the sense of Dreyfuss. For example, one can quickly mock up a user interface for a personal database application using a presentation tool like Macromedia Director and investigate whether the basic tasks people want to perform with such a tool are accessible and appropriately structured. But the prototyping approach also can incorporate a style of system development in which a running prototype is created fairly early in the development process and then changed in response to user evaluations and other feedback during the process. The final design can then be the version at the end of this process. One of the benefits of such an approach is that early evaluations are not limited to user interface mock-ups, which may have little real functionality and may even look and feel quite different from actual final system. The multimedia project was an example. Through prototyping, we may be able to observe some of an artifact's short-term consequences directly.

However, many important consequences for people appear only through the course of extended use. When a personal database is used daily for a year, we are likely to find that the basic tasks have changed, and perhaps in ways that are or are not consistent with the core functionality provided by the system. If we think of each design project as an isolated activity, we will not be able to manage or address long-term consequences such as these. Each time we design something, we will not know enough and not be able to see enough. However, few system designs are completely novel, and we do know some things about human activity and experience that appear to be relevant across many types of situations. Thus, there is the possibility of what might be called cumulative design, in which we observe the human impacts of past designs through time and attempt to direct that knowledge toward guiding the development of future designs.

Design Is Hard

The six properties of design problems help to explain why design problem solving is hard. The designer is asked to improve a problematic situation in the world, though essential and problematic features of the situation are rarely detailed in advance. If the designer can accurately characterize the problem situation, he or she must discover and pursue effective moves to transform the situation, mitigating the original problem while introducing a minimum of new problematic side effects. The moves are not given in advance, and in general, so-called weak problem-solving techniques are inadequate. The goal or solution state for the problem-solving process is not specified in advance either, and conventional techniques for specifying solutions often introduce errors. It is common that features in the design solution have subtle mutual dependencies and multiple consequences, involving trade-offs in functionality and usability. The design process depends on the integration of a variety of skills and perspectives, but most design techniques and representations exclude crucial stakeholder constituencies. Finally, the design product has a variety of impacts on people and their organizations, many of them unforeseen and even deleterious. Moreover, many undesirable consequences emerge only after a design product is fielded and put in regular use.

Our discussion of these six characteristics also suggests a way forward: *a working design representation tied more directly to situations of use.* Design moves and the analysis of their potential consequences, side effects, dependencies, and trade-offs must more directly refer to the original problematic situation and the envisioned solution situation. This is basically what scenario-based design is: descriptions of the original problematic situation and the envisioned solution situation are treated as technical design representations; they are explicitly analyzed and manipulated in the design process. Through the balance of this book, I develop a particular approach to scenario-based design, one that addresses the six properties.

While it is true that contemporary design work often incorporates some notion of scenario—that is, employs descriptions of current and envisioned use—it also is true that scenarios are often used ineffectively or inarticulately. For example, in the multimedia project, an initial vision scenario was created; indeed, it was a rather engaging video. However, it was not created by the developers, but rather commissioned by the project management. It was not used as a technical representation, but as a marketing presentation to garner resources. In the library project, the developers made reference to users and use, but they did this on an ad hoc and post hoc basis, justifying decisions they had already taken or had come to from other considerations. Both of these projects involved scenarios, but neither is an example of scenario-based design.

3

Scenario-Based Design

Designers of information systems and applications face the challenges all other designers face. The problems they address become definitively analyzed only by being solved; appropriate solution methods are never givens, but are confirmed by being tried out; solutions must be implemented in order to be specified. These designers face convoluted networks of trade-off and interdependency, the need to coordinate and integrate the contributions of many kinds of experts, and the potential of unintended and untoward impacts on people and their social institutions. Beyond all this, they face the likelihood that changing cultural and technological circumstances will obviate any solution they develop before it can be deployed.

Most engineering methods belong to the methodological tradition that seeks to *control* the complexity and fluidity of design through techniques that filter the information considered and decompose the problems to be solved. Scenario-based design techniques belong to a complementary tradition that seeks to *exploit* the complexity and fluidity of design by trying to learn more about the structure and dynamics of the problem domain, trying to see the situation in many different ways, and interacting intimately with the concrete elements of the situation.

In scenario-based design, descriptions of how people accomplish tasks are a primary working design representation. Software design is fundamentally about envisioning and facilitating new ways of doing things and new things to do. Maintaining a continuous focus on situations of and consequences for human work and activity promotes learning about the structure and dynamics of problem domains, seeing usage situations from different perspectives, and managing trade-offs to reach usable and effective design outcomes (Carroll 1994, 1995).

What Are Scenarios?

Computers are more than just functionality. They unavoidably restructure human activities, creating new possibilities as well as new difficulties. Conversely, each context in which humans experience and act provides detailed constraint for the development and application of information technologies. In analyzing and designing systems and software, we need better means to talk about how they may transform and be constrained by the contexts of human activity. This is the only way we can hope to attain control over the "materials" of design. A direct approach is explicitly to envision and document typical and significant activities early and continuingly in the development process. Such descriptions, often called scenarios, support reasoning about situations of use, even before those situations are actually created.

Scenarios are stories—stories about people and their activities. For example, an accountant wishes to open a folder on the system desktop in order to access a memo on budgets. However, the folder is covered up by a budget spreadsheet that the accountant wishes to refer to while reading the memo. The spreadsheet is so large that it nearly fills the display. The accountant pauses for several seconds, resizes the spreadsheet, moves it partially out of the display, opens the folder, opens the memo, resizes and repositions the memo, and continues working. This is about as mundane a work scenario as one could imagine. Yet it specifies window management and application switching functionality vividly and pointedly: people need to coordinate information sources—to compare, copy, and integrate data from multiple applications; displays inevitably get cluttered; people need to find and rearrange windows in the display.

Scenarios highlight goals suggested by the appearance and behavior of the system; what people try to do with the system; what procedures are adopted, not adopted, carried out successfully or erroneously; and what interpretations people make of what happens to them. If the accountant scenario is typical of what people want to do, it substantively constrains design approaches to window management and switching.

Scenarios have characteristic elements (Propp 1958). They mention or presuppose a *setting*. For the accountant scenario, the setting is an office, with a person seated in front of a computer. The setting includes the relative positions of the folder and spreadsheet. The scenario implies further setting elements by identifying the person as an accountant, and the work objects as budgets and memos.

Scenarios include *agents* or *actors*. The accountant is the only agent in this example, but it is typical of human activities to include several to many agents, each typically with *goals* or *objectives*. These are changes that the agent wishes to achieve in the circumstances of the setting. Every scenario involves at least one agent and at least one goal. When more than one agent or goal is involved, they may be differentially prominent in the scenario. Often one goal is the defining goal of a scenario—the answer to the question, "Why did this story happen?" Similarly, one agent might be the principal actor—the answer to the question, "Who is this story about?" In the accountant scenario, the defining goal is displaying the memo in such a way that both the memo and budget can be examined. A subgoal is opening the folder in which the memo is located, and a further subgoal is moving the budget to allow the folder to be opened.

Scenarios have a plot; they include sequences of *actions* and *events*, things that actors do, things that happen to them, changes in the circumstances of the setting, and so forth. Particular actions and events can facilitate, obstruct, or be irrelevant to given goals. Resizing the spreadsheet and moving it out of the display are actions that facilitate the goal of opening the folder. Resizing and repositioning the memo are actions that facilitate the goal of displaying the memo so that it can be examined with the budget. Pausing is an action that is irrelevant to any goal, though it suggests that the accountant's goal-oriented actions were not completely fluent. Notably, actions and events can often *change* the goals—even the defining goal—of a scenario.

Representing the use of a system or application with a set of interaction scenarios makes that *use* explicit, and in doing so orients design and analysis toward a broader view of computers. It can help designers and analysts to focus attention on the assumptions about people and their tasks that are implicit in systems and applications.

Scenario representations can be elaborated as prototypes, through the use of storyboard, video, and rapid prototyping tools. They are the minimal contexts for developing use-oriented design rationale: a given design decision can be evaluated and documented in terms of its specific consequences within particular scenarios. Scenarios and the elements of scenario-based design rationale can be generalized and abstracted using theories of human activity, enabling the cumulation and development of knowledge attained in the course of design. Thus, scenarios can provide a framework for a design-based science of human-computer interaction.

By making *use* the object of design, scenarios can be tools to address the fundamental issues about design raised in chapter 2. The balance of this chapter reviews some key challenges for design work and illustrates for each the benefits of a scenario-based approach.

Challenge: Design Action Competes with Reflection

There is a fundamental tension between thinking and doing: thinking impedes progress in doing, and doing obstructs thinking. Information technology designers are skilled practitioners performing complex and open-ended tasks. They want to reflect on their activities, and they routinely do reflect on their activities. However, people take pride not only in what they know and learn, but in what they can do and in what they actually produce. They know from experience that it is impossible to fathom all potential consequences and interdependencies, and they can be frustrated by problem clarification and discussion of alternatives. They want to act—to make decisions and see progress.

In the multimedia education project, the design team was tackling a large and ill-defined problem. The team included a variety of specialized expertise in natural language processing, multimedia authoring, and user interface design, and had broad goals and interests. At the start of their work, they held regular and lengthy meetings to develop a singular vision and a comprehensive plan. They seemed to enjoy the early brainstorming meetings, but increasingly felt it was time to get going, although many issues remained open. They shifted into action mode at the expense of reflection and coordination; the weekly team meetings were quietly canceled. In the end several groups within the project pursued poorly integrated subgoals.

Donald Schön (1983, 1987) has discussed this conflict extensively in his books on reflective practice. For example, he analyzes a coaching interaction between two architects in which the student presents a design concept for a school building involving a spiral ramp, intended to maintain openness while breaking up lines of sight (she calls the idea "a Guggenheim"): "When I visited open schools, the one thing they complained about was the warehouse quality—of being able to see for miles. It [the ramp] would visually and acoustically break up the volume" (1983, p. 129). The coach feels that she needs to explore and develop her concept more thoroughly, noting that a ramp has thickness and that this will limit her plans to use the space underneath the ramp. He urges her to draw sections but without bothering to justify this advice to the student, to allow her to see the rationale behind his advice. As Schön (1987) puts it, he does not reveal "the meanings underlying his questions" (p. 132).

Schön regards this as a hopeless confrontation in which no progress can be made on the particular design project or the larger project of understanding how to design. Both the student and the coach are willing to act publicly and to share actions, but neither adequately reflects on their own or one another's values and objectives. Reflection is not always comfortable; it forces one to consider one's own competence, to open oneself to the possibility of being wrong. As Schön (1987) put it, "The interactions I have suggested emphasize surfacing private attributions for public testing, giving directly observable data for one's judgments, revealing the private dilemmas with which one is grappling, actively exploring the other's meaning, and inviting the other's confrontation of one's own" (p. 141).

Reflective activities in information system design often occur decoupled from action. Design review meetings allow a project team to take stock of progress by working through a set of requirements, a progress report, a specification, or to exercise a prototype. Such reviews can facilitate design work in many ways, clarifying problems, moves, goals, trade-offs, and so forth. However, design reviews remove designers from the day-to-day context of their work to facilitate reflection. They provide an opportunity to stop design work as such and reflect on interim results. Reviews do not evoke reflection *in the context of doing design*. Moreover, design reviews typically focus on enumerating and defining features and functions, as opposed to reviewing the potential use of a system.

Box 3.1
Scenario of use for a multimedia educational system

Harry is interested in bridge failures; as a child, he saw a small bridge collapse when its footings were undermined after a heavy rainfall. He opens the case study of the Tacoma Narrows Bridge and requests to see the film of its collapse. He is stunned to see the bridge first sway, then ripple, and ultimately lurch apart. He quickly replays the film, and then selects the associated course module on harmonic motion. He browses the material (without doing the exercises), saves the film clip in his workbook with a speech annotation, and then enters a natural language query to find pointers to other physical manifestations of harmonic motion. He moves on to a case study involving flutes and piccolos.

Evaluation is another important reflective development activity, and one that often does address use directly, but evaluation tends to occur late in the system development process, and thus also is largely decoupled from design action. Schön's notion of reflection-in-action is an approach to design activity itself, as contrasted with iterative feedback cycles of design activity followed by reflective analysis in design reviews or evaluation.

Scenarios Evoke Reflection in Design

Constructing scenarios of use as focal design objects inescapably evokes reflection in the context of doing design. The scenario in box 3.1 succinctly and concretely conveys a vision of the system—in this case a vision of student-directed, multimedia instruction. It is a coherent and concrete vision—not an abstract goal, not a set of requirements, not a list of features and functions. Elements of the envisioned system appear in the scenario embedded in the interactions that will make them meaningful to people using the system to achieve real goals—perhaps revelatory, perhaps cryptic, but definitely more than just technological capabilities. For example, the role of natural language query is exemplified as a means of locating further case studies that illustrate the principles of harmonic motion.

The scenario emphasizes and explores goals that a person might adopt and pursue, such as watching the film clips twice or skipping the exercises. Some of these goals are opportunistic, such as investigating the Tacoma Narrows Bridge collapse because of experience with a totally unrelated bridge collapse or deciding to branch from bridge failures to flutes. The scenario implicitly articulates the usage situation from multiple perspectives: the student stores and annotates a video clip with speech, raising specific requirements for user interface tools and presentation as well as for particular data structures and memory. The scenario impels the designer to integrate the consideration of such system requirements with consideration of the motivational and cognitive issues in education that underlie the person's actions and experiences.

Schön (1983) drew an important contrast between merely creating or identifying elements of the problem context and "giving them reason." He characterized design as inquiry and the designer as "a researcher in a practice context" (p. 68). From this perspective, the designer's domain expertise is both a prerequisite and a potential liability. Having a category or a label with which to "understand" a situation often establishes an insurmountable obstacle to achieving an innovative understanding. In the Guggenheim example, the student sees the design only as a geometry affording patterns of light and sound. However, in her sketches, the Guggenheim analogy is static; it is a design answer that fails to evoke critical questions about the space underneath the ramp.

Creating and using scenarios pushes designers beyond static answers. The Guggenheim is an environment for walking and sitting underneath the ramp, among other activities. Embodying the activities of the Guggenheim space instantly raises questions about the space. The scenario in box 3.1 conveys the functionality of the system through vivid details about how a person will access that functionality and what a person might experience in doing so. This emphasis on raising questions makes it easier for designers to integrate reflection and action in their own design practice.

In strategic management, scenarios have played this sort of role. For example, Wack (1985a, 1985b) describes the use of scenario-based planning in Royal-Dutch Shell in the early 1970s. By developing a set of future scenarios, Shell was able to anticipate the emergence of OPEC, including the oil crisis of the 1973 and the oil glut of the early 1980s. Wack (1985a) concluded that the use of scenarios allowed Shell managers to raise questions, challenge assumptions, and understand the dynamics of the business environment "more intimately than they would in the traditional planning process" (p. 74).

In human-computer interaction, scenarios have been used in many system development activities. They are widely used for planning and describing evaluation test tasks (Roberts and Moran 1983) and task-oriented instruction and other user support (Carroll 1990a). They are used to specify usability goals in design (Carroll and Rosson 1985), and to frame design rationale (Carroll, Kellogg, and Rosson 1991) and design reviews (Karat and Bennett 1991). However, most of these uses are pursued in isolation from one another and from *acts* of design. That is, most uses of scenarios in human-computer interaction are not coordinated with one another and occur prior to or after design itself.

Schön (1983) emphasized that effective reflection and action must be tightly coupled. A design analysis need not be comprehensive; it need only guide a restructuring of the current situation that can produce new design actions and new insights. Schön contrasted such interactive and concrete "move testing" activity with traditional hypothesis testing in which abstractions are decomposed, instantiated, evaluated, and then either rejected or maintained. His cases are drawn from design domains for which there are rich languages to allow practitioners to create and explore situations quickly, for example, by sketching in architecture. Wack (1985b) also makes the point that effective scenarios must evoke planning and redesign action.

Scenarios provide such a language for the design of human-computer interactions. Kahn (1962), who used scenarios to analyze cold war dynamics, compared the role of scenarios in understanding human action to that of theories of mass and velocity in physics. They allow analysts and designers to sketch interactions in order to probe relationships; they resolve the paradox of reflection and action by providing a language for action that is ineluctably reflection evoking.

Challenge: Design Situations Are Fluid

Design changes the world within which people act and experience, and this changes requirements for further designs. When designs incorporate new technologies and address new arenas of human activity, such as electronic meetings or desktop manufacturing, requirements evolve more rapidly. New design moves and new design goals become possible and necessary to address these requirements. In such cases, there is little technological or social inertia to impede change, and little knowledge or experience to provide overall guidance. Design problems in information technology often change significantly during the course of their own solution process.

The fluidity of information system design is more than merely a source of technical complexity. Schön (1967) observed that in our era, technology undermines the stability of the world. For example, it erodes a manager's concept of "the business I'm in" (p. 195) and a worker's notion of the special skill he or she possesses; it erodes the traditional staging of life into education followed by steady practice. In everyday life, people create illusions of stability to manage their own uncertainty about situations, even if they must adjust their perceptions in order to do this (Nisbett and Wilson 1977). They protect their interpretations by selectively reconstructing their own experience (Erikson 1980). Interestingly, when greater reconstructive effort is required to maintain an interpretation, it is held all the more ardently, even in the face of incontestable discomfirmation (Festinger 1957; Festinger, Riecken, and Schachter 1956). Thus, a typical response to ambiguities in life is to fix interpretations and then defend them as long as possible.

The analogous response to the fluidity of design situations is top-down design and systematic decomposition. Designers fix a top-level concept based on their initial understanding of a design problem. They decompose this overall concept into concrete, enabling subgoals, as in Simon's house. If the top-level concept subsequently turns out to have been a favorable choice, this is called inspiration. However, this approach trades flexibility to avoid uncertainty; the top-level concept will often turn out to have been a premature commitment, painting the design into a corner from which it cannot address requirements that emerge through the course of the design process. Schön (1967) observed that decomposition is useful chiefly through the *side-effects* of eliciting and focusing concrete action, and thereby reducing uncertainty. But he warned that this approach frequently strangles innovation.

Designers almost always design something. If their need for stability induces them to close their designs prematurely, to cease reflecting and critiquing, to declare victory, they may produce a solution for only the first few requirements they encounter. However, struggling against premature commitment is difficult because it is such a general psychological strategy for managing uncertainty in life.

Scenarios Are at Once Concrete and Flexible

To manage an ambiguous and dynamic situation, one must be concrete but flexible—concrete to avoid being swallowed by the indeterminacies, flexible to avoid being captured by a false step. Scenarios of use reconcile concreteness and flexibility. They are concrete in the sense that they simultaneously fix an interpretation of the design situation and offer a specific solution. The scenario in box 3.1 specifies a particular usage experience that could be prototyped and tested. At the same time, scenarios are flexible in the sense that they are deliberately incomplete and easily revised or elaborated. In a few minutes, a piece of the scenario could be rewritten (for example, stipulating a system-initiated prompt for the associated course module on harmonic motion) or extended (for example, the objects in the scenario could be described as anchors for a variety of link types).

Scenarios embody concrete design actions and evoke concrete move testing on the part of designers. They allow designers to try things out and get directive feedback. But their flexibility facilitates innovative and open-ended exploration of design requirements and possibilities, helping designers to avoid premature commitment. This allows designers to manage the three difficult properties of design that Reitman (1965) emphasized: incomplete problem requirements, little guidance on possible methods, and open-ended goal states. Scenarios are Dreyfuss's clay mock-ups for the domain of interaction design.

The power of scenarios to convey concreteness through tentative and sketchy descriptions derives from the way people create and understand stories. Like the strokes of an expressionist painting, scenarios can evoke much more than they literally present. The human mind seems especially adept at overloading meaning in narrative structures, in both generation and interpretation, as illustrated by the remarkable examples of dreams (Freud 1900) and myths (Lévi-Strauss 1967). Indeed, dreams and myths are universal tools for coping with uncertainty. Part of their power stems from being recalled and discussed throughout a community. In a more modest scale, design teams can do this too. Sharing and developing scenarios helps to control the uncertainties inherent in the work, while strengthening the team itself.

Indeed, Simpson (1992) identified overspecification of scenarios as a potential pitfall. And several writers have emphasized the importance of descriptive and memorable names for scenarios (Schoemaker 1995; Simpson 1992; Wack 1985a). Once the scenario has been developed, a vivid name is often enough detail. In strategic management, scenario-based planning and analysis has been found to be most useful when uncertainty is high, there are strong differences of opinion about courses of action, and communication is poor (Schoemaker 1995).

Managing complex and fluid problem spaces with concrete scenarios is a natural approach. Designers already do it—both the library and multimedia system projects used scenarios. However, the role that scenarios play in design is often ad hoc, casual, fortuitous. Even when they are used deliberately, scenarios are rarely used systematically or comprehensively to support coordinated reflection and action. Yet it is a small step from current practice to exploit more thoroughly the possibility of keeping design commitments provisional, and thereby evoking further innovative ideas, through deliberate sketchiness.

Challenge: External Factors Constrain Design

Designers must have constraints; there are just too many things that might be designed. Requirements, if they can be identified accurately, are clearly the best source of constraints because they indicate what sort of design work is needed. But there are many other sources of constraint external to the design problem. The current state of technology development, for example, makes some solutions impossible and others irresistible. Designers cannot use technology that does not yet exist, though their work often drives technology development toward possibilities that are barely within reach. Conversely, designers and their clients are caught up in the technological zeitgeist, biased toward making use of the latest gadgets and gizmos, perhaps even when these novelties are not really appropriate to serve the user's needs. Finally, designers are biased toward employing technologies they have used before and are part of their personal design palette. Technological possibilities are a sort of window within which design work occurs.

Many external constraints in design originate in the organizational structures within which design work is embedded. Development organizations often systematically confuse clients with users, taking client concerns as user requirements. Certain types of assumptions and arguments may be favored in the business cases that underwrite design projects. For example, the multimedia project overemphasized technological objectives and constraints, uncritically assuming that students and professors would rather send video messages to one another than meet face to face. In the 1970s, it was often asserted that executives would never use a keyboard, and this became a working assumption. Such underlying attitudes restrict the designer's opportunity to understand and respond to the actual problem situation.

Organizations also specify work procedures that constrain designers. In information system development, it is still typical for design teams to work within some sort of waterfall framework, handing off documents and partial results to other groups. It is difficult to ensure adequate coordination and transmission of key information in such processes (Poltrock and Grudin 1994). Indeed, procedures involving hand-offs of responsibility and control often make it *more* difficult for people with different kinds of expertise to work together effectively. For example, it is not uncommon for "user interface" and/or "usability" to be broken out as separate subprocesses in a waterfall; this has the effect of removing or subordinating interaction design with respect to the design of system functionality. Since it is common for new requirements, methods, and goals to emerge in later stages of system development, waterfall procedures typically entrain iterations of reworking. Management structures are not part of the design problem, but they constrain how designers can work on problems.

Further external constraints arise in deploying new technology. The people who commission or select new technology are frequently not the ones who will use it, and the people who acquire and use new technology are not the only ones affected by its use. In the simple case, the technology may be difficult to use or just ineffective in the situations for which it has been acquired. But there are many further possibilities. Other tasks and activities that the users engage in, or the tasks and activities of other people in the organization with whom the users interact, may be detrimentally affected by the technology. The technology may indirectly exacerbate or expose problems in the organization itself; it may even become a lightning rod for organizational disputes that have nothing to do with any relevant task or activity.

External constraints are the larger context of design and use. Designers must cope with the current state of technology, their own work organization, and the wide-ranging and continuing impacts their work can have on client organizations. The key risk posed by external constraints is that they can distract designers from what is essential and tractable in the design project: addressing the internal constraints of the problem, the needs and concerns of the people who will use and experience the design result.

Scenarios Promote Work Orientation

Scenarios are work-oriented design objects. They describe systems in terms of the work that people will try to do as they make use of those systems. A design process in which scenarios are employed as a focal representation will ipso facto remain focused on the needs and concerns of prospective users. Thus, designers and clients are less likely to be captured by inappropriate gadgets and gizmos, or to settle for routine technological solutions, when their discussions and visions are couched in the language of scenarios, that is, less likely than they might be if their design work is couched in the language of functional specifications (Carroll and Rosson 1990).

Kahn (1962) emphasized the utility of deliberately envisioning and analyzing extreme cases in order to stimulate broader imagination of a range of future possibilities. Scenario-based analysis helps organizations to steer between the twin risks of overconfidence—attempting to change or accomplish too much, and conservatism—attempting to do too little (Clemons 1995).

Scenarios can help to integrate the variety of skills and experience required in a design project by making it easier for different kinds of experts to communicate and collaborate (Clausen 1993). Among the developers, scenarios can ease problems associated with handoffs and coordination in the design process by providing all groups with a guiding vision of the project goal to unify and contextualize the documents and partial results that are passed back and forth. Such a systematic use of scenarios was notably lacking in the multimedia education project.

All stakeholders speak the language of scenarios. Thus, employing scenarios as a focal design representation facilitates participatory design (Kyng 1995; Muller et al. 1995). But beyond merely allowing users and other clients to participate, scenarios help to keep technical considerations regarding use first and foremost in the face of potentially distracting considerations stemming from the organizations of the developers and the users. Supporting direct participation of users and other client stakeholders is a proactive approach to untoward organizational impacts that may obtain when the technology is inserted into the work context.

Wack (1985a) reported that a key to the Shell approach was directly involving management in the scenario work. Simpson (1992) found that using scenarios helped to clarify management assumptions in a planning process. Stokke et al. (1991) used scenario-based planning to design a long-range research and development strategy for Norway's state-owned oil and gas company, reporting that the methodology was simple and transparent, the process was highly flexible, scenarios helped keep the stakeholders focused on relevant issues, and that there was a high degree of ownership in the final product. They concluded that adopting a scenario-based method started to transform their company into a learning organization.

Challenge: Design Moves Have Many Consequences

Schön (1983) sees design as a "conversation" with a situation comprising many interdependent elements. The designer makes moves and then "listens" to the design situation to understand their consequences: "In the designer's conversation with the materials of his design, he can never make a move which has only the effects intended for it. His materials are continually talking back to him, causing him to apprehend unanticipated problems and potentials." Thus, the systems engineer and the librarian made the move of spooling print jobs and then noticed the (apparently) unanticipated potential of redistributing the entire on-line reference system. When a move produces unexpected consequences, and particularly when it produces undesirable consequences, the designer articulates "the theory implicit in the move, criticizes it, restructures it, and tests the new theory by inventing a move consistent with it" (Schön 1983, p. 155).

A classic design rationale method for representing design conversations is the issue-based information system (IBIS) of Rittel and Weber (1973). This approach describes the design process as a graph of issues arising, each pointing to positions, or alternatives, enumerated as responses, each of which in turn points to arguments for and against that position. In this approach, it is relatively easy to trace single-issue threads, but more difficult to understand why a given alternative (that is, a design element) makes sense in the context of the many issues it may simultaneously address, and the many arguments that bear on it with respect to those issues.

Every element of a design, every move that a designer makes, has a variety of potential consequences. Spooling the local printer output downstairs to the mainframe computing facility had the direct consequence of freeing some floor space near the terminals in the library reference-circulation area. And it also integrated the mainframe facility into the library's on-line reference system, albeit quite loosely. This integration, in turn, suggested the possibility of a more central role in which the mainframe would act as the reference system client for the whole research center.

This design had wide-ranging impacts on the software for accessing on-line references, on the use of library and reference material, and indeed on work responsibilities and social interactions through the research center. The new design distributed access to on-line reference databases through the center. This entailed that the computing center's mainframes, and not the library's terminals, would manage access to these databases. This reallocated work among several groups in the research center staff: the reference librarians ended up with fewer face-to-face reference searches, but the computing center staff ended up with a new function to support. And it affected a myriad of other tangential interactions and activities—for example, carrying out reference searches from one's own office diminishes opportunities for chance encounters with colleagues in the library.

Many of the most common planning techniques are ill suited for problems in which many uncertainties must be simultaneously understood and managed (Schoemaker 1995). Contingency planning examines the impact of one binary uncertainty at a time—for example, what options do we have if we can spool printer output? Sensitivity analysis examines effects of parametrically changing one variable at a time, keeping all others constant—for example, how many additional local print jobs can we expect if the research staff increases by 5 percent? Simulation models make contingency planning and sensitivity analysis more tractable, but the downside they entail is a potentially huge outcome space with little semantic structure.

Designers need a language for keeping track of the conversation with the design situation, for recognizing and addressing the numerous trade-offs and dependencies among elements of the design problem. They need techniques for comprehensively managing of design moves, consequences for software, for directly supported tasks and activities, for work organizations, and for incidental social interactions.

Scenarios Have Many Views

Scenarios of use are multifarious design objects. They allow designers to explore joint impacts of sets of uncertainties. They support changing the values of several key variables at a time to describe new states that may arise after major shocks or deviations in key variables. They give interpretations to patterns or clusters of possible outcomes, concretely structuring the outcome space. And they describe designs at multiple levels of detail and with respect to multiple perspectives.

A scenario can briefly sketch tasks without committing to details of precisely how the tasks will be carried out or how the system will enable the functionality for those tasks. The multimedia education scenario in box 3.1 is at an intermediate level, with some detail regarding task flow, but it could be elaborated with respect to Harry's moment-to-moment thoughts and experiences in order to provide a more elaborated cognitive view, or with respect to individual interactions to provide a more detailed operational view. Alternatively, the scenario could be presented from the point of view of someone watching Harry, perhaps in order to learn how to operate the system. It could be elaborated in terms of Harry's organization, emphasizing the broader context of his activity—the people with whom he works and the goals they are jointly pursuing. It could be elaborated in terms of hardware and software components that could implement the envisioned functionality in order to provide a system view. Each of these variations in resolution and perspective is a permutation of a single underlying use scenario. Indeed, the permutations are integrated through their roles as complementary views of the same design object.

Scenarios can leave implicit the underlying causal relationships among the entities in a situation of use. For example, in box 3.1 the envisioned speech annotation capability allows adding a personal comment without the overheads of opening an editor and typing text. However, the annotation is noncoded and thus cannot be edited symbolically. These relationships are important to the scenario, but often it is enough to imply them. Similarly, scenarios can explicitly detail temporal relations, as in a Gantt chart, or they can leave sequence and duration vague, as in box 3.1. This is an aspect of the property of being concrete but rough.

Sometimes, however, it can be useful to make these relationships explicit. For example, in another scenario of use, Harry may wish to collect and revisit the set of film clips he viewed and annotated as "breakthroughs in forensic engineering." Unfortunately, his noncoded voice annotations cannot be searched by string. Thus, this new scenario would end in failure. To understand and address the variety of desirable and undesirable consequences of the original annotation design move, the designer might want to make explicit the relevant causal relationships in these two scenarios, thus providing yet another view of the envisioned situations, as shown in box 3.2.

Scenarios can help guide the designer's move toward consequences of differing types. For example, the data structures for the workbook might differentiate between annotated and nonannotated items, allowing annotated items to be retrieved and browsed as a subset. This would not allow Harry to retrieve the set of items with a particular annotation directly, but

Box 3.2
View of the multimedia education scenario sets of consequences associated with
the orientational video clip and the speech annotation capability

---

A video clip of the Tacoma Narrows Bridge collapse
+ provides an engaging introduction to a course module on harmonic
motion
+ evokes curiosity and self-initiated learner exploration
− may not sufficiently motivate a learner to attempt the course module
Speech annotation of a saved video clip
+ allows easy attachment of personal metadata
− does not support indexing or search of metadata

---

it would still simplify the search. Alternatively, the search problem might
be addressed directly by speech recognition or audio matching, or by
including the option of text annotation. Each of these alternatives would
entrain different elaborations for both the annotation scenario in box 3.1
and the search scenario just discussed. These elaborations could then be
explored for further consequences and interdependencies.

Thus, one would want to pursue the usability consequences of the
various elaborations, for example, the frustrations of a 90 percent
recognition accuracy. One would want to investigate trade-offs and interdependencies among consequences of different types. The speech recognition capability might resolve the search scenario, but it might entail
prohibitive costs in memory and processing. Including an option of text
annotation might change the annotation task in a subtle way; the person
would be aware when creating the annotations that they will later be
retrieval keys. Providing a finely articulated data structure for the workbook enables flexible organization and retrieval, but at the cost of complexity in the underlying database.

Using scenarios in this way makes them an extremely powerful design
representation. They allow the designer the flexibility to develop some use
scenarios in great detail—for example, the ones that describe the core
application functionality or the critical usability challenges, while merely
sketching other less problematic scenarios. At the same time, they allow
the designer to switch among scenario perspectives and directly integrate,
for example, usability views with system and software views. Such a

flexible and integrative design object is precisely what designers need to manage the nexus of consequences entrained by their design moves.

Challenge: Technical Knowledge Lags Design

Designers often work in domains for which certain critical scientific and engineering knowledge is missing. This is typical in the design of information technology. The multimedia project went forward without good theories about how people work together in networked multimedia environments in general or in educational contexts specifically. There was little science—indeed, little experience at all with such systems to draw on.

Schön (1983) emphasized the "dilemma" of rigor or relevance throughout the professions. He describes the "high, hard ground" where practitioners can make use of systematic methods and scientific theories, but can address only problems of relatively limited importance to clients or to society. He contrasts this to the "swampy lowland [of] situations . . . incapable of technical solution" (p. 42). Here the practitioner can confront the greatest human concerns, but only by compromising on technical rigor. The design and development of technology aspires to occupy the high, hard ground, to apply the current state of science and engineering knowledge systematically, reduce difficult problems to mere corollaries— and then bask in the confidence that deductive science confers on both its practitioners and the recipients of their efforts: science is certainty. But at the same time, technology design and development is ineluctably driven to pursue novelty and innovation, and thereby to slip continuingly into the swampy unknown regions.

It can resist this only through self-destructive willfulness. During World War II, operations research developed from the successful application of mathematics to modeling battle situations like submarine search. After the war, the field expanded its interests to management problems in general, and successfully produced effective formal models for relatively bounded problems like managing capital equipment replacement or investment portfolios. However, it generally failed in complex, less well-defined areas like business management, housing policy, and criminal justice. Remarkably, the response of the field was largely to focus attention on the relatively simple problems that suited the mathematical models (Schön 1983).

Russell Ackoff (1979), one of the founders of operations research, lamented the inability and disinterest of the field in addressing the "turbulent environments" of the real world: "Managers are not confronted with problems that are independent of each other, but with dynamic situations that consist of complex systems of changing problems that interact with each other. I call such situations *messes*. Problems are abstractions extracted from messes by analysis; they are to messes as atoms are to tables and charts . . . Managers do not solve problems: they manage messes" (pp. 99–100). This quotation evokes the story in which a man loses his car keys one night, but decides to search for them not where they were dropped but under a nearby streetlight *because the light is so much better.* The man will not find his keys, and Ackoff analogously worried that solving operations research problems will not lead to "designing a desirable future and inventing ways of bringing it about" (p. 100).

The challenge is to build hard ground in the swamp of real design problems. If we never build abstract and generalizable theories of design domains, every design project must start from scratch. A beacon for this is the Catgut Society's research on the physics of violins (Hutchins 1981). At the start of this project, there was good science for analyzing a single vibrating string, but nothing that could analyze vibrating systems composed of strings spanning air cavities partitioned by wooden ribs and bounded by irregularly shaped wooden boxes. Integrating acoustical research with the design of new stringed instruments, the Catgut group scaled the acoustics of the violin to obtain a complete set of eight acoustically balanced instruments, addressing the traditional problems of the lack of a tenor voice among string instruments and the unbalanced sound power of violas and cellos. Through this design work, the Catgut group also created new fundamental knowledge in physics.

Scenarios Can Be Abstracted and Categorized

Although technical design cannot escape Schön's swamp, designers need to extract lessons from their experience to guide their work and improve their practice. If scientific knowledge lags design, then designers themselves must formulate what they learn. Alexander and his collaborators (1977) pioneered this sort of approach to design knowledge in their concept of pattern. This takes the notion of design as inquiry quite seriously and raises the question of what abstractions can support the development and reuse of knowledge in design.

Scenarios keep the designer of information systems and applications in the swamp, connected to the turbulent real world, but by their very nature, scenarios also provide scaffolding to get a view of the design situation from a bit higher up. The roughness of scenarios is, after all, a homey kind of abstractness. A scenario is a "middle-level" abstraction (Mills 1959) of a set of possible interactions. For example, the scenario in box 3.1 could guide the design of a multitude of information systems. Documenting and explaining a scenario provides an account of a class of possible situations; this creates a generalized design object that can be immediately employed in further design work by being elaborated in various ways. For example, the scenario could be developed as a "protective" scenario, anticipating risks associated with decisions, or as an "entrepreneurial" scenario, codifying new strategic opportunities (Wack 1985b).

But this is only the simplest sense in which scenarios can be used to develop design knowledge. Scenarios exemplify particular themes and concerns in work and activity situations. Thus, Schwartz (1992) describes three main "plots" for strategic management scenarios: winners and losers, challenge and response, and evolution. For example, winners and losers plots assume a zero-sum game for resources or success. He recommends that each of these main plots be instantiated in projecting possible futures in organizational planning and that analysis of given scenarios always include a diagnosis or declaration of the scenario type.

In one of the scenarios for a multimedia education system discussed earlier (see box 3.1), a person is at first opportunistically exploring an information structure, but eventually adopts a particular interest that guides his exploration. In another scenario, a person wishes to search and organize information that has previously been browsed. Described at this level of generality, these are not scenarios unique to multimedia education systems or even to computers. They are general patterns for how people work with information. Therefore, it is likely that some of the lessons learned in managing the "opportunistic exploration" pattern or the "searching under a description" pattern in the design of any given situation might be applicable to the subsequent design of other situations. Such a taxonomy of scenarios would provide a framework for developing technical design knowledge.

Scenarios can also be classified in terms of the causal relations they comprise. In box 3.1, for example, providing speech annotation simplifies the actions needed to personalize a piece of information. In this causal relation, the consequence is the simplification of organizing and categorizing, a general desideratum in designing interactive systems. Generalizing the relation in this way allows the feature associated with the consequence (in this example, speech annotation) to be understood as a potential means for that consequence and employed to that end in other design contexts. There is, of course, no guarantee that the generalization is correct; that can be settled only by trying to use it and succeeding or failing. The point is that such candidate generalizations can be developed from scenario descriptions.

The generalization of the causal relations comprising scenarios can also be carried out across features. Speech annotation of data helps people create a personalized view of their information. But this relation holds independent of whether the data are annotated by speech, text, or handwriting. Understanding the relation more generally allows designers to consider any medium for annotation as a potential means of facilitating a personalized data view.

Scenarios can also be taken as exemplars of model scenarios; for example, box 3.1 illustrates a model of opportunistic control. Harry pursues the link from bridges to piccolos, because that is the aspect of the information that interests him. The system was designed to support this style of use; to that extent it embodies a model of opportunistic control. Other models are possible, of course; many instructional systems would require a student to complete the current module before allowing a branch to related material in some other module. Seeing the scenario in box 3.1 as an opportunistic control scenario allows the designer to benefit from prior knowledge pertaining to this model and to contribute further design knowledge of the model based on the current project.

Designers are not just making *things*; they are making sense. Particularly in technical design it is not enough for them to master a craft practice, for there is no stable craft practice in design domains like information systems and applications. The turbulence of technology development leaves little unchanged but, particularly in the short run, little resolved. We may expect that conventional science will eventually systematize technical knowledge in new domains, but we also know that it typically will do so after the wave of technological innovation has swept onward. The challenge for designers is to learn as they go.

Toward a Scenario-Based Framework for Design

In the large, information technology appears as a coevolution of tasks and artifacts. People engage in tasks and activities. They make discoveries and encounter difficulties. They experience insight and satisfaction, frustration, and failure. At length, their tasks and experiences help to define requirements for future technology. Subsequent technological tools open up new possibilities for tasks and activities, new ways to do familiar things, and entirely new things to do. They entrain new skills to learn and perform, new opportunities for insight and satisfaction, and new pitfalls of frustration and failure. Ultimately the new tasks and new technology become a baseline, helping to evoke requirements for further technology development. This pattern, schematized in figure 3.1 as the task-artifact cycle, emphasizes the dynamically moving window of technology development within which technical design occurs (Carroll, Kellogg, and Rosson 1991).

The task-artifact cycle is pervasive in information technology. Consider the spreadsheet. The first electronic spreadsheet, VisiCalc, was brought to the market in 1979. It clearly embodied a simple yet powerful response to a set of extant tasks: table-based calculations. Placing the spreadsheet in an electronic medium permitted accurate calculation and convenient handling. And it did much more. It opened up important new possibilities for table-based calculation tasks. Electronic spreadsheets facilitated projective analyses (what-if reasoning about altered conditions and abductive reasoning from a desired result to conditions that could produce it). People using electronic spreadsheets could easily alter values and recalculate. Indeed, spreadsheets even afforded a kind of ad hoc work integration: people could type a memo describing an analysis right into a spreadsheet cell (Mack and Nielsen 1987).

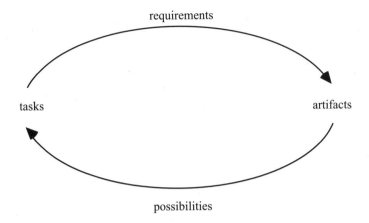

requirements

tasks   artifacts

possibilities

Figure 3.1
Task-artifact cycle. Tasks help articulate requirements for new technology that can support them; designed artifacts create possibilities (and limitations) that redefine tasks

This evolution of spreadsheet tasks can be viewed as successively altering requirements for spreadsheet systems. In the early 1980s, Context MBA provided integrated support for windows, graphing, word processing, and file management—for example, displaying the spreadsheet in one window and a graph of selected cells or a report in another. Lotus 1–2–3 introduced natural order recalculation (in which cell dependencies determine the order of recalculation), easing the overhead of what-if explorations. These advances, in turn, can be seen as encouraging further task evolution. For many office workers, the spreadsheet environment became a fulcrum for a myriad of activities: planning, communicating, accessing information, reporting, and presenting. It is now typical for spreadsheet systems to support multiple windows, integrate support for text and graphics, and share data with other programs. Many spreadsheets offer a range of recalculation options to facilitate projective analysis; some offer a "solver" function that takes a specification of a desired result and suggests how to obtain it.

Scenario-based design provides a framework for managing the flow of design activity and information in the task-artifact cycle. Scenarios evoke *task*-oriented reflection in design work; they make human activity the

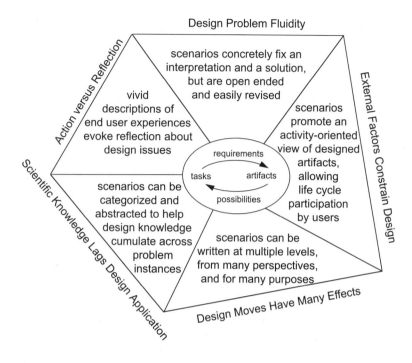

Figure 3.2
Challenges and approaches in scenario-based design

starting point and the standard for design work. Scenarios help designers identify and develop correct problem *requirements* by being at once concrete and flexible. They help designers to see their work as *artifacts-in-use* and, through this focus, to manage external constraints in the design process. Scenarios help designers analyze the varied *possibilities* afforded by their designs through many alternative views of usage situations. And scenarios help designers cumulate their knowledge and experience in a rubric of *task*-oriented abstractions. This is depicted in figure 3.2.

Design is a world that is part art and part science. It is a world of uncertainty and opportunity, a world in which sorcerers cast sweeping spells, often with great fanfare, though the spells generally fail. It is a world in which there is much talk of sound engineering practices, sometimes even of *formal* methods. Few, however, can bear to plod through the rote discipline of top-down structured decomposition toward what they know will be only mediocre results. Nevertheless, as managers and teachers, they may even encourage others to follow such methods, knowing that they will not do so, that they probably cannot do so.

To manage messes, we must come down from the clouds of pedagogical engineering and enter the swamp of real activity—in which new domain knowledge must be discovered in order to understand needs and objectives, in which design moves must be concrete to be evaluated and revised, in which every move taken potentially affects every other move, and in which diverse skills and perspectives are required to plan, execute, and evaluate every move. It is an interesting swamp; most designers would not wish to live anywhere else. We may come to know it better and cope with it better through a more explicit scenario-based design practice.

4

Example: Video Information System

In August 1991, I was presenting a paper at a conference in Edinburgh, Scotland. The topic was the "historical" nature of human-computer interaction—the notion that the concepts, even the facts, in human-computer interaction change as the social and technological context changes (Carroll 1991). Standing at the podium, I decided to build a video information system of designers telling their stories, a documentation system containing informal material about a development process as it occurred through time. Such a system could be a tool for investigating and perhaps managing the historical nature of human-computer interaction design.

A few weeks later, we had formed an ad hoc group to build such a system. It included Mary Beth Rosson, Sherman Alpert, and Mary Van Deusen, at that time the video production guru at the IBM Watson Center (about a month later we were joined by John Karat). Our initial inspiration was to develop a system similar to one worked on by our colleagues (Frishberg et al. 1991). Their project, "John Cocke: A Retrospective by Friends," consists of a database of stories about IBM Fellow John Cocke's thirty-five year research career told by his friends in video clips. The stories are indexed in various ways to support specific navigation and query (such as finding out about the development of the reduced instruction set computer RISC architecture), but people could also just browse and gradually see a picture of John Cocke, the man, emerge from the various views.

Such systems create a new kind of history. Traditionally, people have gathered around campfires and kitchen tables to listen to a single telling of a tale, perhaps by someone who had directly experienced the events in the tale, perhaps by someone who had heard the tale before and was passing it along. In hypermedia folklore, we hear many different tellings of the tale, each from the perspective of one of the principals in the events of tale. This is truly revolutionary; it democratizes history by eliminating singularly privileged perspectives. The John Cocke application brings a man's story to life in a way that could be achieved only if one were to travel the world interviewing the people who knew John Cocke and shared his life.

We decided to use these ideas to develop a kind of design history. Instead of a purely retrospective approach, as in the John Cocke application, we wanted to collect materials starting from the inception of a system development project, focusing on designers' reflections about their own planning and implementation activities while they were still engaged in those activities. We saw this as a response to Curtis, Krasner, and Iscoe's (1988) field study of the software design process, which had identified a need for tools to support knowledge sharing in organizations as a means to facilitate the utilization of knowledge across an organization, but also to bring people together and help them to accommodate change better.

Raison d'Etre

We quickly identified an interesting and amiable design team to work with—a group seeking to create a multimedia platform for network-delivered engineering education. The team incorporated specialists in multimedia, natural language processing, human-computer interaction, object-oriented software, as well as educational technology consultants outside IBM and a large publishing company as a customer-partner. (Part of the story of this group's project was discussed in chapter 1 and subsequently.) In the first few days of October 1991, we initiated a round of videotaped interviews to document the project near its inception. We queried the designers not only about their current activities and concerns, but also about how they saw the prospects and directions of the project and its accomplishments thus far *from that point in time.*

We classified and rated the thousands of video clips we collected through the next year. We were impressed throughout with the goodwill and the candor of the designers. It was fascinating stuff: because each interview was couched in the present tense, reviewing clips across interview rounds created a kind of persistent present that seemed to make the data more vivid and intrinsically interesting.

We designed a simple presentation system for our video database: Raison d'Etre (Carroll et al. 1994). The user interface presented a collection of buttons. Across the top of the display were buttons corresponding to each of the design team members. Across the bottom of the display were buttons corresponding to the project time line—the three interview rounds we ultimately carried out with the team members. In the middle of the display were five buttons depicting our five top-level database topics: Looking Backward, Project Vision, Looking Forward, Human Issues, and Technical Issues.

Looking Backward provides access to database entries bearing on project accomplishments and the reflections of team members on previous points in the design process. The Project Vision topic accesses specific technical views of the project (such as its potential impact on students and teachers, its possible significance for computer science) as well as high-level views of the project's potential impact on groups of people or on society. Looking Forward includes what still lies ahead—anticipated problems, changes, and outcomes. Human Issues refers to data bearing on group dynamics, personal relationships, communication, and collaboration. Technical Issues consists of project history and rationale in the more conventional sense, that is, relating to specific design characteristics and concerns, such as the possibly alternative views regarding specific design points and their resolution. Due to the obvious richness in such broad categorizations, we also developed subtopics for Technical Issues and Human Issues.

One interacts with this system by selecting sets of buttons to build a graphical query. For example, one or more team members might be selected with one or more reference times; then queries including any of the five topics will retrieve only clips relevant to those topics and spoken by any of the selected persons and occurring in any of the selected phases of the project. At any point in the query specification, one can ask for clips; figure 4.1 illustrates the playout of a video clip in Raison d'Etre.

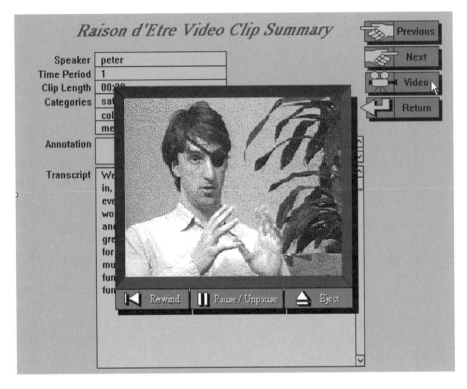

Figure 4.1
Video clip of developer explaining projct activities from Raison d'Etre

Raison d'Etre seemed to give us interesting access to project history. For example, the set of key issues for the project we studied changed over time. In part, we were led to the five database categories because finer-grained taxonomies of our materials seemed ephemeral. In the first round of interviews, for instance, the chief technical issue that the team discussed was the nature of the initial proof-of-concept prototype. However, Prototype did not seem to be a lasting major category; subsequently the team articulated the more detailed and lower-level technical concerns that came up in the course of developing the prototype and follow-on development.

The watershed events that create a team out of a collection of diverse individuals and a project vision out of sometimes disparate motivations and goals are profoundly important, yet they are ephemeral. In the first round of interviews, many of the designers told us the story of a dinner they had shared after a particularly long and tiring team meeting. In the dinner conversation, it came out that all of those present were deeply concerned about the state of education in American society, and in their different ways each saw the project they were working on as a personal commitment to contribute something to the future of education. This was expressed with an intensity that really comes across in the video clips.

In subsequent interview rounds, new, more contemporaneous events were naturally more salient to the designers. They were moving on to technical issues involving databases, information retrieval, and user interface presentation and controls. The educational vision was still there, still galvanizing the team members, but it was part of their shared history by that point, and as such not likely to be talked about. Time is critical. One has to capture history as it happens to capture it easily or, in many cases, to capture it at all.

In the first round of interviews we collected several accounts of how the team had selected a sample content domain for their proof-of-concept prototype: nuclear power plant engineering. These accounts were personalized in interesting ways. From a team member more identified with project vision and management, we got a rationale in terms of social and pedagogical values; from a team member more identified with implementation, we got a rationale in terms of availability of multimedia data and amenability of available data to the mechanisms of the prototype.

Interestingly, only a month later the team changed their sample domain due to problems with data availability and worries about social controversy. In the second round of interviews, we were able to gather a solid and broad-based rationale for the new sample domain. The previously tight rationale for the now-rejected domain was no longer observable with the fidelity observed in the first round. In fact, some designers' stories seemed to forget that there ever had been another domain. That early rationale became a priceless moment in the history of this design project, yet if we had conducted retrospective interviews at the close of the project only, we would not have seen it.

The balance of this chapter describes our Raison d'Etre project as an example of scenario-based design. In this project, we were chiefly interested in investigating and creating a video design history system, but we also wanted to learn more about scenario-based design.

Clarifying Design Concerns and Objectives

From the very start, everyone on the team we studied was enthusiastic about the notion of a design history system. This enthusiasm seemed to have three sources. First, the team members seemed to share our intuition that encouraging and supporting reflection and a sense of history within a design team would create the possibility of better collaborations and better design results. Second, everyone was especially excited about pursuing this through a database of video clips—notably perhaps, the project we studied was itself focused on supporting video information systems. Indeed, we joked at one point that our project history system should be implemented on the system platform produced by the team whose project history was being documented. Third, the project members simply enjoyed talking about their accomplishments—their collaborative interactions and their goals, for example. They seemed to enjoy our attention and the sanctioned opportunity to sort some of it out. As the team members told their stories, they often stopped to comment that these reflections were useful *to them*—that is, they had not yet fully appreciated the significance of their own experiences until they made them explicit (see Orr 1986).

Our team—the one creating the design history system—experienced similar scenario-based epiphanies. We had started with a fairly vague vision: the notion that project history could be a resource for designers and the model of the prior John Cocke system. Our own design work focused immediately on enumerating and developing potential scenarios of use, and within these, potential issues and opportunities. The list of placeholders in box 4.1 is drawn directly from the first page of our design notes. It was the first thing we did.

Creating and developing scenarios helped us in several ways. First, the scenarios helped us to become a design team. Our project was essentially exploratory; we were seeking problems and solutions at the same time. It was also a skunkworks—that is, no one on our team had the design history system as his or her principal job responsibility. The project was never officially chartered, and it had no budget or staffing; only two of the

Box 4.1

Design scenario sketches for Raison d'Etre. This list of possible scenarios to develop is reproduced from the first page of our design notes (from September 1991).

How does one create a workgroup that works?—the user is interested in the collaborative dynamics of design teams, perhaps in relating this example to social psychological abstractions

How do design projects get done?—the user is interested in seeing system development exemplified with more concrete detail than the idealized descriptions of textbooks

What type of system is this, what might it do for me, why would I want to use it?—the first-time user may be unsure what goals are appropriate, and needs to be able to discover this from the system itself

What is the role of lexical networks in the project?—seeking information pertaining to a specific technical issue, which may in fact have its own subhistory and a set of related topics

Why did the design team abandon the bridge failure domain?—focus is a particular design decision, though in this case a major event in the design process

What was Bonnie's role in September 1991?—the user selects the "people" button, and then selects the "Bonnie" button and an early point on the project time line

How did Bonnie's role change between September and December 1991?—query Bonnie's role at two points on the time line, as above (perhaps we need an absolute scale on the time line for such scenarios, but I think that users will care more about relative times within the project life cycle)

How did Ben and Bonnie work together during the spring of 1992 (e.g., on what problems and issues)?—

Compare what Peter said the November 1991 prototype would be like in September 1991 with what he said it was like in December 1991—

What was the consensus view about the project in October 1991?—the user selects an early point in the time line and then browses around under various topics and people

Compare the consensus view about the project in October 1991 with the consensus view in June 1992—the user selects and browses two points on the time line, as above

Compare Mike's attitude toward Donna's tools with Donna's attitude toward Mike's tools—the user pursues Mike's attitude (for example) and then initiates another search for the comparable information about Donna (perhaps finding a bit of data that explicitly contrasts the two, but more likely having to integrate the information for him or herself)

Box 4.1
(continued)

Compare the change in Mike's attitude toward Donna's tools between October 1991 and June 1992 with the change in Donna's attitude toward Mike's tools during the same time period—

Make a report on a search episode—the user wishes to create a report, perhaps just saving the results of a query or a set of queries with a name or description, perhaps designing a presentation sequence (will people want to do this?)

---

five people on the team had a line management relation. We were participating out of interest, not management direction. Projects like this can wander and dissipate very easily. The scenarios quickly gave us a notion of what we were doing, and helped our early brainstorming hang together between meetings.

The scenarios also helped by making it easier for us to plan what we would do instead of prematurely diving into its execution. From the start, we felt the pressure of time and opportunity. We did not know exactly what we wanted to do. We interviewed the members of the multimedia education project, but were still uncertain as to what piece of their needs corresponded to support for the project history. Yet we could see that the history of their project was well underway; they were having meetings and developing plans, and we were *not* capturing any of it! The scenarios allowed us to get going—to develop and explore our design space, but with the least possible degree of commitment. They gave us something concrete to work on, while keeping us from wastefully diving in before we understood what we needed to do. We found that the shorthand descriptions in box 4.1, probably because they had been generated collaboratively, were detailed enough to support subsequent analysis and development discussions.

Creating scenarios also helped us get technically focused. At the outset of the project, we sounded the mantra of supporting design team reflection. But when we brainstormed possible usage scenarios, we quickly generated major reformulations in our own vision. We deliberately couched our scenarios at the basic level, that is, the level at which an agent's goals and actions are experienced by that agent (we adopted this use of the term *basic* from Rosch et al. 1976; see also Carroll and Rosson 1992). This orientation made salient to us the question of why design team members would want to reflect; this question, in turn, led us to generate scenarios addressing the use of Raison d'Etre for situated design education: the system presents an explorable case study. Looking back, it seems that we might also have been led to these educational scenarios both by the fact that the multimedia education project we were studying was itself focused on such scenarios and by our worries that our project would lag theirs too much to provide a resource to them during their design work.

One of the most important uses of these early scenarios was to help us design interview questionnaires for collecting video clips. We wanted to allow members of the multimedia education project to speak about the issues and episodes important to them. But we also wanted to exert some guidance, both to ensure broad coverage of each individual's perspectives and experiences and to make sets of clips among different individuals more comparable. The scenarios helped us with both. We prepared an open-ended set of questions about individual perceptions of project roles, attitudes toward collaboration, the overall project vision and its evolution, the current prototype, the domain for the test module, and specific technical issues like multimedia tools and lexical networks; these are evident in box 4.1.

This first phase of scenario development occupied the first few meetings; it easily fit into the slack time involved in setting up videotaping sessions with the team members.

Envisioning Alternative Situations

In the initial videotaping session, we collected over eleven hours of material from the ten principal team members. The interviewing process itself, and the many hours we spent as a group screening and discussing this videotape, immersed us in the technical problems and social interactions of the multimedia education project. It both grounded us and encouraged us in developing our starting set of scenarios. We tried to sketch out in more detail the things people might do with a project history system, the ways they might go about doing those things, and the contrasts between such possibilities and the current practices we could see.

As the initial set grew, we revisited these scenarios, testing our conception of what we were doing, trying to stretch it to help us better articulate the design problem and the means and solutions we were developing. For example, we became very impressed at how easy it is to collect relatively huge amounts of video and at how difficult video is to handle. It cannot be conveniently searched in the way that a textual database can be, and each clip must be viewed in real time. This led us to develop the scenarios in box 4.1 with a presumption that for most queries, there would be a relatively large number of hits. Thus, we identified the management of large sets of hits as a key technical issue: how to report or display such sets, how to allow people to browse them, whether to provide preview access to sets of hits, and so forth. We identified and developed new scenarios to describe these issues, such as the "Looking for the fast-forward button" scenario in box 4.2.

We began to consider user interface presentations and interactions more specifically. For example, in "Orienting to the project" in box 4.2, a first-time user is learning what kinds of information the system can provide, what kinds of queries can be put to it. We presumed a somewhat sophisticated user, but one for whom using the system would be casual. Thus, we were led to envision a simple, iconic interface in which queries are visually specified by selecting combinations of team members (that is, the speaker in a clip), topics (looking backward, looking forward, project vision, and various technical and human issues), and points along a project time line.

Working with these scenarios helped us discover new functional requirements for the project history system. For example, "What is the project all about?" in box 4.2 is a further development of "Orienting to the project," but it focuses on a particular issue: a sequence of individual queries and returned video clips might not integrate into a coherent concept of the project. The person might still be wondering what the point of the project was even after hearing many specific stories and reflections from team members. This scenario motivated us to consider incorporating a series of system demonstrations in the video database, that is, we decided to include a formally narrated, integrative project

Box 4.2
Envisioning the scenarios more vividly to develop interface and interaction ideas
(based on design notes from November 1991)

Looking for the fast-forward button
Walter has been browsing some clips pertaining to the project manager's
views of the lexical network as they developed through the course of the
project. One clip in particular seems to drag a bit, and he wonders how to
fast forward through the rest of it—perhaps he can just stop the playout?

Orienting to the project
Harry has just joined the project team; his manager suggested that he
should work with the project history to get familiar with what has happened up to now, and what the current challenges are. Looking at the home
screen, Harry sees a set of labeled person icons across the top, a group of
five icons in the middle—labeled Project Vision, Technical Issues, Human
Issues, Looking Forward and Looking Backward, and a rainbow ribbon
along the bottom, labeled with project phases. All of these appear to be
selectable buttons. In the upper-right-hand corner of the display is a button
labeled Find Clips.

What is the project all about?
Betty is a designer, but not a member of the project team. She is browsing
the technical issues with the goal of learning something from the way
various technical issues were handled in the project. She finds a variety of
interesting tidbits on lexical browsers, multimedia authoring tools, and so
on. But she has difficulty seeing how the different pieces fit together as a
coherent project.

Creating a perspective on the design history
Paul is browsing clips related to the use of Smalltalk as a prototyping tool.
He notices that several of these refer to a software framework for user
interface prototyping; apparently, this was a sideeffort or some related
work carried out by members of the project team. Paul marks these clips
and assigns the new group the name "Interface Framework." He continues
adding clips to the group, and then adds the group name to the Technical
Issues submenu.

demonstration for each time period—a kind of official progress report. This could both provide integrative context for the individual stories and reflections and serve as a sounding board for the various personal perspectives.

The fourth scenario in box 4.2, "Creating a perspective on the design history," is an authoring scenario, not a browsing scenario. The user marks clips relevant to a specific interest and creates a new subtopic in the database. This actually changes the system that subsequent users would experience. In September, we had listed a variant of this scenario with a parenthetical question, "Will people want to do this?" By November, when the scenarios in box 4.2 were generated, we were growing more confident of our design concept—enough to take the possibility of user authoring more seriously.

The course of scenario development illustrated in box 4.2 involves elaborating initial scenario sketches, as in box 4.1, and expanding the initial set of scenarios envisioned. A systematic approach to doing this is to generate problem and vision scenarios for the "same" goals, in order to force out the design issues that differentiate them (Carroll 1994). Consider again scenarios for "orienting to the project." The scenario in box 4.3 is a more detailed view of how this scenario might run *before* the deployment of a project history system. It describes the problem or opportunity that occasioned the design.

In the scenario, a new design team member, Harry, attends his first team meeting and hears the project leader run through an overview pitch. The scenario is a vivid and succinct description of a person getting oriented to the work in progress of a design team. One can use it as part of a requirements analysis, to identify problem areas and opportunities for design work. For example, Harry leaves the meeting with a clear understanding of the project vision, but a one-sided understanding. The other team members were excited and supportive of the manager's project pitch, but not at all skeptical or critical. This raises the design question of how the person might have been supported in the goal of getting a more balanced or more complete introduction to the project.

Having observed or conjectured the development team meeting scenario, we would search deliberately for further scenarios that complement or compete. In this case, we generated the "meet various team

Box 4.3
The development team meeting scenario

- Harry, a curriculum designer, has just joined a project developing a multimedia information system for engineering education. Lewis, the project manager, has suggested that he attend the design team's weekly meeting to start getting up to speed on project status and direction.
- Lewis is reviewing a presentation he will make to upper management. Lewis sketches the project vision as a new world of collaborative and experience-based technical education via the use of media across high-bandwidth networks. In this vision, engineering students work on case studies incorporating social as well as technical issues from the very start of their education.
- The talk develops a walk-through in which two engineering students collaborate across a high-bandwidth network, using a multimedia database to study a variety of technical, legal, and social details pertaining to an accident at a nuclear power plant. After analyzing the case study, the students create a multimedia report, including recommendations for improving the power plant's design and operation.
- The discussion is highly animated; everyone is offering suggestions about the presentation. Some of it seems a bit quixotic, but it's very inspiring as to the future of engineering education. Harry notes that there is little detail on the students' curriculum, and clearly sees how he can begin contributing to the project.

---

members" scenario, in which the new team member meets first with the project leader and then subsequently with the various other team members, but in each case in a one-on-one meeting (box 4.4). This is a very different experience from the "development team meeting" scenario: the new member hears many differing views of the project needs and priorities. At the end, he probably has gathered a much richer picture of the project but a far less clear impression of what to do. At the end of the sequence of meetings, the new team member may feel the need to schedule a second round of meetings to clarify questions raised by one person about something another person had said in a prior meeting.

As we designed the Raison d'Etre system to support the work of development teams, these two scenarios and the task-level conflicts and trade-offs they embody provided a very different type of guidance from purely functional requirements like "search by author" even though the same underlying issues are at stake. The contrast between the

Box 4.4
The meet-various-team-members scenario

- In his first meeting with Lewis, Harry gets an overview. He learns that the reason for selecting nuclear power plants as a content domain for the prototype course module is social relevance and timeliness. The earlier content domain was bridges, which seemed somewhat dry by contrast. Lewis sketches the project vision as a new world of collaborative and experience-based technical education via the use of media across high-bandwidth networks. In this vision, engineering students work on case studies incorporating social as well as technical issues from the very start of their education.
- A few days later, Harry meets a team member, Walter, to discuss the state of work on the video database and the collection and digitizing of new video materials. Walter mentions that the change of content domain from bridges and bridge failures to nuclear power plants was motivated chiefly by the availability of better video and other information. He reveals that the first candidate domain was searching and sorting algorithms, which was amenable to visualization through animation, but not rich enough in terms of extant text and video sources.
- To Walter, the project is a great opportunity to make his work concrete. He explains, in some detail, the challenges of integrating text from diverse sources (in diverse formats) and of collecting and organizing video to press laser disks.
- Harry is somewhat confused about what the project is really seeking to accomplish. What should he read up on to prepare? He worries about balancing the objective of working social issues into the instructional exercises with that of emphasizing browsing and authoring multimedia documents. After a few days, he decides to schedule a meeting with Lewis to get more guidance. In the office, he hears that the content domain has now changed to airport design.

"development team meeting" and the "meet various team members" scenarios clearly involves the question of who is the "author" of the information the new member is exposed to, but it is much more than merely a question of the syntax for specifying queries. Another way to develop complementary or competitive scenarios is to reconstruct a scenario from another agent's point of view—for example, writing the development team meeting scenario from Lewis's perspective.

We used a set of requirements scenarios to reason toward a scenario specification of a design. Thus, we used the "development team meeting"

Box 4.5
The browsing project history scenario

• Harry browses the project video history. Sets of clips are categorized under major iconically presented headings; under some of these are subcategory menus. He selects the Lewis icon from the designers, the Vision icon from the issues, and an early point on the project time line. He then selects Play Clip and views a brief scene in which Lewis describes his vision of the project as enabling a new world of collaborative and experienced-based education.

• Harry selects Technical Issues (instead of Vision) and from its submenu, he selects Course Topic. Lewis explains why bridges and bridge failures is a good choice: it's a concrete problem, accessible to anybody and yet seriously technical; it can be highly visual—as in the famous Tacoma Narrows film. Harry selects a point on the time line further along in the project history. Lewis explains why nuclear power plants are such a good choice for the course topic: socially urgent and seriously technical.

• Harry selects Walter from the designer icons. Walter explains his reasons why nuclear power plants is a good course topic: lots of good video, lots of popular-press text, and lots of technical debate.

• Harry selects various combinations: other designers besides Walter and Lewis on these same issues and times, and other times and issues for Walter and Lewis. He begins to appreciate the project vision more broadly, attributing some of the differences to individual interests and roles in the project team. He begins to see the course topic issue as a process of discovering and refining new requirements through active consideration of alternatives.

---

and the "meet various team members" scenarios to clarify requirements (such as the problem of getting information from only the team leader or from various members but thrashing) and then tried to construct further scenarios that could address these requirements. In this manner, we constructed the "browsing project history" scenario (box 4.5) in which the new team member accesses stored video of various team members' commenting on the project vision, status, needs, and current direction. The video clips he browses were created at various points through the history of the project, so the new team member can gather an impression not only of where things stand currently in the project—from each of the individual perspectives of the various team members—but also of how these individual views evolved, and what people on the team thought about various issues before events overtook them.

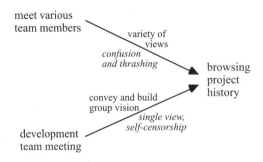

Figure 4.2
Scenario-based design argument from problem-requirements scenarios to a vision-specification scenario

This specification scenario addresses the issues raised in the two requirements scenarios. The "development team meeting" issue of hearing only the manager's perspective—and the possibility that this creates a normative bias among the team members, implicitly suppressing divergent views—is addressed by making it just as easy to access the perspectives of other team members. Yet the desirable property of conveying, and potentially strengthening, the group's vision is preserved. The "meet various team members" issue of thrashing is addressed by making it easy to switch back and forth among the video clips from various team members. Indeed, access to a variety of views is enhanced; one can switch among time frames as well as team members to explore historical factors in the project, something one could never do without such an information system. This scenario-based design argument is visualized in figure 4.2.

This is an example of the task-artifact cycle, discussed in chapter 3. The "meet various team members" and "development team meeting" scenarios are descriptions of current tasks. By analyzing the issues implicit in these tasks, as schematized in figure 4.2, one can reason toward new artifacts that help address these issues by enabling transformations of current tasks. Ultimately, a project history system will enable tasks and practices beyond those its designers imagined, and will raise new issues too.

Managing Consequences and Trade-offs

Every design move has many consequences. Spooling local printer output frees up floor space in the library but also enables a different access paradigm for the on-line reference system. Scenarios are good at vividly capturing the consequences and trade-offs of designs at various levels of analysis and with respect to various perspectives. Any scenario text leaves many things implicit; for example, the "looking for the fast-forward button" scenario in box 4.2 does not tell us why Walter felt that the video clip dragged. This property of being concrete but rough is one reason that scenarios are so useful.

In many cases it can be important to be able to enumerate the causal factors and relations that are left implicit in scenario narratives. In the "looking for the fast-forward button" scenario, one of the most important causal relations is relegated to the background of the actual text. It is the dual nature of video data: very rich and intrinsically appealing to viewers, yet difficult to search or scan.

We can isolate such relations in a simple schema:

{some design feature}
+ causes {desirable consequences}
− causes {undesirable consequences}

The schema makes salient the trade-offs associated with a design feature in a particular scenario context by enumerating its upside and downside consequences. The schema can be instantiated for the "looking for the fast-forward button" example:

Video Information claim: video information
+ is a very rich, intrinsically appealing medium
− is difficult to search, and must be viewed linearly in real time

We call these schemas *claims*: they are implicitly asserted by designs in which they are embodied; we call the approach of developing causal analyses of usage scenarios *claims analysis* (Carroll and Kellogg 1989; Carroll and Rosson 1991, 1992). One can identify claims by systematically posing elaboration questions about the agents and events in a scenario (Carroll and Rosson 1992). Thus, one can ask why the clip seems to drag; an answer is that the video must be viewed linearly in real time, even if the clip is lengthy. This raises the question of how viewers can streamline lengthy interactions, for example, through search. But searching noncoded data like video is not a solved problem; indeed, the lack of search mechanisms for video data comprises another downside.

These questions lead us to ask why one would want to use video data in the first place; an answer is that video data are visually rich and appealing to viewers, evoking attention and empathy. In Raison d'Etre we wanted to show how team members felt about the stories and reflections they contributed to the project history, not merely say how they felt. For this, we needed to use video.

Other elaboration questions one can pose about the "looking for the fast-forward button" scenario motivate further claims. For example, why would a person want to fast-forward through a clip? An answer is that adding such a capability mitigates the downside that video information must be viewed in real time. But it is not a comprehensive solution, since fast-forwarding typically accelerates speech to the point of intelligibility and destroys the sense of the real-time visual information. Would the fast-forwarding capability be effective for mitigating the real-time play-out constraint? The relevant trade-offs are summarized in the Fast-forward claim:

Fast-forward claim: fast-forwarding video information
+ allows the viewer to more rapidly scan and evaluate clips
– destroys intelligibility of the soundtrack and the "feel" of the real-time visual information

We could go on—for example, elaborating the "looking for the fast-forward button" scenario with respect to the particular implementation of user interface controls for fast-forwarding: a button, a slider, a frames-per-second prompter. And this detailing also might lead us to consider alternative approaches, such as storing only key frames, and not video clips, with the audio. These alternatives each raise further questions about causal relations implicit in the scenario, which could be articulated as further claims.

The claims developed as answers to elaboration questions are hypotheses about the underlying causal relations in the scenarios—the analyst's hypotheses about why and how an observed or envisioned scenario of use could occur. The objective of raising these questions and articulating hypothesized causal relations is to open up a process of critique and refinement, to help designers interrogate and explain key scenarios in enough detail that they can be interpreted, revised, and perhaps discarded as the design proceeds. This analysis is not intended merely to rationalize the personal intentions of the designers. A simple way to guard against this is to make sure that claims brainstorming forces out at least some upsides and downsides for every design feature that is analyzed. At the worst, one will generate some trivial upsides for fundamentally problematic scenarios and some trivial downsides for essentially unproblematic scenarios.

Any scenario can be unpacked in this way. For example, "what is the project all about?" in box 4.2 raises questions about how a pool of separate video clips can be used to build an understanding of a project's technical rationale and design process:

Stand-alone Clips claim: decomposing the project history into a pool of stand-alone video clips
+ facilitates analysis of the system from diverse perspectives
+ engages the person by allowing him or her to "construct" an overall view of the technical rationale and design process from diverse pieces
− people may find it difficult to integrate conflicting bits of information into a coherent overall concept

The "orienting to the project" scenario in box 4.2 raises a variety of potential elaboration questions: What might Harry's manager be expecting him to gain through interaction with the project history system? Why are the various buttons grouped as they are in the interface? What do the labeled person buttons convey to people? Is the issue of choosing between Mike's and Donna's multimedia authoring tools a technical issue or a human issue, or both? What does the time line ribbon convey to people? Where is October 10 1991, on the time line? How would a person find information relating to current project challenges? What will people expect to happen when they select Find Clips? The trade-offs that bear on addressing these questions can be organized into claims—for example:

Control Panel Interface claim: a simple control panel interface
+ directly conveys the content categories of the database
+ encourages direct interaction
− precise and/or complex queries may be difficult to articulate directly

Human Issues claim: the Human Issues button, the team members' buttons, and the appearance of team members in the clips
+ suggest questions about collaborative dynamics among team members
− may evoke questions for which there is no information in the database

Time Line claim: the time line interface control
+ encourages a user to take a historical perspective, to consider historical or process issues
− the time periods may not resolve the history finely enough
− the relative model of time may not support the user's concerns (e.g., a "when" question)

Causal claims analysis of scenarios is a refinement of the more informal, more purely scenario-based design analysis sketched in figure 4.1 above. In the Raison d'Etre project, we used claims analysis for relatively more detailed consideration of critical scenarios, or for cases in which a scenario analysis left open questions. The claims in box 4.6 more explicitly highlight the issues raised earlier in the purely scenario-based analysis of boxes 4.3, 4.4, and 4.5. These three scenarios, and their claims analyses, are particularly interesting because they comprise a kind of focused design argument. They emphasize the continuity between the *problem* and *vision* scenarios, and the design transformation that relates them.

For each individual scenario, one can pose a set of elaboration questions. For the "development team meeting" scenario, one could ask how the talk builds group vision, why the manager does all the talking, whether everyone in the project team really agrees, and so forth. And from these, one can build claims as possible explanations for why the scenarios run as they do. There may be a tendency to see the scenarios describing existing situations as *only* problem statements, that is, as mainly downsides, and the scenarios describing envisioned situations as *only* solutions, that is, as mainly upsides. This is an oversimplified view of the progression from problem scenarios, like boxes 4.3 and 4.4, to vision scenarios, like box 4.5. We do not want to merely beg the design question. For this reason, it is very useful to ensure a balanced analysis of all the scenarios. Having done that, we can extract cross-scenario themes for the entire ensemble. It is important to convey and build a group vision, but troublesome if any one team member exerts too much influence on the vision; it is useful to be exposed to a variety of views, but it takes time and effort to do this, and there is no guarantee that the various views will add up.

Making such design arguments and the transformation of the issues (for example, in the envisioned "browsing project history" scenario)

Box 4.6
Causal relations implicit in the three scenarios

Overview Pitch claim: An overview pitch of project status and direction
+ efficiently conveys and builds the group vision
− creates normative averaging and power bias distortions

Piecemeal Understanding claim: Pursuing questions of project vision,
status, and direction through a series of interactions with colleagues
+ accesses a variety of views
− takes a lot of time and effort
− can cause confusion and thrashing

Browsing History claim: Browsing a video database of statements, stories,
and reflections of team members
+ conveys/builds group vision
+ accesses a variety of views
+ provides direct and flexible access to views
+ clarifies and enriches answers to queries via lots of collateral information
− the query categories may not fit the user's goal
− the amount of information to be browsed may overwhelm people

---

explicit helps make the design of scenarios more cumulative and audi-table. One can directly view and compare the considerations that moti-vated the design work and the hypothesized result of the design work: normative averaging and power bias distortions, search time and effort, potential for confusion and thrashing. As we develop and begin to implement the new design, we can evaluate it with respect to the specific claims that were analyzed. We have also found that making a causal analysis of one scenario can often clarify the need for considering and designing one or more other scenarios, thus helping to elaborate the overall design.

Finally, this type of approach emphasizes the open-endedness of the design process. Design does not stop with a project history browser. Some of the issues addressed in the design may turn out to have been addressed inadequately. And new issues may arise. In box 4.6, we noted concerns that the amount of information to be browsed might quickly overwhelm people and that the query categories (looking forward, project vision, and so forth) might not fit users' actual goals.

Claims analysis provides only heuristic explanations of user interac-tion. Their utility in system design derives from directly linking features of a designed situation with people's activities and experiences. However, this can be an oversimplification. Some causal relations between features of situations and consequences for people in those situations may not be first order; they may derive from interactions and side effects, but be important nonetheless. The hope is that when such interactions arise, we might improve the chance of noticing them and beginning to fathom what is going on if we are keeping explicit account of what we expected would happen. If something is clearly working or failing, we have a basis for making credit (or blame) attributions to features of the design; we have a starting point for systematically revisiting our decisions and understanding other situations that guided us to those decisions.

Creating and Using Design Knowledge

Design reasoning is often quite local. designers address subsets of known requirements and then set aside tentative reasoning and partial results in order to explore other, hopefully converging, subproblems—recall, for example, the library design problem described in chapter 1. Creating an explicit analysis of the causal relations in scenarios can extend the scope and depth of a scenario analysis. It provides a working design representation to preserve and integrate interim considerations and conclusions. Indeed, the scope of such reasoning can extend beyond the current design project: we can view and reconsider the causal analyses of prior projects that might be relevant to what we are doing.

In this way, scenarios support a principled approach to the traditional technology development paradigm of craft evolution. Our design of Raison d'Etre was in many ways a direct emulation of the John Cocke application. However, the evolutionary process in this case was not articulated only at the level of the artifact itself; it was self-consciously guided by analytic consideration of the scenarios we wanted to address and those we wanted to enable. We managed these scenarios and claims to elaborate our design systematically—for example, coming to recognize it as an educational design tool, as well as a documentation tool. In the end, we had made a deliberated evolution of John Cocke, an explicit development of the prior system backed up with extensive use-oriented rationale.

A designer's chief interest must be the project at hand, and therefore, in claims analysis, for scenarios pertaining to that particular design. But some of the analytical work any particular design context is more widely applicable. For example, the Video Information claim expresses general relations regarding the use of video, relations not specifically bound to the "looking for the fast-forward button" scenario or the Raison d'Etre system. The next time one considers incorporating video information into a system design, the trade-offs enumerated in this claim will be relevant. The work we did, or that someone else did, to understand and articulate these relations can be of direct use in the future.

In a modest sense, this is an example of what might be called design-based science. Recall the work of the Catgut group in integrating fundamental investigations of acoustics with the design of novel stringed instruments (Hutchins 1981). What we are observing here is essentially the same thing. Some aspects of even the most specialized information systems are general, *if we take the trouble to draw out the generalizations.*

We can generalize scenarios or claims developed for specific design projects by trying to see them as instances of types. For example, the "what is the project all about?" scenario can be seen as an example of opportunistic interaction. The person explores information about people and issues by responding to whatever buttons or other interface mechanisms are encountered, trying to construct an understanding through a series of experiments. We can contrast opportunistic interaction scenarios with scenarios in which the user has a guiding goal and takes a series of actions intended to attain the goal. Thus, search scenarios contrast with opportunistic interaction scenarios in that the person is by definition seeking something in particular.

If one makes an analysis of an opportunistic interaction scenario, some part of the work one has done may generalize to other instances of the type. Indeed, this was precisely our own experience with opportunistic interaction scenarios. We had identified opportunistic scenario patterns in studies of the use of office systems years before we worked on Raison d'Etre (Carroll and Mazur 1986; Mack, Lewis, and Carroll 1983). Because of this prior work, we expected that one common usage scenario for Raison d'Etre would be one in which people directly browsed and experimented with the interface controls to discover what information and functionality was available in the system. This generalized opportunism scenario is always in the back of our minds in designing user interfaces and applications.

Claims also can be generalized. Claims about similar user consequences or similar artifact features can be grouped together. We have already discussed the Video Information claim as a potentially general relation with implications for any video information system. The Control Panel Interface claim can also be seen as an instance of a more general claim—one about simple, direct manipulation interfaces. Such interface designs are cognitively transparent and invite experimentation. On the other hand, it is not possible to express much variety or subtlety through such interfaces. This is a very general design trade-off that impinges on most contemporary user interface design.

The Stand-alone Clips claim is an instance of a more general claim about piecemeal information. When the chunks of available information are quite small and only loosely structured, the person has the opportunity to construct meanings actively, to put together diverse views of the data in potentially novel ways. On the other hand, the person may not always be able to make satisfactory sense of a vast and unstructured field of data. Again, this is a highly prototypical trade-off in design. There is a fine line between challenging and engaging the user with stimulating cognitive tasks and overwhelming him or her with tasks that are too difficult.

Integrating the generalization and refinement of knowledge employed and attained in design with design work itself is perhaps the strongest implementation of Schön's (1983) view of design as inquiry. The design argument behind the "browsing project history" scenario provides a good illustration. One generalization of the Overview Pitch claim in box 4.6 is the Social Conformity claim:

Social Conformity claim: Articulating one's beliefs and engaging in action in a social context
+ provides a highly responsive setting for testing and refining one's beliefs and behavior and for building group consensus
− encourages actions and beliefs that are group normative and consistent with the actions and beliefs of powerful others (such as group leaders), and thereby can inhibit diversity

Couching the relation at this level engages a huge research literature from social psychology detailing a variety of factors that create social influences (Allport 1920; Asch 1958; Cartwright 1968; Latane 1981; Lewin 1953; Milgram 1968; Schein, Schneier, and Barker 1961).

Being able to generalize a design argument in this way provides a framework for adducing relevant science. Perhaps even more important, it provides a framework for adducing the results of design inquiry *to* science. Thus, a current theoretical formulation of social influence states that the pressure to change one's attitudes or actions is proportional to the product of the strength, the immediacy, and the number of social interactions aligned with change (Latane 1981). In this formulation, the concept of immediacy does not provide for electronic immediacy, as in a video information system or electronic conferencing system. Thus, the design and use of a system like Raison d'Etre can directly bear on extending the science base of social psychology to new types of social interactions made possible by new technologies.

Articulating the underlying issues in a design also helps to define more explicitly the space of near-neighbor artifacts related to any given design. During the early 1990s, many projects investigated group history and memory systems. These systems had in common an interest in gathering and presenting design documentation from a variety of different persons. Most focused on documentation at the level of individual features or elements. Some were essentially FAQ (frequently asked question) systems, on-line help for new users (Ackerman 1994); some were hierarchical catalogs of use experience with particular design elements (Terveen, Selfridge, and Long 1995), and some integrated rationale and construction at the level of features (Fischer et al. 1992). None focused on personal information or organizational dynamics as a part of project history, or on differences in interpretation of the "same" information (see also Zimmerman and Selvin 1997).

The point of generalizing scenarios and claims is not to undermine the creativity of design, to presume to reduce design to mere instantiation of general scenarios and claims. Making design too simple is not the problem. The problem is making it manageable at all. The purpose of generalizing scenarios and claims is to enhance the tractability of design, to provide a way of learning from design experiences, from prior design results. Technical knowledge always underconstrains design. It does this even in relatively well-worked realms, such as the design of a new word processor. It does this even more severely in the design of novel systems, such as our design of Raison d'Etre. Nevertheless, there are always existing situations, general scenarios, relationships involving potential consequences for use. If we can manage this prior knowledge and bring it to bear on our design problems, we can increase our chance for success.

Our claim is that scenario-based design facilitates generalizing and reusing design knowledge at the right level of abstraction for productive design work: the level of tasks that are meaningful to the people who perform and experience them. In this sense, the roughness of scenarios discussed in chapter 3 is a useful kind of abstractness; it allows scenarios to be both concrete and generalizable.

Staying Focused on People and Use

Because our project was a skunkworks, without staff or budget, the chief external constraint we faced was a lack of resources. The use of scenarios helped our loosely bound group to establish and maintain a project direction. A particularly challenging external constraint we faced was the lack of enough disk storage to build the video database. Indeed, one could see this constraint alone as a show-stopper; we were, after all, designing a video information system. Focusing on the interaction scenarios made it obvious to us that we should develop an initial text-based prototype. We recognized that many of the scenarios we wanted to support could be implemented and evaluated with text transcripts standing in place of their video clips. This allowed us to finesse building the digital video database and to get concrete feedback on our user interface design. We did this in the spring of 1992, months before we were able to obtain enough disk storage to begin building the video database.

Later, when we had a running video-based prototype, we returned to our scenarios to evaluate the performance of the system in the kinds of scenarios for which it had been designed (Karat et al. 1995). Because of delays in our own work and the short life of the project we studied, this evaluation actually proved to be quite retrospective: eighteen months after the target project had been canceled. But we were interested to find whether a system like Raison d'Etre could possibly be a tool for designers to manage their collaborations, could support communication of information and perspectives among team-members, and could enhance collaborative dynamics.

We carried out a "think-aloud" study, asking eight of the original team members to work with the system while making a running commentary of their goals and plans, actions and reactions. First, we asked each designer to recall information on selected topics; we prompted them, "What did you think about <some issue>?," "What did <someone else> think about it?" Next, we asked each to explore this topic using the system. Finally, we asked each to assess the information provided by the system on the particular topic, and the access to and presentation of that information in the system. Each of these sessions took about two hours.

Our plan was to guide the designers to explore a range of topics in this manner, including at least one technical issue, at least one human issue, and at least one general issue (for example, "How did the issues identified when team members looked ahead in the project actually work out?"). However, we observed more spontaneous use than expected, and often did not need our preplanned task suggestions. In general, team members liked the system and suggested many ways in which something like it might support their design work. They created their own stories by selecting among speakers, topics, and times in a variety of ways.

Many of the behaviors and judgments we observed bear out and elaborate the claims we identified. Recall, for example, the Video Information claim. There was abundant evidence that the designers appreciated the richness of video. After reading the text of a clip, one of the designers said, "Let's see with what conviction he says this," and then viewed the video. Another read the transcript and then viewed a "frustration" clip, commenting, "You couldn't get 'frustration' out of that unless you sat down and looked at it." Another said: "I learn a lot looking at myself"; still another said that the video "made the information worthwhile."

The designers also emphasized the downside content of the Video Information claim: "It is more informative to see people, but it takes longer." Most developed a strategy of initially scanning at least some of the transcript before deciding to view the video. Some referred to the length of clips, more readily viewing briefer clips, but first reading the transcript for lengthier ones. Some referred to the content of clips, tending to read technical clips ("I'm more interested in what they are saying than how they said it"), but to view human issues clips ("some stuff I just want to see").

The prominent time line in the user interface called attention to project history and seemed to be easily understood and controlled. However, the very coarse and purely relative model of time presented through this interface control was in other respects not satisfactory. In many cases, the designers had trouble deciding within which of the three interview rounds a clip or topic might have occurred, but at the same time they were able to produce lots of temporal information (such as the approximate date or various contemporaneous events). This convinced us to use absolute, not relative time (for example, we labeled a time period as First Quarter 1992 instead of just as "second of three") and incorporate temporal landmarking (to indicate in the time line dates of certain watershed events) in a subsequent design history system (Carroll et al. 1995).

A variety of observations bear out and elaborate aspects of the Browsing History claim. The team members we studied felt that Raison d'Etre could help teams manage a variety of their activities. Interestingly, one of the chief roles they saw for systems like Raison d'Etre was in design education. They judged that using such a tool could "significantly" decrease the time it takes new members to attain familiarity with technical issues and social aspects (personalities, collaborative dynamics), that it could "speed the transition to productivity," as one person put it. One designer, playing the role of a new member, explored a technical issue and discovered a somewhat negative comment about the approach to that issue advocated by another member. He commented that if he were in fact new to the project, he "would want to go and talk to him about that as soon as possible."

The designers felt that Raison d'Etre could enhance communication between management and other members of the team. We observed clear tendencies for nonmanager team members to explore what their managers had to say, particularly about the project vision, and for managers to see what the people reporting to them had to say, often checking what their frustrations were. Most team members agreed that these were things people would find out by directly asking, but it seemed clear that this did not happen in every case. "I never knew he thought that" (a response to a clip from one of the managers) and "That may have been more of a problem than I thought" (a response by one of managers to a clip from a designer reporting to him) were examples.

The designers also agreed that the system could help maintain focus and group vision in a distributed team. They commented that Raison d'Etre might help "to make sure people understood what the project direction was," that is, to help keep a team focused on common goals, and that the system would be useful in "keeping track of issues that were outstanding." They particularly emphasized the potential utility of such a system for supporting reflection within the context of design work. "There are times when you want to go back and remind yourself what was said and done. Seeing people talking about it themselves adds an extra dimension, a feel for the process leading up to the decision."

Because scenarios are rich descriptions, they may be better at evoking images, reactions, and new lines of thought in designers than function-level requirements. We have found it very natural to use scenarios genera-tively. Even a relatively small set of such scenarios can provide lots of direction in a design project (Carroll and Rosson 1990). Just a single scenario is an obvious and immediate design resource. It highlights the goals of people in such a situation, some of the things a person might do, aspects of the activity that are successful and erroneous, what interpreta-tion people make about what happens to them.

This chapter described our efforts to take scenarios more seriously in design, managing usability and usefulness by making *use itself* a design representation. We used scenarios to describe existing situations as design problems and opportunities, to codify and analyze requirements, and to plan envisioned situations. We found it useful and convenient to integrate the development of requirements and specifications in this way. We also used scenarios to communicate the concerns and objectives of our project among ourselves and with the team we studied, from whom we obtained content material for our system and by whom our system was to be used. We found it worthwhile to maintain diverse perspectives, even on fairly central issues. We analyzed some of these scenarios in terms of underlying trade-offs and consequences for the people in Raison d'Etre usage situations. We were able to generalize claims embodied in our scenarios, and implicit in our design. Finally, we used scenarios both to design our evaluation study and interpret its results with respect to design rationale.

I hope the Raison d'Etre example makes more concrete both the challenging properties of design problem solving, described in chapter 2, and the ways that scenarios can help address the challenges of design, described in chapter 3. This is not to say that Raison d'Etre is representative of all software design, or that it is a paragon of what design work can be. Its role here is to illustrate and to raise questions. The next several chapters describe a more developed example of scenario-based design from a different domain of interactive software systems.

5

Example: Programming Tutorial and Tools

Much of our design work in the past fifteen years has addressed instructional problems. We have pursued the grail of making people wise very quickly, of helping them to develop practical computer skills and enjoy doing so. The principal design example we consider through the next several chapters is an instructional system called MiTTS (Minimalist Tutorial and Tools for Smalltalk). MiTTS is a discovery learning curriculum aimed at supporting experienced procedural programmers who are just getting started with object-oriented programming in the Smalltalk language (Goldberg 1984; Goldberg and Robson 1983). A key element of the MiTTS design is to involve learners immediately in the realistic task of analyzing and enhancing a small graphical application—to allow them to learn by doing.

The tutorial was designed to balance the pedagogical objectives of providing directive guidance for people undertaking this technical learning task and providing encouragement to them for initiating, pursuing, and evaluating their own learning goals. Thus, we attempted to make our instructional materials sparse, using explicit step-by-step procedures only when a task was very complex and very novel. To assist learners in tracking their progress in our relatively open-ended instructional tasks, we provided considerable checkpointing information, as well as a variety of error recognition and recovery support.

MiTTS employs a spiral curriculum design (Bruner 1966) in which learners explore a particular example application several times in successively greater depth. First, they analyze the application at a purely functional level; that is, they analyze the relations among software design objects without examining the Smalltalk code that implements these objects. Next, they analyze the application along with its user interface, still at the functional level. They then analyze the application code, and implement an enhancement to this code. Finally they analyze and enhance the user interface code. At the end of the tutorial, learners are given several new projects, along with very open-ended suggestions for ways in which to test and expand the skills and knowledge they have acquired from the tutorial.

MiTTS incorporates two interactive programming tools. The Bittitalk Browser simplifies the Smalltalk class hierarchy browser by providing access only to project-relevant structures and code (Rosson, Carroll, and Bellamy 1990). In the early spirals of the curriculum, the tool hides the code details to encourage learners to focus on the overall functional design. A second tool, the View Matcher, specializes the Smalltalk system debugger tool to coordinate multiple run-time views of the example application. It specifically leverages the prior experience that procedural programmers have with procedure call stacks as a vehicle for learning about object message passing (Carroll et al. 1990).

Design Context

The direct inspiration for the MiTTS project came from a specific usage episode. In early 1988, I was relaxing with a simple chess program—the one bundled with TurboPascal. The program's evaluation metric for planning its moves was tragically flawed; in certain circumstances, it would impetuously sacrifice a rook for a pawn. There was no apparent strategy behind this behavior, no hope of gaining an advantage; it merely extended the game by one move, and more definitively settled its outcome. This is the kind of incident that makes people want to study artificial intelligence. What kind of otherwise-sensible rules could combine to produce this bizarre play?

TurboPascal obligingly provided source code for the chess program, which made it possible in principle to pursue this question. Of course, the program was relatively large and complex and had very few in-line comments. Finding and understanding the code for wasting rooks would be a classic case of 1970s-style noninteractive debugging: reading the text, making changes, recompiling, testing, and iterating. A further complication was that I was not a Pascal programmer, though I knew similar procedural programming languages. More decisive complication was that this was 1988, and too late in the history of the world to be spending time on noninteractive debugging.

This episode became a touchstone design scenario for us and was incorporated into our thinking about the problem of teaching object-oriented software technology to experienced procedural programmers. In the late 1980s this was an outstanding technical problem in the software industry, particularly in IBM, where I was employed at the time. When we started the MiTTS project, many procedural programmers were being asked to adopt the object paradigm, but many difficulties were reported. We read and heard many stories about confident and experienced programmers' plunging into self-study tutorials, only to give up in frustration after several hours, still wondering, "Where is the application code?" The object paradigm, in which program control is distributed across a set of tightly encapsulated and high-function software objects, was alien to experts in procedural design.

In our lab, we observed and interviewed programmers who had been working to learn the Smalltalk language and environment (Campbell 1990; Nielsen and Richards 1989; Rosson and Carroll 1990; see also O'Shea et al. 1986). We identified several key issues in terms of typical scenarios of Smalltalk programming skill (Campbell 1990). One issue was the novelty and complexity of what needed to be learned. The language itself is easily understood; anyone with programming language background can learn the basic syntax within a few minutes. However, to use Smalltalk fluently, a programmer must become familiar with a huge class hierarchy and with the tools of a sophisticated interactive programming environment. New programmers often became lost in the hierarchy or spent considerable time in unfocused exploration of the interactive tools.

Programming in Smalltalk consists of orchestrating the interaction of computational "objects." Classes are abstract objects that define the generic behaviors (methods) and attributes (variables) of their instances. A message sent to a class object triggers the execution of a corresponding class method; most class messages are instantiation requests, creating new instances of the class. Instances are specified by their classes, but can also inherit behaviors and attributes from their superclasses—classes higher in the hierarchy. Messages sent to instances trigger the corresponding instance methods. Typically, instance method execution results in state changes (changes in the values of instance variables) as well as in additional messages being sent to other objects (objects accessible to the sender by means of instance variables or global variables). Programming in Smalltalk is adding, refining, and testing classes and methods in the class hierarchy.

Smalltalk's interactive environment encourages a programming process that integrates analysis, design, and implementation. Identifying relevant objects and their message protocols is a major programming task. The central tool is the Class Hierarchy Browser, which provides editing access to all objects, including those that define the language and the environment. Smalltalk also includes an interactive Debugger that allows programmers to decompose nestings of message sends in various ways, and an Inspector that provides access to the structure of current instances (recall the specification of the debugger in box 2.3). In a typical scenario, a Smalltalk programmer might execute test code in a Workspace, observe its direct results in the behavior of an application object, explore the stack of messages sent in this episode using the Debugger, inspect objects that were created using the Inspector, and edit code in the Class Hierarchy Browser.

Figure 5.1 shows a Smalltalk session in which a programmer is using the Class Hierarchy Browser and the System Debugger to work with a graphical gomoku game. The programmer is debugging a method that takes a selected square for the player. The programmer has caused a halt in execution by inserting the expression `self halt` at the beginning of this squareSelected: method, and is browsing the method execution stack and instance variables. For example, the variable `square`, which identifies the square the player has selected, has the value "4@4." This square is still vacant in the game board; the halt was encountered at the beginning of the squareSelected: method.

A second issue we identified was *motivation*. Experienced programmers came to the Smalltalk environment excited about its reputation as a platform for rapid prototyping of graphical applications. However, the user interface functionality in Smalltalk comprises some of the most

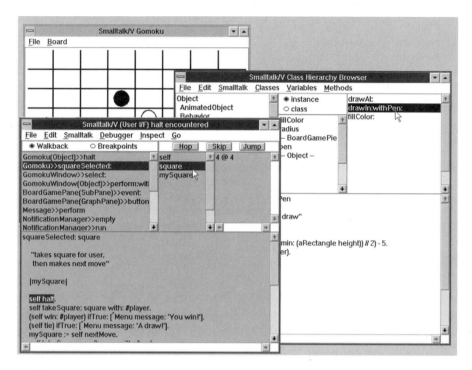

Figure 5.1
Smalltalk session illustrating the Class Hierarchy Browser and System Debugger tools

complex code in the system, and ironically, new programmers are advised to set aside their driving interests in prototyping and user interfaces, and instead spend days or weeks learning about fairly traditional data structure classes like Collection and Array. Many programmers found this demoralizing.

A third issue concerns the importance of *design*. For most language-learning situations, an experienced programmer already has relevant design knowledge, which can be applied to problems in the new language. In our case, prior knowledge of the object-oriented design paradigm was precisely what was missing. The key to building object-oriented applications is learning to distribute functionality across a set of cooperating objects. To learn to do this, programmers need to see and analyze paradigmatic object-oriented designs and attain familiarity with a sufficient variety of software components so that they can generate their own designs. However, most learners, and most instruction in object-oriented design, began with the simpler task of analyzing and building individual objects. Unfortunately, this approach often deferred design concerns so long that programmers began falling back on their prior design experience before they ever grasped the essence of the new paradigm.

Design Analysis

Scenarios helped us to clarify our design concerns and objectives for MiTTS. They included Smalltalk learning scenarios we observed in our laboratory, those we gathered reports about from colleagues in IBM and elsewhere, those we inferred from reading Smalltalk tutorials, and our own touchstone scenario. This material was a mixture of problem statement (circumstances we wanted to transform and improve through design, and vision statement) and learner activities we wanted to emphasize and support.

We were struck by the prescribed learning scenarios built into the tutorial for the most popular version of Smalltalk (at that time), Digitalk's Smalltalk/V. These tutorial scenarios were designed to lead the programmer through a series of step-by-step exercises and an assortment of analogies to procedural programming concepts, as suggested in box 5.1. Message sending among objects is indeed a crucial concept in Smalltalk, and the exercise does provide a means of beginning to fathom it. But the activity is quite trivial for an experienced programmer. For us, this scenario foregrounded and concretized the objective of designing instructional tasks that are meaningful and significant to the learner.

We reworked our touchstone scenario, focusing attention on how interactive investigation of intriguing program behavior could become an effective learning activity. This led us to consider building example applications that deliberately incorporated quirky behaviors, and software tools and interactive documentation to guide analysis and redesign activities. Indeed, this initial reflection on the scenarios we had observed, inferred, and experienced pretty much defined our design approach. Our conjecture was that the Smalltalk learning issues of complexity, motivation, and design could be addressed by creating instruction centered on debugging and modifying small but intriguing interactive applications.

Box 5.1
Activities from Smalltalk tutorial (Digitalk 1990, pp. 45–46).

- Chapter 3: The programmer reads that objects and messages are the basis for Smalltalk computations; that global and temporary variables will be introduced.
- The programmer reads that objects are analogous to pieces of data in other languages, and sees examples of strings, integers, characters, and arrays.
- The programmer reads that you send messages to objects in order to make things happen in Smalltalk, that messages are similar to function calls.
- The programmer evaluates three correct expressions (e.g., 20 factorial).
- The programmer evaluates an incorrect expression: "20" factorial.

This design analysis did not pop out of thin air. Our reflections on the Smalltalk scenarios extended a foundation of instructional design work we had carried out through the prior decade. In the early 1980s, we had discovered that new users of information systems often suffered not from too little support but from too much of the wrong kind of support. We had noticed that people often experience profound difficulties in using what seem to be carefully designed materials. We came to view this not merely as bad design, but as indicative of a fundamental paradox of sense making (Carroll and Rosson 1987): to be able to interact meaningfully, a person must develop relevant skills and understanding, but to develop skills and understanding, a person needs to engage in meaningful interaction.

The paradox of sense making essentially tells us that some of the very things that make human intelligence so awesome—capacities that create order out of rich and chaotic situations—can manifest as formidable problems in using ostensibly well-crafted instruction and documentation. For example, people can learn by doing (which is great), but they often act too impulsively. People can learn by thinking and reasoning, by creating and testing their own hypotheses about how things work. However, they often focus too narrowly, too shallowly, or on the peripheral aspects of situations they are trying to analyze. People learn through working toward goals that are meaningful to them, but they tend to compromise on rote steps and overlook small details—which is less of a problem in the physical world than it is in the relatively brittle electronic world. People learn by analogy and assimilation, building on their prior knowledge in developing new understanding. However, what they already know often conflicts with what they are trying to learn. People learn by recognizing, diagnosing, and recovering from their own errors; errors are an extremely important learning opportunity. However, errors can be subtle and can tangle into situations no beginner can realistically hope to analyze or correct.

We developed the minimalist approach to exploit human sense making in the design of information (Carroll 1990a, 1998). For example, in response to the apparent preference people have for learning by doing, the minimalist approach urges that designers ensure that people can quickly begin acting, working on realistic projects. It responds to the predilection of people to learn by thinking and reasoning by urging that designers rely on people to do just that. It responds to the need people have to learn through working toward goals that are meaningful by embedding information to be learned in real tasks. It responds to the tendency people have for building on their prior knowledge by specifically trying to take advantage of what learners already know. And it responds to the fact that people often learn from mistakes by supporting and managing error recognition, diagnosis and, recovery.

All designers build on their prior work. In our case, design reflection was guided by cumulative work. We had a library of specific presentation techniques and learner activities from our tutorials and other instructional systems. These projects had also been generalized into principles of learning and designing to support learning. Thus, we were able to analyze and reconceive our Smalltalk scenarios in very specific directions: to support rapid engagement in and learner-initiated reasoning about realistic programming tasks. We wanted to take advantage of what learners might already know, but also ensure that error recognition, diagnosis, and recovery would be tractable and valuable.

Envisionment: Bittitalk Browser

The first scenario we envisioned for what ultimately became MiTTS was a reworking of the TurboChess touchstone scenario (box 5.2; see Carroll 1990a, pp. 267–272). The scenario is an improvement in that the pro-

Box 5.2
A MiTTS touchstone design scenario

- The programmer plays gomoku, noticing that occasionally the program makes a double move.
- The programmer steps through the execution of the game, reading the code for methods placed in the execution stack.
- One method accesses a variable named "steal," skipping the player's move whenever steal is equal to zero.
- Further investigation reveals that steal is an instance of Counter, initialized with a value ranging from 1 to 5, and decremented on each move.
- The programmer removes all reference to steal and saves the changed method. The game plays without stealing moves.

---

grammer is able to investigate the intriguing behavior of a gomoku game interactively. This investigation involves systematically reading through the code for methods in the execution stack, inspecting instance variables, modifying method code, and testing. It is learner initiated and requires creative problem solving. It also depends on prior programming knowledge, for example, knowledge about types of variables and flow of execution. It constitutes a paradigmatic, albeit simple, cycle of real Smalltalk programming, not merely a practice exercise.

This scenario is a concrete response to concerns about trivial and rote learning activities, such as that in box 5.1. But it is also rough: it was only the beginning of our design. For example, the scenario in box 5.2 addresses our original concern about learner motivation, but does not address concerns about complexity. The programmer (apparently) has to deal with all of the Smalltalk tools, the Debugger, the Inspector, the Class Hierarchy Browser, and workspaces. It only tangentially addresses concerns about design. The programmer is working with a design, but at a very low level and with a rather brute-force approach (merely removing references to an unwanted function).

One line of envisionment we pursued with respect to the complexity issue was the Bittitalk Browser. Code development in Smalltalk involves the navigation, understanding, and modification of a huge hierarchical class and method library. The central tool for this is the Class Hierarchy Browser. To learn anything significant about Smalltalk and to do anything significant with Smalltalk, one needs to use this tool. However, the view of Smalltalk provided by the Class Hierarchy Browser is that of a huge indented list (figure 5.1). The version of Smalltalk we were using in 1988 included over fourteen hundred system-defined methods; since that time the basic system has grown substantially. And of course any Smalltalk programming has the ineluctable effect of increasing the number of classes and methods.

From the standpoint of our touchstone design scenario, this is a nightmare. Smalltalk "programs" are ensembles of objects, distributed throughout the class hierarchy, that work together by means of message passing to produce computations. The various participating objects are each defined within the class hierarchy, but they are not differentiated in any way from all the other objects defined there. Thus, finding out why gomoku makes a quirky move is potentially far *more* difficult than it would have been in Pascal. In Pascal, one at least knows exactly where to find the relevant code. In Smalltalk, finding the relevant code is a major part of the task.

The Bittitalk Browser, designed in collaboration with Mary Beth Rosson, Rachel Bellamy, and Eric Gold, segregates the objects participating in an application by providing a filtered view of the Smalltalk class hierarchy. The Bittitalk Browser *is* a Class Hierarchy Browser, but one in which only the classes and methods tagged as belonging to a given application are displayed. This is a simple idea, but it has dramatic effect on the touchstone scenario. For example, in a blackjack game we built for instructional purposes, the Bittitalk view included forty-two methods; it filtered out 97 percent of the methods in the class hierarchy, methods irrelevant to understanding the blackjack application.

Figure 5.2 shows a Bittitalk Browser opened on the blackjack game. The upper left pane of the browser displays a filtered view of the Smalltalk class hierarchy, providing access to the classes relevant to the blackjack game. The BlackJack class is selected. The upper right pane of the browser displays the instance methods for the selected class; the hitMe method is selected. The lower pane displays the Smalltalk code that implements this method. This code reveals, for example, that the hitMe method sends the message takeCard: to the player if the Boolean player-

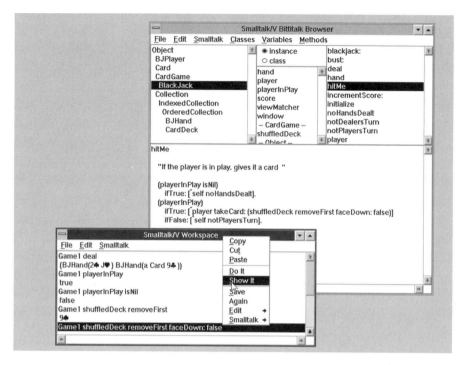

Figure 5.2
The Bittitalk Browser provides a view of the Smalltalk class hierarchy including only the classes and methods that play a role in the given application

InPlay is true. The message has as its argument the first card of a shuffled deck, dealt face up. As can be seen in the Workspace tool, the card the player got was the nine of spades.

We developed the Bittitalk Browser concept by systematically analyzing a space of techniques for controlling the complexity of user interfaces (Carroll and Kellogg 1989; Carroll, Kellogg, and Rosson 1991). We of course knew function dimming, as used in the Macintosh interface: dimmed functions are displayed as gray in menus, but cannot be selected (that is, executing selection actions has no effect). We analyzed this as a good technique for experienced computer users: menus have consistent layouts, but syntactically inappropriate functions cannot be accessed. We had developed the function-blocking technique in earlier work (Carroll and Carrithers 1984): blocked functions appear in menus and can be selected, but the selection of a blocked function merely evokes a message stating that the function is not available. As in the case of function dimming, the user can pursue other actions. We analyzed this as a good technique for learners: specific feedback is provided indicating that the selection was successful, but that the function is not appropriate in this circumstance—perhaps provoking further analysis. We chose a stronger approach, that of function hiding: classes and methods were selectively removed from the user interface. We wanted to protect learners from the consequences of errors, but also to conceal initially the sheer number of classes and methods to avoid intimidating or distracting them.

In inventing the Bittitalk Browser, we were chiefly guided by the complexity issue. Displaying only a small number of classes and methods makes the indented list representation of the class hierarchy a manageable view of the relevant code. A programmer who wishes to explore the blackjack game in order to understand various aspects of its behavior can browse the code implementing the methods for each of the blackjack classes, and trace the message-sending relationships among the classes to unpack the computations underlying game-level behaviors. This is just not a reasonable beginner task when hundreds or thousands of classes and methods are displayed.

Our development of the Bittitalk Browser idea also helped us with respect to the design issue. Given a Bittitalk Browser, programmers might choose to hand-simulate simple executions, not even involving the interactive Inspector and Debugger tools. This suggests a scenario variant of box 5.2 in which the programmer studies the static code structures in order to understand and modify the program. Such an activity might be a very powerful way to help programmers more directly appreciate the design of the game objects, as opposed to their run-time interactions, as detailed in the Debugger. On the other hand, this line of thinking also underscored for us the importance of highly paradigmatic example applications. Object-oriented software typically models its application domain. Thus, the objects of the blackjack game design are players, hands, cards, decks, blackjacks, and so forth. But it is not always obvious what should be an object; for example, should the player and the dealer be separate objects, should the dealer be a specialization of player, or should the dealer be incorporated into an overall game object?

Envisionment: View Matcher

The View Matcher was our most direct attempt to envision the scenario in box 5.2; it was our most direct attempt to address the motivation issue. Our idea was to coordinate the Smalltalk Class Hierarchy, Debugger, and Inspector tools within a single window. The programmer can interact with a graphical application and at the same time browse various aspects of the running code that implements the application—for example, the stack of methods currently executing and the source code and instance variable values for the currently selected method in the stack. The programmer can edit the code for a method and immediately see the changed code and its effects on subsequent application execution. We hoped that supporting scenarios like box 5.2 with a single, integrated browser would make the various tools more accessible and that coordinating the tools would help programmers learn through their experiences.

We developed several prototypes of the View Matcher; figure 5.3 displays the version incorporated in MiTTS. The Application View in the upper right displays the blackjack game's user interface, a menu bar and listpanes for the current player and dealer hands. The View Matcher does not alter the graphics or execution of the application it presents; the Application View runs in its own window and acts exactly as it would were the application to be started without the browser.

In the upper left is the Stack View, displaying the methods currently waiting to execute. As in the Debugger, the parenthesized names to the left of the angle brackets in the method stack specify the classes that define these methods. So, for example, a BJWindow object inherits performMenuItem: from the ApplicationWindow class description. The names to the right of the angle brackets are the names of the methods that are being invoked. The View Matcher updates the Stack View whenever the expression `self viewMatcherHalt` occurs in the currently executing method.

The stack can be displayed in two modes, Animate and Halted Stack (selected via the menu bar). Halted Stack mode stops the application each time a `self viewMatcherHalt` expression is executed. The learner may select "resume" in the Stack View's pane menu to continue, or may explore the state of the application using the other View Matcher views.

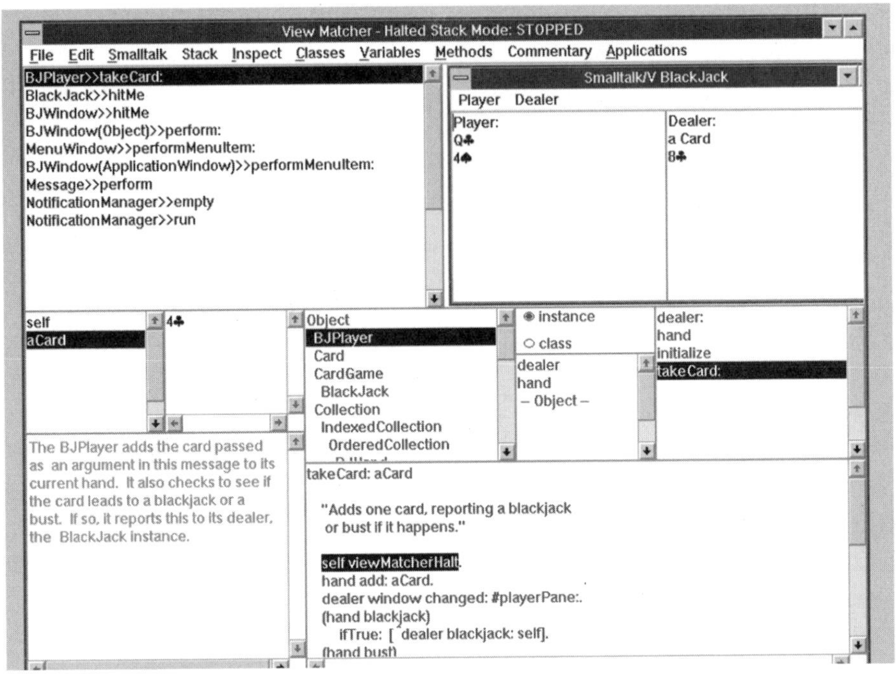

Figure 5.3
View Matcher

Animate mode displays the same method stack as Halted Stack mode, but places each method on the stack as it begins execution and removes it when it finishes execution. Thus, the learner can interact with the application without Halt interruptions and "watch" the execution of each user interface interaction (at the level of message sends). Animate mode serves as an orientation to the more analytical, but also more tedious, explorations afforded by Halted Stack mode.

The panes in the bottom right of the View Matcher comprise a Bittitalk Browser. In this Bittitalk View, only the classes pertaining to the application are displayed (the classes for the blackjack game model and user interface). The two panes immediately beneath the Stack View comprise the Inspector View. The left-hand pane displays, for a selected method, the method's receiver and the temporary variables. Selecting an item in the left-hand pane results in the value of that item being displayed in the right-hand pane (in figure 5.3 the value of aCard is the four of clubs). As in the Debugger, instance variables of the receiver of the current message may be accessed by inspecting it.

Smalltalk methods sometimes include a comment describing their behavior, but these are of limited use in discerning the role a method plays in a specific application context. We incorporated a Commentary View into the View Matcher (bottom left), coupling a natural language explanation with the Smalltalk code representations in the Bittitalk View. The comments provide functional role information oriented to the programmer's interaction with the application and to the relations between classes and methods in application execution (for example, relations between the application model and the user interface). Commentary can be provided when an application is installed in the View Matcher. However, people using the View Matcher can also add their own notes to (or substitute their own notes for) the initially provided commentaries.

Actions in one View Matcher view can have direct consequences for other views. In the Stack View, selecting a method causes all other views to display their view of the selected method. For example, the Inspector View displays the method's receiver and temporary variables; the receiver is selected and its value displayed in the right-hand pane. At the same time, the Bittitalk View displays the method code and its location in the hierarchy; the code currently being executed is highlighted in the method text pane. The Commentary View displays relevant commentary. The learner can explore the Bittitalk View directly, that is, without making a selection in the Stack View. In this case, the method selected in the Bittitalk View would determine the coordinated views (the method previously selected in the Stack View becomes grayed out). More powerfully, the chain of execution can be traced by selecting methods in the Stack View in turn, understanding these methods through the use of coordinated views, and making changes to methods in the Bittitalk View to observe effects on application execution.

In developing the View Matcher design, we worked with several specific scenarios. For example, the original design did not permanently display an Inspector and did not incorporate a Bittitalk Browser (Carroll; 1990a). As we worked through usage scenarios, we concluded that these views would be useful to programmers trying to analyze running code. We also focused on just what programmers would learn from given View

Matcher interactions. For example, the steal scenario in box 5.2 motivates the programmer to analyze a series of messages and learn about the Counter class. We developed two additional scenarios in which the programmer learns how point-and-click and text entry interactions are reported to the application model and how the model updates the user interface display (Carroll et al. 1990). Both of these key scenarios were similar to the touchstone scenario in that the learning activity was motivated by a realistic programming challenge.

In inventing the View Matcher we were addressing the motivation and complexity issues. In part, we did this by reframing the problem. We took a strongly minimalist view of basic concepts and skills. We assumed prior knowledge about problem solving with formal representations; knowledge about functions, variables, control relationships, and so forth—even some awareness of object-oriented software concepts like message passing and inheritance. After all, the View Matcher was designed for experienced programmers; we took the sketchiness of box 5.2 seriously. We focused on supporting immediate, concrete programming activity, interactive analysis, and enhancement of a running application that could show programmers how Smalltalk computations work. The learning activities in the View Matcher *are* the prototyping activities that new Smalltalk programmers want to undertake.

The View Matcher recruits the resources of the system itself as the basis for an integrated, exploratory learning environment. The tools employed in the View Matcher *are* the major system tools of the Smalltalk environment. Permanently displaying and jointly updating a tiled palette of these tools helps programmers find the tools and understand how they work. This simplified view of the Smalltalk environment provides scaffolding (Bruner 1973) for subsequent interactions with the full system environment.

Easing the complexity of the Smalltalk environment also helps to ease the complexity of the Smalltalk language. For example, polymorphism and dynamic binding are central to Smalltalk. The response of an object to a given message can vary depending on the class of that object, which is not fixed until run time. Accordingly, a static analysis of methods associated with an object often cannot unambiguously determine which other classes of objects it interacts with during the course of a particular computation. These techniques are especially prominent in the coordination between application models and their user interfaces. The View Matcher permits an application to be browsed as it executes, allowing the interface protocol dynamics to be interactively browsed and analyzed. This illustrates how our evolving touchstone scenario led us to address issues that were not, and indeed could not have been, part of the original analysis of the TurboChess scenario.

Development: MiTTS

The touchstone scenario—analyzed as a minimalist instruction scenario and then envisioned with the Bittitalk Browser and the View Matcher—helped us to identify key issues and define our design approach. But the touchstone scenario is just one view of the tip of an iceberg. There are other instructional scenarios and other instructional contexts in which to analyze and develop the touchstone scenario. We were particularly interested in permuting the touchstone scenario into the context of a tutorial package. The Bittitalk Browser and the View Matcher were initially conceived as stand-alone tools for guided exploration; we wanted to investigate roles for them in a minimalist curriculum for Smalltalk.

In a tutorial scenario, specific goals and activities are suggested to learners. The minimalist approach emphasizes active learning. It streamlines read-only activities by building on the learner's prior knowledge of real tasks and relying on learner discovery. This tutorial context is very compatible with programming work in general and with the touchstone scenario in particular. We wanted to design tutorial activities that are strongly work oriented. We had already studied many minimalist tutorial scenarios in domains other than Smalltalk programming; thus we had in hand a model for developing minimalist scenarios and a stake in assessing and further developing the model through developing and evaluating a specific case (chapter 8 develops this point in more detail).

The MiTTS curriculum is a structured programming project. The learner does real programming work in the sense of understanding and developing software that does something meaningful. Reading about the syntax of message sending or about the distinction between classes and instances can enable real programming work, but is not itself real work.

Similarly, practice exercises on the creation and manipulation of Collections or Bags (Smalltalk system classes) in a Workspace with no task-oriented agenda for their use and exploration of various system tools for the sake of learning how they work can enable real work but are not themselves real work.

The project in MiTTS is a blackjack game, designed to be simple to understand and modify, fun to use and explore, and paradigmatic with respect to important characteristics of Smalltalk (such as the use of inheritance, different kinds of instance variables, and message sending) and its environment (Inspectors, Debuggers, the Class Hierarchy Browser). We hoped that most programmers using MiTTS would already be familiar with blackjack and would thereby be able to focus on the Smalltalk-specific aspects of the game and to leverage their knowledge of the game to investigate the program. For example, we expected this prior knowledge to help learners orient to the application model entities (CardGame, BlackJack, Card, CardDeck, Hand, BJplayer, etc.).

One of the key ideas in MiTTS is that of a spiral design (Bruner 1966). Learners successively revisit the blackjack project in increasing depth. This is schematized in box 5.3. In the first tutorial topic, learners use a Workspace and the Bittitalk Browser to explore the blackjack model; they create a BlackJack game object and play a game by sending messages to it. They do not see Smalltalk code; the methods in the Bittitalk Browser are defined only by method comments; the code is not displayed. In the second topic, learners explore the interactions between the model and its user interface. They use the View Matcher tool, but as in topic 1, do not see Smalltalk code. In both of these first two instructional topics, the learners can focus on only the software design–level interactions among methods and classes, since they have no access to the code.

In the second two topics, we provided access to code. In topic 3, learners use a Workspace and the Bittitalk Browser to enhance the blackjack game, analyzing and modifying the code in game object methods (a method is the code evaluated when a message is sent). In topic 4 they again expand their focus to the game plus its user interface; they use the View Matcher to understand the code-level mechanisms of this interaction and to introduce and verify changes in the user interface code.

The sequencing of activities in MiTTS is overdetermined; we wanted to demonstrate two important concepts of Smalltalk programming practice

Box 5.3
Four instructional topics of the MiTTS curriculum

	Topic 1	Topic 2	Topic 3	Topic 4
Activity	Explore blackjack game; create BlackJack object and play game by sending messages to it	Explore game plus its user interface; observe message passing behind user interface interactions	Enhance blackjack game; analyze and modify game object methods	Enhance game plus its user interface; analyze and modify user interface display
Tools	Workspace and Bittitalk Browser; object and method names, but no code	View Matcher; object and method names, but no code	Workspace and Bittitalk Browser; code accessible	View Matcher; code accessible

simultaneously. First, having learners initially work on the blackjack project on a purely functional basis—that is, without access to code—implicitly conveyed to them that this is possible and productive. Programmers play and analyze the game by creating objects, sending messages, and observing the results. By abstracting away from execution details, this activity emphasizes design-level thinking. In subsequent topics, we spiraled back through similar activities but gave learners access to the code. This sequencing demonstrates the paradigmatic relationship between design and implementation in Smalltalk programming: the priority of design.

A second lesson conveyed by the sequencing of topics is the distinction between an application model and its user interface. This distinction is one of the fundamental architectural ideas of Smalltalk, but it is enforced only by the design of the class hierarchy and good programming practices. The conventional wisdom is that the model and user interface should be separate, they should communicate only through standard protocols, and the design of the model should determine or constrain the design of the user interface (Goldberg 1990). MiTTS itself models this programming practice by having programmers work first with a model-only application view and then subsequently with the model plus user interface. This is the relationship between topics 1 and 2, and between topics 3 and 4, respectively.

The overall sequencing of topics 1 through 4 is a very constrained scenario structure. Within the bounds of this overall structure, we wanted MiTTS to be very lightweight, brief, and practical—just enough to get programmers going on their own. We challenged ourselves to produce a basic foundation of Smalltalk programming skill within four hours. The instructional manual we designed for the four topics was only thirty pages long. The introduction, for example, was a single page, most of it directed at preparing the learner to accept the idea of learning by doing at a fast clip. The text for each topic was kept to an absolute minimum, incorporating only as much explanation as was needed for learners to accomplish and make sense of the overall programming tasks. We wanted to rely on learners to reason and improvise. For example, a hint appears: "If you bust, you can reevaluate BJ deal to start a new hand." The learners have evaluated code, but to use the hint, they need to recall on their own that doing so involves selecting an expression and executing the Show It command.

We included open-ended questions and activities within each topic. We directed learners to the Stack View, suggesting that other information displayed in the View Matcher (the commentary, the method comment, and code) could help them interpret the stacked messages. Indeed, the entire topic of inheritance was treated in this fashion; although passing mention was made of inheritance in working with the blackjack game, direct exploration of the inheritance relationships implicit in the Black-Jack class structure was encouraged only through a few open-ended suggestions at the end of the first topic. Topic 5 is an advanced "on your own" piece (not described in box 5.3) that users are given to take away with them; it includes a refined version of our original gomoku project and a bibliography database project.

By walking through the tutorial topics and testing them, we were able to anticipate potential problem spots. We used checkpointing descriptions to help learners coordinate their activity with the state of the system. Immediately after an instruction (for example, "Click twice at the beginning of the line"), we provided a description of what the screen should look like (e.g., `Game1 := BlackJack newGame` becomes highlighted"). In general, when learners were asked to perform an action, the corresponding explanation began with a simple description of what the consequence of the action should have been (for example, what object should have been returned by sending a message). This was to help them recognize whether they had carried out the intended action. MiTTS also had a general recovery mechanism: all the code required for each topic was packaged on a separate diskette. If an intractable problem was encountered, one could always reload the topic, and begin again.

Deployment and Evaluation

Scenarios do not always run as designed. The real context of work activity is more complex and less deterministic than the scenarios that describe it or envision it. Nevertheless, if a design has been envisioned and planned in terms of activities it will support, it is more evident how to understand and make use of obtained scenarios that depart from the design scenarios.

For example, we observed that programmers had difficulty with Smalltalk's interaction techniques. Our own design concerns were not at this level. However, the mechanics of scrolling or resizing windows often distracted attention from that with which we were concerned: exploration of BlackJack. Our initial response was to refine the introduction of these interaction techniques in our materials. We observed where the need for a technique would first arise and provided succinct hints at just that point in the scenario. We enclosed the hint texts in boxes to increase their initial salience and facilitate later reference. Although this helped, referring back to hints itself was a distraction for learners, and thus compromised the organization of the manual. Ultimately we generated an interaction tips sheet, separate from the manual, which learners could refer to whenever a need arose. In our situation, this seemed to minimize the distraction of interaction techniques and allow the learners to concentrate on programming tasks.

In a spiral curriculum design, each topic builds on previous learning experiences. Thus, the transitions between topic activities are crucial junctures. Our design envisioned how we wanted the topic spiral to work (box 5.3), but the transitions were in fact more problematic than we had anticipated. For example, we initially tried to ease the transition from topic 1 to topic 2 by providing a history mode in the View Matcher. In this mode, the Stack View displayed a history list of messages sent in playing the blackjack game. Our thinking was that this kind of record would be familiar to people who had just finished topic 1, in which they worked with many of these messages. The history list was in fact easy to understand, but it interfered with subsequent View Matcher interactions—that is, with understanding the halted stack mode. This led us to replace history mode with an animate mode: as people interacted with the game, the stack was continuously updated (ironically, this mode had already been incorporated in our earlier, stand-alone View Matcher). Animate mode provided an advance organizer for the halted stack mode used in the balance of the topic 2 scenario; we introduced it with an analogy to procedure calls.

Another example involved the transition from the third to fourth topic. In topic 3, learners see Smalltalk code for the first time and explore the code of individual methods. In the View Matcher scenario of topic 4, the complexity of the situation increased tremendously; the scenario is driven by the message execution stack, in which learners were given access to ten to fifteen related methods at once. This proved to be a significant instructional step. Some programmers we observed responded to the stack by attempting to understand the code comprehensively, reading through every stacked method. Others, perhaps daunted by the prospect of the first approach, ignored all the code. We provided more support for this transition by suggesting a strategy for exploring the stacked methods (that of determining how each message got onto the stack) and by enhancing the View Matcher's user interface to support this activity (by highlighting the message expression that causes a method to be stacked).

MiTTS was designed to guide people simultaneously through a complex learning task and encourage them to initiate, pursue, and evaluate their own learning goals. Thus, our instructions were sparse, providing step-by-step procedures only when a task was complex and novel. To assist learners in tracking their success in open-ended tasks, we provided considerable checkpointing information; we also developed and refined many specific instances of error recognition, diagnosis, and recovery support. These coordination and recovery materials had to be minutely crafted to anticipate the broadest possible range of usage scenarios we encountered or could reasonably anticipate; fine-grained formative evaluations were a key aspect of this.

We were indeed surprised to discover that not all Americans know even the main structure of blackjack, a game we had selected for its universality. It is perhaps the most popular casino card game in the United States and also well known internationally (it's called pontoon in Britain and 21 in some areas of Europe). However, some of the programmers we studied were unfamiliar with blackjack, and so we added a summary of the rules to our tutorial materials.

The process of early deployment and design refinement—often called formative evaluation (Scriven 1967)—was critical to meeting our overall design goals. We realized that the potential efficacy of our design scenarios hinged on addressing a myriad of specific design and implementation issues that became manifest only when we were able to observe and analyze actual learning situations. One of our usability objectives was to provide a meaningful, project-based training experience within a window of four to six hours. We felt that this was the maximum time one could expect an experienced and otherwise busy professional to devote to learning the object paradigm before impatience would outweigh curiosity. Over the course of its development, we distributed MiTTS to more than thirty sites throughout IBM and obtained posttutorial questionnaire data from people who used it. We found that although many people were unable to find an uninterrupted four- to six-hour period, they did in fact complete the tutorial in three to eight hours. This was consistent with our laboratory studies, where despite the additional request to think aloud, people completed the tutorial in four to six hours. All programmer trainees participating in a "class test" of the tutorial at an IBM customer site completed the materials in less than a day of training.

Even more important was our goal of conveying a general sense of what object-oriented programming was all about, to provide an initial training experience that left programmers motivated and confident enough to learn more on their own. Such a training outcome is, of course, difficult to assess. In the IBM programmer questionnaires, for example, learners typically did quite well at describing the design of the blackjack game, but often they reported fairly low confidence about their overall understanding of object-oriented programming and design. The trainees observed at the IBM customer site reported that MiTTS had provided a good introduction, but that they needed to learn much more. One programmer who had encountered the object paradigm as an undergraduate proclaimed, "I learned more here today than in a whole course in school." Another said that he had learned just enough to want to take the tutorial home and learn more. Although such testimonials are only indirect payoff measures, they do capture the essence of what the tutorial is striving to provide.

This chapter has presented a scenario-level view of the MiTTS project. It reemphasizes a point from chapter 3: one of the important properties of scenarios as design objects is that they are multifarious; they are coherent and useful at many levels of detailing and for many design activities. The TurboChess touchstone scenario provided vision, focus, and technical guidance to the MiTTS project. We generated variants of it to explore and clarify the design issues we wanted to address, envision the tools and the tutorial we ultimately designed, and interpret and evaluate our tools and tutorial as vehicles for minimalist instruction. As a result, we found that many individual design decisions were overdetermined. This pervasive orientation and commitment to support and to exploit a typical programming experience gave the MiTTS project a design coherence not attainable by lists of instructions.

6

Usability Rationale

The unadorned scenario-based approach of chapter 5 is simple and powerful. It comprehensively addresses the challenges of design and technology development discussed in chapters 2 and 3, and it provides a foundation for developing further scenario-based techniques for managing and evaluating usefulness and usability in design and development.

Why would anyone want more than a naked scenario? Representing the use of a system or application with interaction scenarios makes that use explicit. It focuses design reflection and supports envisionment and the consideration of alternatives. It helps designers recognize and manage trade-offs and more effectively create and use design knowledge. Above all, it helps designers and analysts to focus attention on the assumptions about people and their tasks that are implicit in systems and applications. But the scenarios themselves leave implicit the underlying causal relations of use: a scenario does not isolate just what it is about people or about a design that allows that scenario to occur.

Indeed, envisioning a better scenario for people may well require making explicit just what it was that needed to be improved in terms of specific consequences for specific activities, how those improvements were attempted in terms of managing or altering consequences, what other consequences might have been entrained as side effects, what trade-offs were confronted and how they were investigated and resolved, and so forth. A direct approach to articulating why scenarios run as they do is to isolate individual causal relationships between features of a situation of use and specific consequences for people and their activities.

In chapter 4, the scenario analysis of Raison d'Etre was supplemented with a more explicit claims analysis. We enumerated specific hypotheses about what features in the designed situations might cause what consequences for people in those situations. This allowed us to identify potentially important causal relations in the Raison d'Etre scenarios that were not necessarily obvious in the scenario narratives—for example, the trade-off that video data are very rich and intrinsically appealing to viewers, yet difficult to search or scan, and the secondary trade-off that enabling fast-forwarding of video information undermines the intelligibility of the soundtrack and the "feel" of the real-time visual information.

It helped to expose conflicts and contradictions among scenarios—for example, between confusion and diverse views in "meet various team members" and possibly oppressive coherence in "development team meeting." And it allowed us to recognize general patterns and social mechanisms that were important in these scenarios, such as the Social Conformity claim—articulating one's beliefs and engaging in action in a social context provide a highly responsive setting for testing and refining one's beliefs and behavior, and for building group consensus, but encourage actions and beliefs that are group normative and consistent with the actions and beliefs of powerful others (such as group leaders), and thereby can inhibit diversity.

Figure 6.1 visualizes the relation between unadorned scenario-level design and analysis and relatively more explicit claims-level design and analysis. Both levels of design reasoning seek to manage the evolutionary task-artifact cycle (figure 3.1) in order to impose some measure of use-oriented deliberation on the process of technology development. As sketched in the discussion of the Raison d'Etre project, we want a scenario-based design process in which it is possible to integrate scenario-level envisionment and analysis with more detailed and focused reasoning: claims analysis.

The argument made in chapter 3 is that scenarios are a consummate management tool for technical design; we are not questioning that conclusion now but rather elaborating it. We want to be able to switch between relatively more holistic scenario-based design and analysis (the outer cycle in figure 6.1) and relatively more detailed design and analysis (the inner cycle) as necessary and appropriate. In the next several chapters, we continue to enlarge the scope and ambition of the scenario-based design approach, to show that scenarios can be a fulcrum for a variety of design and development activities.

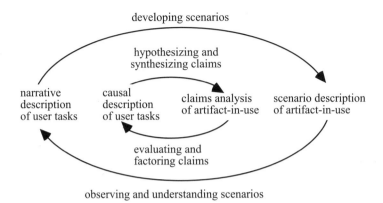

developing scenarios

hypothesizing and
synthesizing claims

narrative
description
of user tasks

causal
description
of user tasks

claims analysis
of artifact-in-use

scenario description
of artifact-in-use

evaluating and
factoring claims

observing and understanding scenarios

Figure 6.1
Managing the task-artifact cycle at the levels of scenarios and claims

Claims and Requirements for the Touchstone Scenario

The scenario in box 6.1 is a variant of our enduring touchstone scenario: the activity of playing with a blackjack game raises questions about how the game updates its user interface display, questions that are not easily answered as the programmer explores Smalltalk code using the Class Hierarchy Browser.

The programmer does succeed in finding the BlackJack class in the code hierarchy but cannot find a method with a name that suggests display responsibilities, in either that class or its superclass CardGame. The programmer broadens the search and subsequently does find a method named "open" that creates an instance of the class BJWindow. The substring "window" looks promising, and the programmer decides to examine the BJWindow class and its methods. Ultimately, the programmer does find a "display" method in BJWindow's superclass Application-Window, but the method's code makes no reference to BlackJack, and the programmer cannot determine whether this method is indeed used by the blackjack application.

This scenario recalls the three issues we originally wanted to pursue in the Smalltalk domain. The first was the complexity of the class hierarchy and Smalltalk environment: the programmer has trouble finding what is relevant, reads a lot of code, and finally cannot answer the original query. No system tool other than Class Hierarchy Browser is employed. The

Box 6.1
Analyzing card-hand display

A colleague has given the learner an example application, a blackjack game. The learner plays the game, and wonders how it does its display updates. The learner opens a Class Hierarchy Browser, but is unable to find anything that looks like a "display" method in either the BlackJack class or its superclass CardGame. Eventually the learner discovers an "open" method whose code creates an instance of the BJWindow class. The learner finds a "display" method in BJWindow's superclass ApplicationWindow, but sees no reference in its code to the BlackJack class, and has no idea how to tell whether it is actually used by the blackjack application.

second issue was the motivation of programmers toward rapid prototyping of graphical applications: the programmer is pursuing a user interface query, but in the end actually discovers nothing about how user interfaces are implemented in Smalltalk. The third issue was the importance of design in object-oriented programming: the programmer chases objects that participate in the blackjack game one at a time, diving into the code for particular methods, but never glimpsing the design of which the objects and their methods are merely parts.

We can further detail the design issues embodied in the scenario by developing a claims analysis, as shown in box 6.2. Claims are identified by systematically posing elaboration questions about the events in the scenario: Why did the programmer look for a display method in the BlackJack and CardGame classes? Why was the initial search limited to these two classes? Why was the programmer interested in the reference to the BJWindow class in the open method? Why did the programmer search the ApplicationWindow class for a display method? Why couldn't the programmer tell whether that display method is used by the blackjack application? This analysis identifies two particular features of the scenario, as causally implicated in its outcomes: "search in the Class Hierarchy Browser" and "tracing references to classes in the code for various methods." For each of these antecedents, the analysis isolates several specific consequences for the programmer.

Searching for code with the Class Hierarchy Browser makes it salient to the programmer that the code library is a class hierarchy and directs

Box 6.2
Claims embodied in the "analyzing card-hand display" scenario

---

Searching for code with the class hierarchy browser
+ directs attention to inheritance relationships among objects
− may reduce attention to other important object relationships (such as sharing instance variables)
− gives no application view in which objects that work together in an application appear together in the code library
− the number of classes in the class hierarchy may overwhelm new programmers

Tracing references to classes in method code
+ allows learners to analyze run-time relationships among application objects
− many run-time relationships are not obvious just from the code as a text (for example, user interface code is especially hard)
− finding a class referred to leaves open how that class works (which in turn involves understanding all of its methods)
− reconstructing a network of class references in various methods may not reveal the overall application design

---

the programmer's attention to inheritance relationships among objects. This is a potentially useful consequence, or upside, for the programmer; it calls attention to the fact that BlackJack is a subclass of CardGame. However, in doing this, it makes other object relationships less salient, in particular relationships in which one object uses another. It is this latter type of relationship that pervades the Smalltalk user interface software paradigm. Thus, the salience of the hierarchy undermines the programmer's efforts to understand the blackjack game as a whole, and in particular how the application manages its display updates. Finally, the sheer number of classes in the hierarchy exacerbates the downsides: it is difficult to find things at all, and particularly difficult to find things that are nonadjacent in the class hierarchy.

The feature of tracing references to classes in method code also has specific upside and downside consequences. It allows programmers to analyze run-time relationships among application objects—basically, by hand-simulating code execution. This is useful as far as it goes, but many run-time relationships are not obvious in the code-as-text. Smalltalk in particular makes extensive use of interpretive techniques like polymorphism and dynamic binding that make hand simulation very difficult. And at best, tracing references to classes will identify further classes that need to be understood, presumably by tracing references to an even larger set of classes. This will lead to lots of incidental learning about Smalltalk, but it is quite divergent with respect to the goal of learning how the blackjack game does its display updates. The network of classes identified will include many that in fact play no role in the application that triggered the original search. Accordingly, the effort of making sense of that network of classes will most likely not reveal the overall application design.

The claims analysis in box 6.2 provides a more explicit and detailed requirements analysis than either the scenario itself or the three orienting issues of complexity, motivation, and design. The claims constitute explicit empirical hypotheses about why and how the scenario in box 6.1 runs as it does. They can be grounded in general psychology. For example, salient structures and displays compel attention, and thereby limit attentional resources for other structures and displays (Kahneman 1973). The class hierarchy "bias" can be seen as a corollary of this principle. Integration for perception and memory is enhanced by having an overview or schema, and impaired by not having this (Ausubel 1960; Bransford and Johnson 1973). The difficulty of understanding a Smalltalk application a class at a time, with no overall application view, can be seen as a corollary of this principle.

Scientific principles are often articulated at too general a level to guide design reasoning directly. However, the context of building a claims analysis can make it clear how to adduce general principles to explain particular causal relationships. The claims analysis is a mediating specialization of the scientific principles, helping to bridge between science and design. The claims ground design decisions and artifact features in science, and thereby make it more feasible to generalize specific design lessons for future reuse (a topic considered in chapters 7 and 8).

In providing an explicit and empirically grounded analysis of the scenario, the claims in box 6.2 provide the foundation for a principled requirements analysis. The link from a claims analysis to such a requirements analysis is the heuristic of mitigating downsides and strengthening upsides. The claims in the box suggest the following design agenda:

1. Maintain emphasis on hierarchical code views, but support other views as well; for example, provide an application view.

2. Simplify the Class Hierarchy Browser; for example, allow it to reorganize or filter the classes displayed.

3. Strengthen support for analysis of references to classes; for example, provide code simulation or access to running code, versus hand simulation of code text.

4. Emphasize software design; for example, provide a design-oriented view of classes and methods participating in an application.

Designing and Analyzing a New Touchstone Scenario

The claims in box 6.2, and the requirements analysis it entails specify the constraints for designing a "new" "analyzing cardhard display" scenario. Our design solution involved creating the Bittitalk Browser and the View Matcher. The Bittitalk Browser maintains a hierarchical code view, but simplifies this view by filtering out classes and methods that do not participate in the application being browsed. Thus, it provides a hierarchical application view. The View Matcher provides a variety of coordinated views of an application, one of these being the Bittitalk Browser. It supports the strategy of tracing references to classes by providing access to the running code. Our redesigned "analyzing cardhand display" scenario is in box 6.3.

Learners can open an inspector on an object to examine its internal state; in an error situation, they can analyze application functionality in the debugger's message execution stack. They can open multiple tools to compare and contrast different information sources. But managing and integrating all these tools can be complex. This suggests a presentation of Smalltalk that permanently displays and synchronizes these tools with example applications.

The system debugger provides a model, coordinating an inspector and a class browser with the message execution stack. However, the debugger can be overwhelming, particularly for a learner. It is typically encountered in the context of an error; it presents a lot of information about message activity, object states, and implementation; and it is only loosely coordinated with the application. This suggests a design that more tightly couples the application with the system tools: incorporating a permanent

Box 6.3
Redesigned card-hand display scenario

The new user wonders how blackjack displays its cards, and has noticed that in halt mode the game stops before each display update. The person plays the game to such a point, then looks at the information displayed in the various panes. Selecting the top message on the stack (showHand) triggers the display of commentary for that message and selects it in the Bittitalk view, displaying its code. The programmer discovers that this message is sent to the card-hand object when it is time to display its cards. The person infers that this message was sent in the course of processing the next message in the stack, just as would be true for a call stack. The rest of the messages on the stack seem very confusing, involving a number of nonblackjack classes (e.g., TextPane, NotificationManager), but by using the commentary, the programmer is able to see how the responsibility for displaying things is distributed between the window and its components, and the blackjack and its components.

application view, tailoring the information presented in the tools to be application relevant (for example, a class hierarchy that displays only classes and methods used by the application), and providing help texts to support integration across tools.

Chapter 5 argued that the Bittitalk Browser makes the application design more apparent by presenting only the application objects and that the View Matcher supports understanding the run-time dynamics of object communication. We can improve on this analysis by more explicitly specifying the consequences of various View Matcher and Bittitalk Browser features incorporated in the scenario. Box 6.4 presents a claims analysis of the scenario in box 6.3.

This analysis addresses the various elaboration questions that can be posed about the events in the scenario. What interpretation did the programmer make of the halt itself, and of the information in various panes of the View Matcher? Was the programmer surprised or distracted by the halt? Why did the programmer select the message on top of the stack, and what encouraged the inference that that message was sent in the execution of the second message in the stack? What did the programmer conclude about the method, based on the information in the commentary pane? Was the programmer confused at all by the variety of

Box 6.4
Claims embodied in the redesigned card-hand display scenario

Permanent display of multiple views of an application
+ simplifies access to system tools and to application code
+ supports convergent reasoning about how the application works
− does not develop basic skills for accessing and managing system tools

Coordinated updating of multiple views of a running application
+ supports convergent reasoning about how the application works
+ temporally groups information, helping people to parse the display
+ directs attention to the code relevant to the application's current state
− may discourage exploration of methods not on the stack or in the Bittitalk Browser
− too much information changing at once might be confusing

The View Matcher break points
+ parse application execution into coherent episodes for analysis
− may interrupt interaction sequences
− it can be difficult to make sense of an application in the midst of a message send

An application-filtered Class Hierarchy Browser (Bittitalk Browser)
+ focuses attention on inheritance relationships among application objects
+ encourages and supports opportunistic analysis of the application design
− may reduce attention to other important object relationships (such as sharing instance variables)
− other classes in the class hierarchy cannot be accessed

The object communication summarized in the message execution stack
+ helps learners to decompose application functionality
+ supports transfer from procedural programming experience
− the object communication can be quite complex
− learners may rely on a procedural model of computation to interpret the stack

Access to objects in the inspector
+ allows learners to interrogate, track, and experiment with instance variable values

Application-specific commentary for each message in the stack
+ supports an application-oriented interpretation of object communication
− is not general and may not apply well to other applications

events in the View Matcher that were triggered by selecting the message? Why wasn't the programmer able to understand all of the message sends in the execution stack? Did the programmer want to browse any methods not in the stack or in the Bittitalk view? How did the programmer determine the organization of the display functionality? What did the programmer ultimately learn about the Smalltalk language and environment from this episode?

This analysis highlights a set of specific consequences entailed by the core features of the View Matcher and the Bittitalk Browser in this scenario. Most of these involve trade-offs. For example, the permanent display of multiple views in the blackjack game gives the programmer direct access to the Smalltalk system tools, supporting convergent reasoning about how the game works, but because the programmer never has to activate or manage these tools, he or she does not learn how to do this. Synchronizing these views has additional consequences. It temporally segregates information; by displaying the execution stack, instance variables, commentary, and method code pertaining to the current application state, it helps the programmer's focus on understanding that particular execution state. However, extensively structuring access to the Smalltalk programming tools could discourage more open-ended exploration on the part of learners, and presenting many animated code views could itself overwhelm programmers who are just getting started.

The View Matcher break points parse the application into coherent episodes for analysis, but this parsing could disrupt the programmer's work with and analysis of the application; moreover, the task of analyzing an application in the midst of a message send may be rather novel and therefore difficult for programmers. Filtering the Class Hierarchy Browser, that is, making it a Bittitalk Browser, highlights the inheritance relationships among application-relevant classes, presenting an overview of the application design without the distraction of the many classes that do not participate in the application. However, it does not help the programmer analyze noninheritance relations, like sharing instance variables, and it implicitly discourages exploration of the filtered classes.

The object communication summarized in the stack view helps the programmer analyze execution; it is a vast improvement over hand simulation. The stack itself resembles a call stack, with which procedural programmers already have some familiarity. However, the information in the stack is complex, and the similarity of the stack with a call stack could induce programmers to reply to much on procedural programming concepts. The inspector view makes it easy for programmers to access and monitor the instances involved in the message send currently selected in the stack. The commentary view provides an application-specific interpretation of the selected message send; however, because the commentary is application specific, it may not transfer well to uses of the selected method in other application contexts.

Why would one want to make a claims analysis for a design scenario, as in box 6.3? Isn't the work already done? Managing the task-artifact cycle is not a linear endeavor with starting and ending points. As schematized in figure 6.1, design work is never "done." There will always be a further development, a subsequent version, a redesign, a new technology development context. The design scenarios at one point in time are the requirements scenarios at the next point in time. The scenario in box 6.3 will need to be further specified in order to guide implementation and deployment effectively. It can be useful to unpack the implicit trade-offs that inhere in the design, to keep track of them as the design is developed: lower-level, downstream decisions could make things slightly better or slightly worse.

Figure 6.2 traces the flow of part of the design argument regarding the "analyzing card-hand display" scenario. In the original scenario (figure 6.1), the programmer wondered about display updates but was able to make little progress; the dominating Class Hierarchy Browser view of the code design focused attention on inheritance relations (see box 6.1). We reasoned from this that coordinating access to the message execution stack with access to the class hierarchy could help programmers analyze run-time relationships as well as inheritance relationships; it could mitigate the downside of a dominating Class Hierarchy view. We designed a new situation (box 6.3) in which the programmer can more conveniently explore the execution of the code, for example, discovering the showHand message. Finally, we analyzed this design solution, noting that while it addressed one of our original concerns, it introduced additional complexity (box 6.4).

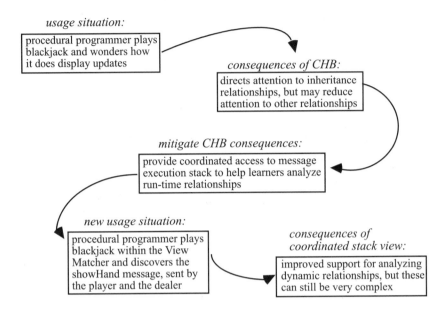

Figure 6.2
Portion of the design argument for the View Matcher, regarding consequences of the Class Hierarchy Browser (CHB) for the "analyzing cardhand display" scenario

As we implemented, deployed, and evaluated the View Matcher, we kept this possible downside in mind, trying to mitigate it in our implementation and determine its actual magnitude in use. For example, incorporating the commentary view reduces the complexity of interpreting the stack, though it adds a complication of its own (that the method-oriented documentation it provides is also application specific; box 6.4).

Identifying Appropriate Goals

Not every programmer will come to Smalltalk through an experience like the touchstone scenario. In many cases, people have a specific high-level objective—perhaps to learn about object-oriented design, or to try user interface prototyping—but no specific project in mind. The initial usage scenarios for these people are fundamentally different from the "analyzing card-hand display" scenario. Box 6.5 is an example of a type of scenario we observed among procedural programmers trying to get

Box 6.5
Starting up Smalltalk scenario

A new Smalltalk programmer sees "Graphics Demo" in the File menu, and reasons that a demo might be a good way to see what Smalltalk is all about. The programmer runs several of the demos. It turns out that the demos have some flashy graphics, but you basically sit back and watch. The programmer wonders what you can do with the demos, and where the demo programs are. The programmer returns to the File menu and tries "Browse Classes"—recalling that classes is an important Smalltalk concept; the class hierarchy browser appears. After making a few random selections here, the programmer sees what appears to be Smalltalk code. After several minutes browsing classes, the programmer discovers the class Graphics Demos. It includes several large methods, each corresponding to one of the system demos. The programmer excitedly begins studying these to see how graphical applications are written in Smalltalk.

---

started quickly with Smalltalk (note that, as in the touchstone scenario, no one uses the instruction manual!).

As usual, we can interrogate the events of the scenario better to expose the causal dynamics that underlie these events. For example, why did the programmer select demos (demonstration programs)? How might watching demos support learning about Smalltalk? How might it fail to support learning? Why did the programmer wonder what to do with the demos and where their code is? Why did the programmer open a Class Hierarchy Browser? What did the programmer learn from studying the demo code? The claims analysis in box 6.6 is a summary of the result of such elaboration questioning.

The appearance of functions like "Graphics Demo" and "Browse Classes" in the File menu (and, for that matter, "New Workspace"—another function in the File menu that did not happen to play a role in this scenario) conveys that these are useful and appropriate initial activities. The new Smalltalk programmer is invited by both the names of these functions and their positioning in the menus to pursue these activities as initial goals. In this sense, the design of the Smalltalk environment embodies claims that these are appropriate initial goals. Put the other way around, if these are not appropriate defining goals, then why are they prominently listed in the most prominent menu?

Box 6.6
Claims for the "Starting up Smalltalk" scenario

Discovering "Graphics Demo" on the File menu
+ suggests that running a demo is an appropriate initial goal

Running the system demos
+ captures the interest of programmers
+ motivates programmers to learn by doing
− noninteractive demos offer little for the programmer to do
− programmers may have difficulty finding the demo code

Discovering "Browse Classes" in the File menu
+ suggests that reading Smalltalk code is an appropriate initial goal

Browsing and studying demo code in the Class Hierarchy Browser
+ establishes basic Smalltalk programming skills
+ provides model applications for programmers to analyze and extend
− may reduce time spent on instantiating and analyzing objects (e.g., in a Workspace)
− the demos are not paradigmatic Smalltalk applications

However, as described in the other two claims of box 6.6, these activities have both upside and downside consequences for programmers. Running the demos is intrinsically interesting and motivating, but the demos are somewhat disappointing in that they allow almost no interaction; they are merely scripts that play out. They are also somewhat frustrating in that the code for the demos is not immediately available for analysis and experimentation. Similarly, studying code in the Class Hierarchy Browser helps to build core Smalltalk skills and provides programmers with models to work with and emulate in their own code. But code reading is not a very active way to learn; contrast it to experimenting with objects in a Workspace. The demo methods are also extremely nonparadigmatic as Smalltalk applications; they are implemented as single methods rather than as model-view ensembles. They provide very poor learning models.

The claims in box 6.6 should be seen as an empirical theory of the events and experiences in the scenario of box 6.5. As in the earlier examples, this theory can be grounded or empirically justified in psychology. The claims are an analytic elaboration of the observed scenario, integrating direct observations with causal hypotheses as to why and how the observations occurred. The two claims hypothesizing that the discovery of a function in a menu tends to entrain selection and exploration of that function are examples of opportunistic planning (Hayes-Roth and Hayes-Roth 1979): as people plan their own activities, they often respond locally and immediately to opportunities the environment presents to them. Animated color graphics are intrinsically motivating to people; they draw attention and encourage action (Malone and Lepper 1987). The upsides of running the system demos can be seen as a corollary of this more general principle. The upside of the browsing and studying demo code claim exemplifies the principle of modeling: people who are unconfident or inexperienced in a domain tend to seek and emulate models that they take to be paradigmatic (Brown 1973).

The scenario and claims analysis of "starting up Smalltalk" entrains a design agenda based on the heuristic of enhancing upsides and mitigating downsides:

1. Directly convey appropriate initial goals through the kinds of functions easily accessed.

2. Capture interest and intrinsically motivate programmers with highly interactive applications involving dynamic graphical displays.

3. Ensure that example applications have paradigmatic software designs and that their code is easy to access and coordinate with their interactive behaviors.

The design solution is a scenario meeting these requirements (box 6.7).

In the redesigned scenario, the View Matcher environment provides easy access to a blackjack game—a simple application, highly interactive, interesting enough (we hope) to evoke motivation, deliberately designed to exemplify both object-oriented software design and the Smalltalk model-view paradigm for user interfaces. The default state of the View Matcher coordinates the application only with a Bittitalk view of the application classes, though even this level of coordination makes the blackjack code immediately accessible. Halt mode dynamically coordinates the running application with an animated view of its method execution stack, stopping at predetermined points where an important game or display computation takes place.

Box 6.8 presents a claims analysis for the redesigned "starting up Smalltalk" scenario. As before, we tried to focus on the downsides that

Box 6.7
Redesign for the "starting up Smalltalk" scenario

A new Smalltalk programmer sees "blackjack" on the View Matcher menu, and reasons that it might be an enjoyable and useful way to learn what Smalltalk is all about. The game window opens within the View Matcher environment. The programmer plays several games, noticing that apparently relevant classes (e.g., BlackJack, Card) appear in a coordinated browser. The programmer selects several classes and methods, and browses code, before returning to the View Matcher menu to select "Halt Mode." Now, the View Matcher dynamically displays a list of methods (the same ones that appeared in the browser). The dynamic updating of this list ceases just as the game is about to deal a new hand. Selecting a method in the list, the programmer notices that the browser is updated to select that same method and that a paragraph of documentation appears in the lower-left pane. The programmer tries several other selections and decides to try to make sense of these various sources of information.

---

accompanied and could undermine the upsides of our design scenario. Filtering classes could limit programmers too much, providing access to system tools might deter programmers from learning how to set up the Smalltalk environment on their own, playing blackjack could be so interesting and motivating as to distract programmers from learning, or the many dynamic tool views could be overwhelming. It is interesting to compare the analysis in box 6.8 with that in box 6.4. There is considerable overlap. Different scenarios emphasize different aspects of a design, but in a well-integrated design, the major elements have consequences across most usage scenarios.

Figure 6.3 maps part of the design argument for "starting up Smalltalk." In the original scenario (box 6.5), the programmer was attracted to the graphics demos. Although this activity was initially engaging, it was not interactive, it provided no guidance to link it to code analysis, and the demos were poor examples of Smalltalk code (box 6.6). Our design work focused on providing more interactive applications that were also better examples of Smalltalk code and better coordination between running applications and their code. In the redesigned "starting up Smalltalk" scenario, the programmer plays with and analyzes a blackjack game using a suite of tools coordinated by the View Matcher (box 6.7). This design

Box 6.8
Claims for the redesigned "starting up Smalltalk" scenario

Discovering "blackjack" in the View Matcher menu
+ suggests that playing the blackjack game is an appropriate initial goal

Permanent display and coordination of a filtered class hierarchy (Bittitalk view)
+ encourages and supports opportunistic analysis of the application design
+ simplifies access to the class hierarchy
− other classes in the class hierarchy cannot be accessed or learned about
− does not develop basic skills for accessing and managing the Class Hierarchy Browser

Playing and analyzing a paradigmatic interactive application (the blackjack game)
+ captures the interest of programmers
+ motivates programmers to learn by doing
+ establishes basic Smalltalk programming skills
+ provides model applications for programmers to analyze and extend
− may encourage context-specific learning
− people may spend too much time using the application and not enough time learning about it
− the game may introduce learning burdens of its own if it is not sufficiently familiar to the learner

Permanent display and coordinated updating of multiple views of a running application
+ simplifies access to system tools and to application code
+ supports convergent reasoning about how the application works
+ directs attention to the code relevant to the application's current state
− does not develop basic skills for accessing and managing system tools
− may discourage exploration of methods not on the stack or in the Bittitalk Browser
− too much information changing at once might be confusing

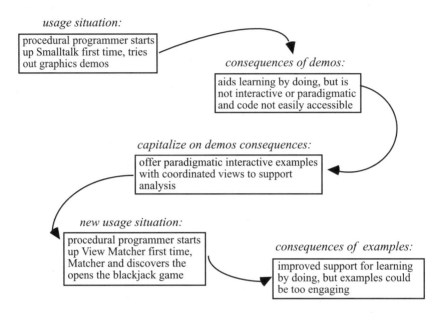

Figure 6.3
A portion of the design argument for the View Matcher, based on analysis of demos and examples in the "starting up Smalltalk" scenario

solution addressed our concerns about providing more effective support for identifying and pursuing appropriate learning goals, but we noted that it incorporated downsides of its own, for example, the possibility that programmers may get so caught up in playing with the game that their motivation to understand how it works is diminished (box 6.8). When we recognized this potential downside of the Blackjack game example, we became more conservative about implementing enhancements to the game presentation, preferring to make the game only moderately engaging.

Sustained Learning

The two scenarios considered to this point describe initial learning activities; they talk about someone who has just begun to learn about Smalltalk and object-oriented programming. Learning something as complex as a programming language and environment is a substantial undertaking that

Box 6.9
Following tutorial instructions to learn about objects and messages

A programmer follows directions to open a text file within the Smalltalk environment and begins reading chapter 3, "Objects and Messages," working through a series of brief sections on simple objects, simple messages, unary messages, keyword messages, arithmetic messages, binary messages, messages inside messages, expressions series, cascaded messages, simple loops, temporary variables, assignment expressions, return expressions, and global variables, plus a short section on how objects and messages are safe. In each section, the programmer reads definitions and then selects and evaluates pieces of code.

For example, in the section on simple messages, the programmer reads that you send messages to objects in order to make things happen in Smalltalk—that messages are similar to function calls. The programmer follows directions to evaluate three correct expressions (e.g., 20 factorial). In each case, the result is displayed. The programmer next evaluates an incorrect expression ("20" factorial); a walkback window appears displaying the title "'factorial' not understood," along with other information the programmer does not understand. The programmer follows instructions to select Close in the System menu of the walkback window, and it disappears.

At the end of the chapter is a section called "putting it all together," in which the programmer sees an example of comments and executes a larger code example.

unfolds over hours, days, weeks. Even if we consider only the challenge of getting started, that is, getting to the point where one can develop further skill on the job or on one's own, we need to consider situations beyond the first few insights and achievements.

The scenario in box 6.9 is a re-presentation of the scenario considered in box 5.1. It describes a situation in which a programmer is in the midst of working through a Smalltalk tutorial. This scenario is extrinsically structured relative to "analyzing card-hand display" (box 6.1) and "starting up Smalltalk" (box 6.5): its structure derives from the ordering of tutorial topics and exercise steps, not just from the goals and reactions of the programmer. In the scenario, the programmer is coordinating sections in an instructional manual with a series of exercises carried out within the Smalltalk environment. Each section is a small, descriptive passage including one or more Smalltalk expressions. The programmer reads the text and selects and evaluates the code. At the end of the chapter, the programmer examines a multiline code example illustrating several of the structures and techniques described.

Nothing goes remarkably well or poorly in this scenario, but still it vividly illustrates what is probably fair to see as the standard design approach to instructional manuals (Gagne, Briggs, and Wagner 1988). The organizing principle for such instruction is the hierarchical decomposition of basic concepts and skills. Thus, the topic of "Objects and Messages" in box 6.9 is analyzed into types of objects and messages, each of which is analyzed into cases and subtypes; for example, "simple objects" includes "strings," "integers," "characters," and "arrays." Learning activities tend to consist largely of rote drill and practice; for example, in the subsection "simple messages," the learner evaluates `20 factorial` and reads that the message `factorial` is sent to the object `20`. The learner is then directed to select and evaluate two other Smalltalk expressions, `'now is the time' size` and `#(1 3 5 7) at: 2`. The first of these merely reinforces the pattern of the factorial case, and the second builds on this type of case to illustrate how messages can take arguments (`2` is the argument of the message `at:`). The claims in box 6.10 summarize the key causal relationships in the "following tutorial instructions" scenario.

These claims answer some of the elaboration questions one can pose for the scenario in box 6.9. Why does the chapter include its various topics? Why are these presented as independent subsections? What does the programmer surmise from following these instructions—about the various topics and about Smalltalk as a whole? What sorts of affect and motivation does the programmer experience while completing the various exercise steps? What kind of "real" programming tasks is the learner ready to perform having worked through this instruction?

As in earlier examples, the practice of being clear and precise as to the potential consequences for people and their activities helps to identify the psychological and social mechanisms that play a role in the scenario. For example, a substantial body of laboratory research on learning describes how component concepts and skills can be assembled to support complex performances (Gagné and Briggs 1979; Singley and Anderson 1989). This literature stresses the importance of juxtaposing descriptions and explanations with the practice activities to which they refer and of repetitively

Box 6.10
Claims embodied in the "following tutorial instructions" scenario

---

Decomposing learning objectives into sections and steps, and directing each of these in turn
+ allows complex concepts and skills to built up from parts
− learners may become impatient and may reject activities that seem trivial or irrelevant
− following steps may not facilitate retrieval and performance in real programming
Keeping directive instructions and learner practice in lockstep contiguity
+ allows the learner to know exactly what to do and when
− does not promote reflection or analysis (the learner may focus too narrowly on each small task)
Repetitive practice
+ clarifies correct discriminations and smoothes performance
− complex programming tasks are not merely scripts

---

exercising these linkages (Lewis and Anderson 1985; Singley and Anderson 1989). But these findings are challenged by research on cognition and education in realistic task domains showing that mere decomposition and juxtaposition of rote learning often fail to evoke the motivation to learn, that rote skills often cannot be effectively engaged in real settings, and that domain-specific planning and problem solving, not conveyed well by rote practice, are essential to real skill (Bruner 1966; Resnick 1987; Voss, Wiley, and Carretero 1995).

Unpacking the design trade-offs in the "following tutorial instructions" scenario highlights the underlying conflict between two major schools of psychological theory. Drill-and-practice designs, such as that illustrated in box 6.9, capitalize on the upsides described by association theories—the view that knowledge and behavior that occurs together will eventually be organized together in the mind (Crowder 1976; Ebbinghaus, 1885; Wasserman and Miller 1997). But as a design foundation, this risks the downsides that constructivist theories described—the view that people must actively create their knowledge and skills by recognizing and pursuing personally meaningful goals (Dewey 1966). Our studies of experienced programmers using the Smalltalk tutorial revealed many episodes in which the downsides in fact prevailed. For example, we observed one

Box 6.11
Redesigned scenario

The programmer is using a workspace and the Bittitalk Browser to work with a function-level view of the blackjack model (that is, exploring the functionality of the game without its user interface, and working at the level of application objects and messages, not their implementations). The programmer follows an explicit instruction to create a new game and deal cards. The programmer reads about messages and return expressions. The programmer reads hints about managing information in the workspace in case it becomes difficult to find. The programmer follows an instruction to find the message that requests the game to give the player an additional card (a hit). The programmer follows instructions to find the message that ends a player's turn and the message that returns the current game score. The programmer follows an instruction to explore methods defined for the four other major model objects: BJPlayer, BJHand, Card, and CardDeck.

---

programmer who was unable to create a new object he needed for a project, although he had been drilled in this skill earlier (Carroll et al. 1993). The rote practice did not transfer to the realistic task.

The heuristic of mitigating or eliminating downsides and strengthening or maintaining upsides in the claims analysis in box 6.10 helped to focus these observations as requirements for further design work:

1. Introduce learners to Smalltalk concepts and skills in the context of realistic programming activities.

2. Provide many opportunities for practice, but also encourage learners to plan and reflect on what they are doing.

The claims analysis in box 6.10, and those described earlier in this chapter, provide constraints on the envisionment of a new scenario. They guide us broadly toward better reconciling associationist and constructivist theories, and specifically toward addressing the problems observed with the Smalltalk tutorial and the design requirements they entail. Box 6.11 is one scenario we envisioned.

In the redesigned scenario the programmer is using Smalltalk tools to study and exercise a blackjack game. The programmer is working with a simplified "view" of the game, the user interface is not included, and the code details have been filtered. The programmer executes a series of Smalltalk expressions to create a new game object and deal cards. Most of the instructions are specified mainly in terms of suggested goals; for example, the programmer is asked to give the player an additional card, but must search in the class hierarchy to find the appropriate message to carry out this function. The claims analysis in box 6.12 summarizes the state of the design argument at the point of envisioning this scenario.

The familiar example of blackjack immediately and concretely conveys the goals of the instructional activity to the learner, motivating and focusing the learner's activity (Bandura and Schunk 1981; Dixon 1987). However, learners could be captured by the familiar activity, interacting with and understanding it at too low a level and with too little reflection (Bruner 1966). The blackjack game is designed to a paradigmatic Smalltalk design, and hence provides a model for the learner's own subsequent design efforts (Brown 1973; Lave 1988). However, a complete application, even a small one, could be too complicated for some learning situations, and there is a risk that some learners might overgeneralize, taking blackjack as a general design pattern for all applications (Holland et al. 1987). Developing a single example in some depth is both a key to this approach and a major consequence of adopting it; depth allows richness in the tutorial, but at the cost of less breadth.

Working with the application model first (that is, without the interface graphics) simplifies comprehension of the underlying design, conveys the distinction between models and user interfaces, and highlights the Smalltalk model-view application architecture. It allows the model-only design to serve as a cognitive scaffold for learning the complete application (Bruner 1966; Papert 1980). On the downside, this staged approach could undermine the motivation of learners who are eager to learn about interactive applications (Weiner 1980) and could encourage overarticulated design styles (Fowler 1998; Vlissides 1998). Presenting goal-level guidance in favor of step-level guidance compels learners to generate plans and hypotheses instead of merely sequences of steps, and thereby helps them think at the level of strategic relationships (Craig 1965; Singley 1990). The downside is that learners might feel anxiety, might fail, or might draw suboptimal conclusions (Holland et al. 1987; Shulman, and Keislar 1966). Finally, supporting error diagnosis and recovery directly assists learners, but more generally helps them better differentiate correct and incorrect performance (Gold 1967; Piaget 1985; VanLehn

Box 6.12
MiTTS claims for "following tutorial instructions"

Exploring a familiar application (the blackjack game)
+ orients and motivates programmers by engaging prior knowledge
– may encourage context-specific learning
– people may spend too much time interacting with the application, and not enough time learning about it

Exploring a paradigmatic interactive application (the blackjack game)
+ provides a model for the design of new functionality
+ provides an appropriate framework for integrating and applying learning experiences
– may be too difficult for learners
– may create a design bias in future projects

Developing a single example in some depth
+ promotes an understanding of the real contexts in which Smalltalk skills are exercised
– the programmer does not see components in a range of contexts

Working with the application model first (without its graphical user interface)
+ simplifies early attempts to understand object-oriented design
+ provides a foundation for subsequent work with the model-plus-interface aggregate
+ highlights the important distinction between application models and their user interfaces
– may disappoint programmers who are eager to learn about graphical applications (the limited tasks may not be experienced as sufficiently meaningful)
– may encourage a programming style that proliferates objects and message-sends

Emphasis on programming goals (sparse procedures) in favor of step-by-step instructions
+ engages learners' attention
+ requires programmers to infer or retrieve connections between goals and methods (thus strengthening connections between their goals and the actions needed to accomplish these goals)
– programmers might not have access to enough information to reason successfully
– programmer may feel anxious about generating the action plans themselves
– the learner-generated procedures may be nonoptimal

Error-specific explanatory material and recovery procedures
+ assist people in making sense of unexpected problems
+ sharpen concept of correct performance
– people not experiencing these specific problems may become confused by the extra information

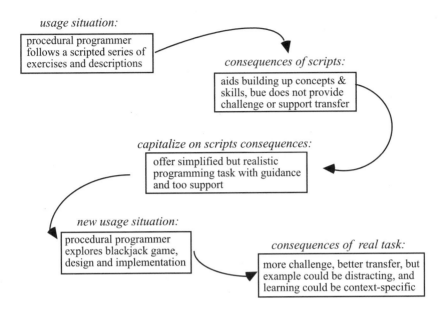

usage situation:

procedural programmer
follows a scripted series of
exercises and descriptions

consequences of scripts:

aids building up concepts &
skills, bue does not provide
challenge or support transfer

capitalize on scripts consequences:

offer simplified but realistic
programming task with guidance
and too support

new usage situation:

procedural programmer
explores blackjack game,
design and implementation

consequences of real task:

more challenge, better transfer, but
example could be distracting, and
learning could be context-specific

Figure 6.4
A portion of the design argument for the MiTTS curriculum, based on the
"following tutorial instructions" scenario

1988). Of course, those who do not make errors could be distracted or confused by the error support information, or perhaps could merely explore the error support material (van der Meij 1994).

Figure 6.4 presents part of the design argument for the "following tutorial instructions" scenario. In the original version of the scenario, the programmer follows a scripted series of exercises and descriptions. These many small elements provide a foundation of Smalltalk concepts and skills, but may leave the programmer unsatisfied, impatient, and not sufficiently challenged. Because the instruction takes place out of a meaningful work context, the concepts and skills may not be recalled or effectively engaged in the real programming situations in which they are required. The design approach was to embed the instruction in a realistic project context; the programmer was provided with a blackjack game, simplified in both its structure and its presentation. With this support, the programmer was able to carry out recognizable programming tasks immediately and to learn in the context of these tasks. This should have resulted in a more challenging and more satisfying learning experience, as well as in better learning transfer to real programming work. However, we also expected that working with a real code example might be more distracting (after all, you can have fun just playing the game) and that at least some of the learning might be context specific (for example, some of the Smalltalk objects that constitute the game, like cards, might not be very generally useful data structures).

The redesigned scenario incorporates many of the ideas central to our minimalist approach to instructional design, as described in chapter 5. For example, it emphasizes immediate immersion in realistic domain activities: the programmer is analyzing and using the Smalltalk objects that constitute a real application. The scenario illustrates leveraging specific prior knowledge. Blackjack is a common casino card game in the United States; most people already understand how the game runs and can use that knowledge in analyzing the Smalltalk code that implements the game. The scenario incorporates opened-ended specification of concepts and tasks, intended to engage learner-initiated problem solving and reflection: the instructions are incompletely specified.

Consequences for Work Groups

The analysis to this point is a *cognitive* view of the tutorial scenarios. The claims enumerated in boxes 6.10 and 6.12 are problem-solving and learning consequences for an individual agent. It is a *distributed* view of cognition (Hutchins 1995) in the sense that the claims analysis of the scenarios assigns roles to entities in the task environment as well as to mental entities like plans and goals, but it is not a social analysis. Only a single person plays a role in the described activity; the activity is described from that individual's point of view.

Typically, however, people work and learn in the context of peers. Indeed, as it turned out, the MiTTS materials were most often distributed to whole work groups within IBM. These organizations had adopted or been assigned the goal of acquiring expertise in Smalltalk programming and object-oriented design. Thus, we were impelled to consider an organizational work view of MiTTS and the scenarios it enables—for example, the case in which variants of the tutorial scenario in box 6.11 occur

Box 6.13
Organizational MiTTS claims for "following tutorial instructions"

Training on one's own
+ eliminates the trainer role
+ mitigates differences among students (self-confident students cannot monopolize learning interactions)
+ allows training in a greater variety of work settings and schedules
+ gives students more autonomy and responsibility for their own learning
− makes it difficult to monitor progress or offer help
− may diminish collaborative interactions among students

Providing a setting for training that is similar to the real work setting
+ supports interaction between learners and their more experienced colleagues
− could create confusion by blurring the distinction between training and working

Basing group instruction on design analysis of a blackjack game example
+ creates a community focus on design and a background of shared design information
− may disturb the division of labor, may not serve or satisfy coders, and may narrow the organization's design view (cf. "seeing everything as blackjack")

---

throughout an organization, with the various learners interacting with one another and with other colleagues.

We and the groups we worked with in IBM initially focused only on the individual-level concepts and skills of Smalltalk programming and object-oriented design, not on the organizational requirements for implementing such an instructional program. This illustrates Goldstein's (1987) observation that "many training programs are based on teaching skills requirements rather than the unspecified and unidentified organizational objectives. Yet, paradoxically, organizations often judge the value of a program on the basis of their own objectives, which were never specified, never considered in the design of the program, and never utilized in designing the evaluation model" (p. 971).

Both the Smalltalk tutorial as we found it and the MiTTS curriculum we created had specific implications for training and work in the organizations that employed these tutorials. Some of these organizational consequences are summarized in box 6.13.

Self-study instruction has many consequences for individual learners. For example, self-initiated planning and error recovery are much more important in these situations than in learning situations managed by teachers. But there are many organizational consequences as well: training on one's own eliminates the teacher role, allows training in a greater variety of settings and schedules, and gives students greater responsibility for their learning. Because the training can be carried out anywhere and at any time, self-study training can make it difficult to monitor student progress or offer help, and it can diminish collaborative interactions among students. These downsides pertain to how the organization provides feedback to its members and facilitates the integration of their experiences.

Learning in a realistic setting has potential consequences for individual learners, as analyzed in box 6.12. But it also has consequences for work groups' incorporating learners and their more experienced colleagues. More and less experienced colleagues can pool their competencies and work together more easily if they are in similar task environments. Thus, training on realistic tasks increases the possibility of collegial coaching. A possible downside is that specious similarities between training tasks and real work activities could mislead colleagues into trying to work together when doing so is not appropriate; for example, inexperienced group members may take initiative in critical work activities before they are competent to do so.

We originally adopted the technique of emphasizing the design of a single, paradigmatic application in order to motivate individual learners and situate their learning in a meaningful task setting. The same feature, however, has consequences for groups of programmers. The blackjack design provided the learner community with a shared paradigm example—a focus for acknowledging and discussing their interests in design. Foregrounding design as a programming activity is very consistent with the object-oriented programming paradigm and thus broadly supportive of the organization goal of adopting that paradigm.

On the other hand, many of the programming groups we worked with incorporated a division of labor in which some members worked at a code design level and others at a coding level. The latter group tended not to see application design as a personal concern because their efforts were

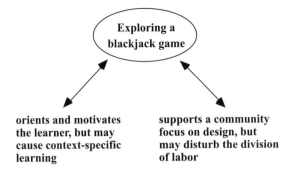

Figure 6.5
Scenarios of use can be developed at both the individual task and organizational work levels.

directed at lower levels of software design (such as optimizing individual algorithms; MiTTS did not address topics of this sort). Perhaps undermining this division of labor is a constructive step toward establishing the object-oriented paradigm, but it was not always perceived as such by the groups we worked with. Also, we observed a tendency for organizations sometimes to make too normative an interpretation of the blackjack game design, taking it as a kind of locally standard template for object decomposition in general. Although we did offer the blackjack design as a paradigm example of object-oriented analysis, it was certainly not a universal design pattern.

Scenarios can be developed and articulated in claims analyses at both the individual task level (as in boxes 6.10 and 6.12) and at the organizational task level (as in box 6.13). The individual task level considers the cognitive, perceptual, and affective consequences for a single individual. The organizational task level considers consequences for a group incorporating multiple persons in a variety of roles, and for the interactions among these persons. This is depicted in figure 6.5.

Note that MiTTS is not "groupware" (Baecker 1993) in the conventional sense of requiring more than one participant. Indeed, one point of the MiTTS example is that most software is ipso *facto* both groupware and individual "cognitive artifact" (Norman 1991), and should be analyzed as both. Even "user-centered" approaches to the design and evaluation of information systems and applications still tend to focus on the task and skill requirements of individuals considered in social isolation, though ultimately the systems and applications that are developed and deployed will be assessed in terms of their ability to satisfy organizational objectives.

The Place of Claims Analysis in Scenario-Based Design

Scenario-based design can be an effective yet flexible tool for making use—that is, for tracking and attacking the myriad and tangled constraints, desiderata, and contextual factors that define the design space for an artifact in use. Developing and maintaining a set of design scenarios addresses many of the key technical problems. Scenarios help designers consider, question, and clarify their concerns and objectives in terms of the use situations that may be created by their designs. Scenarios help designers envision transformations of use situations that could be caused by their designs before those designs are set in stone. Scenarios help designers reason about trade-offs in their designs—about specific usage consequences that might be afforded or obstructed by particular design features or sets of features. Scenarios provide a medium in which design knowledge can be captured, developed, and used by other designers, allowing design work to move from the paradigm of implicit craft evolution toward the paradigms of explicit applied science and engineering. Perhaps most important, scenarios keep design work focused on human activities—increasingly the chance that new technologies will be useful to people and appropriate.

This chapter examined usability rationale, an elaboration of "pure" scenario-based design that makes explicit the potential causal relationships between features of a design and consequences for use. We revisited the MiTTS design case of chapter 5 but tried to probe it more deeply. We illustrated claims analysis as an analytical method for generating and evaluating potential causal relations between design features and use. Where a scenario is chiefly a narrative inventory of the typical and momentous things that people may do and experience, a claims analysis seeks to get at just how a designed artifact suggests to people that they do something one way or another, how it supports and fails to support their efforts, how it signals progress and error. Scenarios are integrated descriptions of what can happen to people and their activities; usability rationale, such as claims analysis, goes beyond this to offer an explanation of the scenarios, an analysis of why the scenarios can occur.

As is true for scenario-based design in general, usability rationale is largely a methodological refinement of design practice that already exists. Many design case studies, particularly in the areas of information systems, applications, and user interfaces, are brimming with usability claims, arguments, and attributions. Often, however, they seem almost unwittingly psychological. For example, descriptions of object-oriented systems typically incorporate assertions about the "naturalness" of this programming and software design paradigm, but without any explicit psychological account of what might be involved in making such an attribution, that is, without saying what it means to be "natural" or what follows from it (Rosson and Alpert 1990). The intent of usability rationale, as described in this chapter, is to achieve greater specificity in appeals to scenarios of use.

Even when appeals to scenarios of use and to their underlying usability rationale are fairly specific, they often innocently conflate the designer's intentions as to how people will engage and experience a design with attested or observable consequences of the design as it is experienced by its users. For example, Smith et al. (1982) discuss the claim that graphical presentation of a user interface metaphor can facilitate learning and use by supporting analogical reasoning. This claim states the intent of the designers and is offered as part of a design memoir. It is useful for designers to capture and report their intentions; after all, these intentions underlie what was done and can provide important insights toward analyzing a design. The usability rationale in Smith et al. (1982) is indeed an example of design memoir that proved to be generally illuminating for user interface design. However, there is a distinction between an intention and a result, between a personal memoir and an objective analysis: intentions are part of the historical context of design work; results and analyses are the explanation. The intent of usability rationale is to achieve greater objectivity and better grounding in appeals to scenarios of use.

A personal memoir of design intention is true merely because the designer had that intention. In contrast, the scenarios and claims of a usability rationale are specific empirical hypotheses that can be evaluated and developed through observation and experimentation. For example, the question of whether permanent display and joint updating of the View Matcher tools support the integration of the information displayed in tools (relative to the baseline integration supported by the Smalltalk environment) can be specifically investigated; particular error patterns can show where and how learners become overwhelmed with the amount of information they need to interpret. Moreover, scenarios and claims articulate *both* desirable and undesirable potential consequences; memoirs are almost always entirely positive discussions of how a good idea was developed.

The features of an artifact-in-use cannot be understood in isolation from the whole design. It is dangerously naive to consider the impacts of a single feature, like a user interface metaphor, without taking that feature in the context of other significant features of the artifact and the situations of its use. Figure 6.2, for example, schematizes a line of reasoning for the touchstone scenario (analyzing a card-hand display). Providing coordinated access to the message execution stack (and other Smalltalk tools) mitigates the prominence of the Class Hierarchy Browser and helps learners attend to run-time code relationships. However, as detailed in box 6.4, many design issues remain open, some of them *caused* by this enhancement (programmers are not challenged to learn for themselves how to access and manage the system tools that provide access to run-time information). Carroll and Kellogg (1989) argue that designed artifacts characteristically embody a nexus of usability claims, not a simple list of independent effects. Claims analysis segregates the causal factors by scenario, highlighting a set of design features and associated consequences in a compact list.

The designers of information systems, applications, and user interfaces are making use as best they can. The memoir of Smith et al. (1982) spawned a voluminous research literature on user interface metaphors and many developments in user interface technology. The point of contrasting design memoir with usability rationale is not to fault early classics but to emphasize that we can and should do better. We can upgrade the somewhat uncritical advocacy of design memoirs to a design-based science that seriously attempts to explain how things work and why by articulating specific and explicit hypotheses that can be evaluated and developed.

The next two chapters pursue this. Chapter 7 addresses cumulation: design arguments of the sort mapped in figures 6.2, 6.3, and 6.4 show how design knowledge develops through direct hill climbing, local improvements to a predecessor artifact-in-use. If we can do better than this, abstracting and generalizing particular usability rationales, we can provide more powerful sources and reservoirs of design knowledge and make design-based science more than merely a figure of speech. Chapter 8 addresses evaluation: scenarios and claims are explicit hypotheses about how artifacts are used and with what consequences for people and their activities. Accordingly, they can provide substantive guidance for designing and interpreting evaluation data. Indeed, they make evaluation work far more valuable by allowing us to attribute evaluation data to general design knowledge, and not only to specific artifacts in specific use contexts.

7

Cumulative Design

The past several chapters demonstrated how scenarios can be used as a central design representation. A key to the scenario-based approach is usability rationale: explicit statements about how particular design elements might affect use. Usability rationale provides designers with a succinct summary of the potentially critical issues and relationships pertaining to a given scenario of use or a set of scenarios. It is a tool that supports the development and evaluation of scenarios within an evolutionary design process, allowing that process to be more systematic, more thoughtful, and more cumulative.

The examples so far have emphasized "hill climbing" from prior design situations: Raison d'Etre provided support for making use of informal project history, and MiTTS provided support for learning Smalltalk programming. In both cases, the design result was achieved by addressing issues identified in direct predecessor scenarios to climb toward better alternatives. Usability rationale was employed as a means of identifying the most important issues to address in doing this.

Hill climbing is often an effective approach to design. Starting from an extant situation of use helps to concretize the design problem immediately. It focuses how to conceptualize the design issues and what sorts of solutions to entertain on the manifest problems and latent opportunities in current practice. This greatly simplifies the space of issues and possibilities that might have been considered, and does so in a way that provides an obvious and prominent role for users and use in the design work. Hill climbing from one situation to another, when it is grounded by explicit scenario descriptions and usability rationale, can make design more productively reflective and more cumulative: prior design work is used technically and articulately, not merely as inspiration. The design reasoning from learning Smalltalk in the unadorned programming environment to doing so with the View Matcher tool demonstrates this.

The strengths of hill climbing are coupled to its weaknesses. When we start with a specific situation of use and ask how it can be improved, there is little chance that our understanding of the design problem, or the solutions we create for it, will be radically innovative. Hill climbing tends to be inertial and myopic; the reasoning is local, from a specific predecessor artifact and its use to a specific successor artifact and its use. Given a lemon, it may produce lemonade, but it does not question whether the lemon was the right starting point. In the worst cases, it optimizes for salient but inconsequential design issues, while overlooking more profound issues.

It is often possible to engage a more powerful kind of design reasoning than hill climbing from a specific predecessor. These are cases in which more than one prior design bears on a project, or in which general types of designs or patterns of preference, need, or activity can be adduced to a project. Expert designers are able to recognize potential connections between a current design problem and various artifacts and use situations encountered in the past. In the context of industrial design, Dreyfuss (1955) referred to these as "survival forms," design elements or patterns worth remembering and reusing. Survival forms are, by definition, only *potentially* relevant, but they are an excellent complement to hill climbing. Where hill climbing focuses on analysis and incremental improvement of a particular use context, survival forms are vehicles for potentially relevant, proved innovations, imported from other use contexts.

Survival forms are generalizations across design domains. The minimalist instructional theory, discussed in chapters 5 and 6, is a design generalization that guided the development of MiTTS. This chapter describes two techniques for systematically codifying and using design generalizations: principled emulation and activity modeling. In principled emulation, the scenarios and usability rationale for a nonpredecessor artifact are adduced to a current design. In activity modeling, aspects of a human practice or activity are encouraged and supported in a current design, based on a usability rationale for that practice or activity. These supplements to direct hill climbing are depicted in figure 7.1.

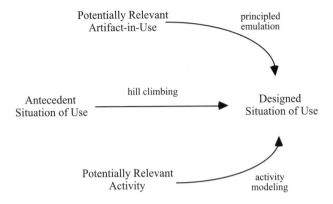

Figure 7.1
Activity modeling and principled emulation complement hill climbing by emphasizing the use of design generalizations

This chapter examines three design projects in which we tried to reach beyond strictly local hill climbing in applying usability rationale. In the first project, we extended the design genre of the View Matcher to the support of a new set of programming tasks. In the second, we developed a new sort of tool for a tutoring system, based on rationale from prior tutoring systems and from observed coaching interactions among teachers and students. In the third, we developed a goal-analysis tool, again generalizing the rationale of prior tutoring systems and extant instructional situations.

A View Matcher for Reuse

When we began to deploy the View Matcher as part of our MiTTS tutorial, several people inquired as to whether we could extend the tool for use in routine programming. These requests were not specific; rather, it seemed that the users appreciated something about the View Matcher approach. We decided that this was indeed an interesting request to try to respond to, perhaps in part because it required us to discover the nature of the request itself.

We decided to focus our redesign effort on facilitating code reuse, because this is so fundamental to Smalltalk programming. Smalltalk provides a rich and extensible hierarchy of classes, and any significant project involves reuse of this code. For example, a manager might want to create a directory associating staff members with descriptions of their special skills and current projects. The manager would want to be able to browse, search, add and remove names, edit descriptions, and so forth. An application like this can be created in ten minutes by reusing the Dictionary, ListPane, TextPane classes.

We decided to address the situation in which a programmer is in the midst of pursuing a programming goal and wishes to reuse code as appropriate in achieving the goal. A programmer engaged in such a task may have several sorts of concerns (Fischer 1987; Raj and Levy 1989). First, he or she may search for a candidate class or classes that could help to provide the required functionality. When a candidate class is identified, the programmer orients more specifically to that class, wondering what it can contribute. If the class looks promising, the programmer will wonder how it can be incorporated into the project at hand. If anything unexpected occurs in working with the class, the programmer will wonder how it works. Finally, if the programmer determines that the class has only some of the necessary characteristics, the reuse project may encompass a concern with how to specialize the class.

We focused on the middle three concerns: those involving questions about the functionality, usage protocol, and implementation of a target class. Based on our experience with Smalltalk and Smalltalk programming, we created a set of reuse scenarios, exemplified in box 7.1, to make these three concerns vivid and help articulate the usability issues of Smalltalk reuse. We also wanted to make use of our analysis of the View Matcher for learning Smalltalk as a starting point for our design of a View Matcher for code reuse.

Two important differences between learning and reuse situations are that the goal in a reuse situation is well defined, and that the agent is assumed to be experienced, fluent at finding and interpreting information in the system. However, analyzing a class in order to reuse it *is* a kind of learning; the programmer learns about a particular class or functionality. The Smalltalk claims we identified for the reuse situation reflect similarities between the two task contexts. For example, as a learner might explore a demo application to learn something about how Smalltalk

Box 7.1

Reuse scenarios for Smalltalk/VPM. The scenarios exemplify concerns that arise after a programmer has identified a candidate class for reuse.

What do Sliders do? A programmer sees Slider in the class hierarchy, and the name sounds as if it might be useful to the current project—a color-mixing application. It is a subclass of ControlBox, which seems consistent with this inference. The programmer takes a look at the messages defined for Slider; they sound as if they involve input handling (e.g., `adjustToMouse:`), but it is not clear how they fit together or what the look and feel of the Slider will be. The programmer tries to find an example instance to work with, asking for "allInstances" of the class, but none exists. Because this is a user interface object, the programmer suspects that it will require considerable set-up to create an example, so finally hunkers down to read through the code.

Hooking up a BoardGamePane: A programmer wants to use an instance of BoardGamePane in a chess game being developed, and needs to know how to connect it to the current objects. The programmer takes a look at the code for BoardGamePane, and sees that it has a boardPane instance variable, and asks for "senders" of the `boardPane:` message, hoping to see situations in which this variable gets set. A long list is returned, but the programmer infers that many of the senders involve other implementations of this message. Scrolling through the list, the programmer sees BoardGameWindow. This class sounds promising, so the programmer goes off to look at its code, to try to figure out how it uses a BoardGamePane.

Analyzing slider scale conversion: The programmer has successfully incorporated three sliders into the color-mixing application, setting them up to have a horizontal layout. As the mouse moves, the slider changes size, but the color output is not right. The programmer puts a halt into the code for adjustToMouse:, and when the application halts, inspects the mouse value, which seems correct. Using the debugger stepping functions, the programmer then traces through all subsequent message sends, checking values at each point to see when the error occurs.

programs work (recall box 6.6), a programmer might send messages to an object to explore its functionality (as in the Sending messages to an object claim in box 7.2). As the first scenario in box 7.1 illustrates, a downside is that the programmer must often create objects from scratch, which can be quite cumbersome (for example, a user interface object that must be connected to several other objects; see Gold and Rosson 1991).

As in the learning scenarios, if programmers can find or create a representative example, Smalltalk encourages them to enlist the system tools in the analysis of the example. Using the debugger, programmers can trace the message-passing activity of an application that uses a target object, to see when and in what context messages are sent to the object, as well as to see what messages the target object sends in fulfilling these requests. The inspector allows them to examine the target object's changing state over time, to understand how the object manages itself in the process of fulfilling requests. Also as in the learning scenarios, it is up to the programmer to set up an informative situation and to extract and integrate the information relevant to the use or implementation of the target object.

As in our learning analyses, the salience of the class hierarchy focuses programmers' attention on inheritance relationships. This has consequences for each of the three reuse concerns. For programmers wondering what a class can do, an inheritance context can be quite helpful. Programmers should be able to predict something about the target class's functionality based on that of its superclass.

Inheritance relations are less directly helpful if the programmer wishes to know how an object is used. What the programmer really needs to know is how other kinds of objects make requests of the target object. In the "Hooking up a BoardGamePane" scenario in box 7.1, the programmer asks for the senders of the squares: message. By examining the code within which a message is sent, the programmer can determine something about the sending context (what kinds of objects send it, and in what circumstances). A downside is that in Smalltalk, a given message name may have multiple implementations (that is, may be implemented differently for different classes), and the implementation invoked in response to a message can be determined only at run time. The sender's query returns a list of all code that includes the message name string, but this list often

Box 7.2
Reuse claims embodied in the design of Smalltalk/V

What do Sliders do?

Sending messages to an object
+ supports discovery of its functionality
− finding or creating a representative instance may be difficult
− trying out individual messages may be tedious and distracting to ongoing work

Descriptive class and method names
+ suggest the functionality provided by a class
− some names may be ambiguous or inappropriate
− object behavior may be too complex to suggest merely with a name

The primacy of the class hierarchy
+ directs attention to inheritance relationships among the objects
− programmers may not be familiar with a class's superclasses
− superclass functionality may not predict subclass specialization

Hooking up a BoardGamePane

Tracing an application's message passing
+ allows programmers to build schemas for use of its components
− temporal integration of requests to a single object may be difficult
− abstraction of communication and control relationships among the objects may be difficult

Halting an application in the midst of receiving a particular message
+ supports functional analysis of the message's role
− it may be difficult to tie this analysis to the visual state of the application

The primacy of the class hierarchy
+ directs attention to inheritance relationships among the objects
− it may reduce attention to sender-receiver relationships

Browsing a class's method code
+ helps in understanding how to use the class
− programmers may be distracted by irrelevant implementation details

Message-naming conventions
+ allow programmers to predict parts of a class's usage protocol
− many message are not covered by convention

Examining the senders of a message
+ supports analysis of the context in which this request is made
− a senders listing may include many false alarms

Box 7.2
(continued)

Analyzing slider scale conversion

Tracking the messages sent and the state changes produced in the process of evaluating a message
+ allows programmers to analyze message implementation
− the programmer must initiate, control, and integrate the analysis
The primacy of the class hierarchy
+ directs attention to inheritance relationships among the objects
− it may reduce attention to other functional relationships, such as those provided through instance variables

---

contains false alarms—code in which this message is sent, but (as it turns out at run time) not to an instance of the target class.

Principled Emulation of a View Matcher

The usability rationale in box 7.2 provides guidance for direct hill climbing to support reuse concerns in Smalltalk better. We wanted to use this rationale in concert with that which we had developed earlier regarding the View Matcher for learning. Much of our design reasoning was by analogy: what are the analogous representative examples to incorporate into a reuse analysis, what should the multiple views of that analysis convey, and how should they be coordinated? To some extent, our ability to reason by analogy in this way indicates that the issues we are concerned with are general: general human propensities and requirements, general limitations of the Smalltalk language environment, and general opportunities for redesign.

The usability rationale for learning Smalltalk and for the original View Matcher highlighted the importance of example applications as vehicles for learning and pointed to issues concerning support for analyzing such examples. Similarly, the usability rationale for reuse in Smalltalk highlighted the potential of analyzing an example application's use of a target object, understanding the context of this use, and analyzing the target object's state and activity over episodes of use. Empirical studies of expert

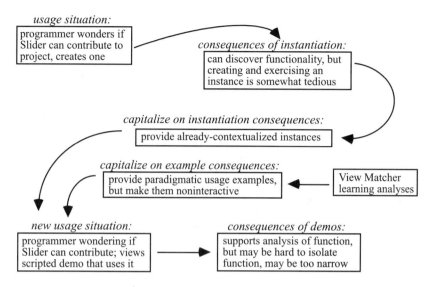

Figure 7.2
Evolution of demos and examples in the View Matcher

Smalltalk programmers showed that example-based reuse was a typical pattern (Rosson and Carroll 1993, 1996a). By analogy, then, we conjectured that a Reuse View Matcher should center on an example application that makes use of a target object and should provide coordinated views to support analysis of this use.

Box 7.2 schematizes the development of usage demos in the Reuse View Matcher both from analysis of reuse in Smalltalk and from analyses of Smalltalk learning.

The claims map in figure 7.2 illustrates how our design of the reuse examples considered not only the advantages of working with an example instance of the target class, but also the usability rationale developed earlier regarding demos and interactive examples in learning. Smalltalk learners are searching for reasonable goals, pursuing goals opportunistically, trying to make sense of things. Smalltalk's demos encourage this mode of learning, but are not paradigmatic code examples and do not provide meaningful activity (recall box 6.6); the View Matcher addresses this downside with its provision of paradigmatic interactive applications (box 6.8). The code reuse situation is different. An experienced programmer seeking to reuse a class is not looking for appropriate goals, but rather is already in the midst of a meaningful project and is seeking specific information about a candidate reuse target. The programmer wants as little distraction as possible from the ongoing project. This suggested to us that appropriate examples for reuse analysis should be scripted (as the Smalltalk demos are).

A key idea in our design approach to the Reuse View Matcher was to provide small, focused examples that are easily accessed and demonstrate core functionality and interactions with other objects, but require little activity on the part of the programmer beyond interpretation. As illustrated by the "What do Sliders do?" scenario in box 7.3, the programmer opens a Reuse View Matcher on an object and runs a demo. The demos illustrate what the reuse candidate can do in various simple application contexts.

Viewing the demos addressed only our first reuse concern. We also wanted programmers to be able to pursue questions about the usage protocol and implementation of reuse candidates. This guided us to a second key idea in our design approach to the Reuse View Matcher. After a demo plays out, the programmer can browse structured and coordinated documentation for that demo context. In the "Hooking up a BoardGamePane" scenario in box 7.3, a programmer wants to know how to connect the BoardGamePane object to game objects. After viewing the demo, the programmer is able to revisit the specific portion of the demo in which the game board was updated. The programmer can study the instance variable and message-sending relationships among the pane, its window, and the window's owner (the game)—in this case, finding that the pane gets game board information from the window, which gets it from the game.

This notion of allowing the programmer to revisit and analyze usage demos led us to envision the Reuse View Matcher as coordinated by the episodes of the demo. Each demo could be expanded into a list of constituent usage episodes (for example, the gomoku game demo could be expanded as "starting up the game," "making a move," and "clearing the board"). The episodes can be expanded in turn to display the requests that are either sent to the target object directly (for example, `boardPane at: aPoint draw: (self convertPiece: aSymbol)`), or that include the target object as an argument. Finally, each message sent to the

Box 7.3
Design scenarios for the reuse View Matcher. The scenarios instantiate the same high-level goals as those used for analysis of Smalltalk in box 7.1, but describe how the goal might be pursued using the new system.

What do Sliders do? A programmer sees Slider in the class hierarchy, and the name sounds as if it might be useful to the current project, a color-mixing application. The programmer opens a View Matcher on it and selects the first example, a football player analysis program. A short demo of the football program is shown, and the programmer sees that sliders are being used to manipulate player characteristics that predict several player success measures. The programmer recognizes that this situation is very similar to the needs of the color mixer, but goes on to view a second demo, an economic simulation in which the sliders interact with one another, constraining each other's values.

Hooking up a BoardGamePane: A programmer wants to use an instance of BoardGamePane in the chess game being built and needs to know how to connect it to the game objects. The programmer opens a View Matcher on the BoardGamePane class and selects the first example, a gomoku game. After watching the demo, the programmer examines the object communication map; the map shows that there is a Gomoku object that points to a GomokuWindow, an instance of a subclass of BoardGameWindow, and that the window points to a BoardGamePane. The programmer wonders how the board updates during a move, and selects the "making a move" usage episode. The analysis of the episode describes how the GomokuWindow updates its BoardGamePane, specifying which graphic game piece to draw in the currently selected square.

Analyzing slider scale conversion: A programmer has successfully incorporated three sliders into the color-mixing application, setting them up to have a horizontal layout. As the mouse moves, the slider changes size, but the color output is not right. The programmer opens a View Matcher on Slider, selects the football example, and expands the "increase player speed" episode. The usage analysis updates to show the messages sent to the slider. The programmer expands the adjustToMouse: message and sees that it involves an internal request for a scale reading. The programmer examines the code for the scale reading, finding an error in the conversion algorithm.

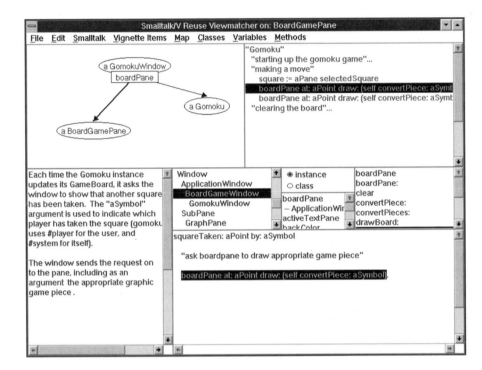

Figure 7.3
View Matcher window for the BoardGamePane class. The usage view is in the upper right, the communication map in the upper left, the class hierarchy view in the lower right and the commentary view in the lower left. The programmer has already viewed the gomoku usage demo and is exploring the messages involving the BoardGamePane in the "making a move" episode. In the communication map, the connection between the window and the subpane has been selected and shows the name of the window's instance variable that refers to the instance of BoardGamePane.

target object can be expanded to display messages the object sends to itself in carrying out the request. (See figure 7.3.)

The usage episodes also coordinate other views of the usage context. The communication map provides a graphic representation of the relevant communication context. At the level of a usage demo, this consists of the relationship of the target object to the controlling objects of the application (for example, showing that boardPane is an instance variable of the BoardGameWindow object, which in turn is an instance variable of the Gomoku object). When a specific usage episode or a message within an episode is selected, the communication map updates as necessary to display other supporting objects. At any time, the programmer can select one of the objects in the communication map and inspect that object's internal state either before or after the point under analysis in the usage view (for example, before an episode begins or after it completes, or before a particular message is sent or after it is evaluated). This information is captured during the demo presentation.

A filtered class hierarchy view is used to show the relevant sender code. When an episode is selected, the browser shows the method code from which this episode was initiated (for example, the gomoku selectedSquare method for the "making a move" episode); when a particular message in the episode is selected, the browser displays the code within which this message was sent (for example, `at:draw:` is sent within the `BoardGameWindow squareTaken:by:` method). The class hierarchy view supports a copy/edit reuse strategy (Lange and Moher 1989) by directing attention to the code in which a message is sent, but may confuse programmers who expect to see the implementation of the message itself.

The commentary view describes the contributions of the target object as a function of the current selection in the usage view, to the application as a whole, more specifically to a usage episode, or even more specifically to the evaluation of a particular message.

As in the case of the View Matcher for learning, the design of the Reuse View Matcher involved direct hill climbing from Smalltalk. We tried to capitalize on the claims of Smalltalk for reuse while addressing their downsides. Thus the usage view is an approximation to the message tracing available with the Debugger, but it enumerates only messages that are sent to the object of interest or include it as an argument. We added to this message trace a presentation that would make explicit the communication and control relationships among the participating objects (the "communication map"). The filtered Class Hierarchy Browser capitalizes on inheritance structure with respect to predicting a target class's functionality but addresses the downside that inheritance reveals little about usage. Because the example application exemplifies use of the target object, exploration of it in the browser will necessarily involve accessing true "senders" code. (See box 7.4.)

Box 7.4
Usability claims embodied in the View Matcher for code reuse

What do Sliders do?

Viewing paradigmatic scripted demos that use a target object
+ helps programmers analyze its functionality
+ minimizes distraction from the ongoing project
− people may have difficulty isolating the target functionality
− the concept induced might be too narrow

Descriptive class and method names
+ suggest the functionality provided by a class
− some names may be ambiguous or inappropriate
− object behavior may be too complex to suggest merely with a name

Hooking up a BoardGamePane

Permanent display and coordination of multiple views of an object's use
+ support convergent reasoning
− novelty of views and amount of information presented may make analysis difficult

Connections between the target object and other objects in a usage episode
+ provide a template for its incorporation into other design contexts
− may convey a fragmented view of the demo application's design

Requests made of an object during a usage episode
+ provide a template for exercising a particular functionality
− may convey a fragmented view of the usage application's activity
− programmers may overgeneralize the details of particular episodes

The episodes comprising a usage demo
+ evoke specific subgoals for analyzing how its components are used
− the demonstrated episodes may limit the range of reuse contexts that are considered
− it may be difficult to connect analysis subgoals to the observed features of the demo

Directing programmers' attention to the code in which a message is sent
+ supports creation of analogous sender code in a new application
− experienced programmers may be disturbed when the browser does not display a message's implementation

Result-oriented commentary for each message in the usage view
+ promotes a functional analysis of the target object's role
− may discourage analysis of how a particular request is fulfilled

Box 7.4
(continued)

Seeing a demo
+ provides an advance organizer for the usage view and communication map
– programmer could fail to see the relevance of the demonstrated behavior to the current project

Analyzing slider scale conversion

Analyzing requests made to self in response to a message
+ supports inferences about message implementation
– may discourage a complete decomposition of the request
Examining the state of relevant objects before and after a message send
+ facilitates analysis of the message's preconditions and consequences
– some consequences may not be apparent in state changes

The design of the Reuse View Matcher also illustrates principled emulation. The Reuse View Matcher is not a successor design for the original View Matcher situation; rather it is a systematic extension of that prior design work to a new situation. To make such an extension, one must recognize that some of the relevant usability issues have been analyzed before and that some of the approaches taken to these issues may be appropriate. The key insight in this case was seeing that multiple coordinated views of an example might be effective, and for reasons we had analyzed before (providing model applications for programmers to analyze and adapt; box 6.8). We were also able to reason from our prior analyses that the role of examples in this new situation might be systematically different (for example, we did *not* want to motivate programmers to practice basic skills; box 6.8).

We created a heuristic mapping between elements of the View Matcher design and rationale, and corresponding elements in the new design. The usage view corresponds to the stack view of the original View Matcher in that interactions with it drive the coordination of the other views. The message execution stack supports learners' decomposition of a running application into its basic transactions (by break points delineating interactions between the underlying application and its user interface), helping them to see how the parts cooperate to produce the overall functionality; it also provides an important path for learning transfer, though perhaps promoting too procedural a view of application activity (box 6.4). In the reuse case, we assumed that experienced programmers are the users, so the transfer consequence becomes less important. We hypothesized that by providing an analysis of the demos into usage episodes typifying the target object's contribution to the application, the tool would support a decomposition that was both more task relevant and more object oriented.

While the analysis in box 7.4 focuses on an individual agent's programming activity and experience, the Reuse View Matcher also has potential consequences for programming organizations. When aggregated, the reuse practices described in box 7.3 imply a group programming practice in which documented examples like the color mixer and the chess game are shared among colleagues. This would have the effect of creating a cooperative software development community. It would facilitate but also standardize—and therefore perhaps limit—the reuse of classes like Slider and BoardGamePane. This causal relationship extends the Example-based Instruction claim of box 6.13.

In this project, usability rationale allowed our design work to be more deliberate and cumulative. Projecting the rationale from an immediate predecessor system and its use makes hill climbing more deliberate and more principled. In this example, we showed that prior work can be extended into new design situations as well. General concepts like paradigmatic examples, view coordination, and filtering were abstracted and generalized from one design project to another. Studies of expert Smalltalk programmers using the Reuse View Matcher indicated that it did support their example-based reuse practices (Rosson and Carroll 1996a). This allows us greater confidence that we are standing on the shoulders of our prior View Matcher design work and the specific claims it embodies, and not merely in the vicinity of prior work. This in turn raises questions and possibilities about design genre (Newman 1988): can we better articulate and more deliberately emulate and develop a View Matcher species of artifacts?

Activity Modeling in the MoleHill Guru

The Reuse View Matcher design project encouraged us to explore further design abstractions based on usage scenarios and usability rationale. Several opportunities to pursue this arose in the subsequent MoleHill design project. MoleHill is an intelligent tutoring system for Smalltalk (Singley and Carroll 1990, 1996; Singley, Carroll, and Alpert 1991). The name "MoleHill" conveys the objective of reducing the "Smalltalk mountain" of novel programming concepts and skills (Rosson and Carroll 1990). Among the system's a variety of integrated tools and resources is the Guru, an animated documentation tool that provides project post-mortem commentary critiquing the execution of a tutorial project (Alpert, Singley, and Carroll 1995, 1999).

The MoleHill project took a very empirical approach to scenario-based design. We observed experienced procedural programmers working on tutorial projects. Box 7.5 summarizes a scenario in which the programmer was to implement a new kind of text pane that displays its input in uppercase. This project involves learning about two key subtrees of the Smalltalk class hierarchy, Magnitude-Character and Window-SubPane-TextPane, and allows the programmer to implement a concrete and usable new Smalltalk object by extending existing system functionality with a minimum of coding. The programmer carries out the project by subclassing the TextPane class and specializing the code that processes character input from the keyboard. Although this project involves writing only a few lines of code, it typically takes an intermediate-level Smalltalk programmer about thirty minutes to find the appropriate reusable components and test the solution.

We carried out a claims analysis of the scenarios we had observed to identify more sharply the design issues to be addressed by MoleHill (box 7.6). We did this by asking questions to elaborate the events in the scenarios. For the UpperCasePane scenario (box 7.5), we asked: Why did the programmer search for relevant functionality while still defining a strategy toward the project? Did anything about the situation make it especially difficult or easy to proceed in this way? What was the programmer thinking about while browsing for relevant classes and methods? Did

Box 7.5
A Smalltalk tutorial scenario "Creating an UpperCasePane."

- A beginning Smalltalk programmer is working through a series of tutorial projects designed to provide initial familiarity with some central classes and methods. The programmer is trying to create a new kind of textpane that displays keyboard input in uppercase.
- The programmer searches for existing relevant functionality, simultaneously trying to define an approach to the project and to identify existing software resources for it. Eventually the programmer locates the methods asUpperCase (in the Character class) and characterInput: (in the TextPane class). The sheer number of possibly relevant classes and methods necessitates considerable browsing in order to do this, and the programmer pursues several incorrect possibilities along the way (the programmer has trouble finding the Character class, later losing track of where it is while browsing in TextPane, and at first considers specializing the appendText: method of TextPane, which does not take a character argument).
- The programmer specializes TextPane by creating a new subclass UpperCasePane, copying down its characterInput: method, and altering one line of the code to transform the characterInput: argument asUpperCase
- The programmer creates and tests an UpperCasePane. The programmer is satisfied with the result and decides to move on to the next tutorial project.

---

the programmer have any particular difficulties with browsing; did he or she benefit from the browsing activity? Why did the programmer pursue several incorrect possibilities when searching for relevant functionality? Why was appendText: considered, and why was it finally rejected? Why did the programmer have trouble finding, and then later lose track of, Character class? Why did the programmer copy down the method code for characterInput:, instead of inheriting the functionality using super? How did the programmer decide to use Character's asUpperCase method? Why does the programmer test only one UpperCasePane, and test only the external behavior of the pane?

The answers to such questions are a set of hypotheses about the underlying causal relations in the scenario—the analyst's hypotheses about why and how an observed (or envisioned) scenario of use could occur. Some of this usability rationale was familiar and anticipated, based on our earlier work with the View Matcher. For example, the programmer in box 7.5 has some difficulty navigating the Smalltalk class hierarchy (recall box 6.2). This suggests that the tutorial might be improved by incorporating an indexing tool.

A more subtle example, but an important one in Smalltalk programming, is that in box 7.5 a method is *copied* to a subclass instead of being specialized to inherit functionality from the superclass. This is a poor programming practice from the standpoint of reuse and system maintenance; it masks the fact that the characterInput: method in UpperCasePane is a variant of the same-named method in TextPane, the superclass of UpperCasePane. Smalltalk provides a mechanism, the special variable *super*, to make such inheritance relations clear; when a message is sent to super, the Smalltalk interpreter looks in the superclass for the code. Thus, one can write the characterInput: method for UpperCasePane to return the value of the expression `super characterInput: (aCharacter asUpperCase)`.

The usability rationale in box 7.6 supports hill climbing of the sort discussed in chapter 6. It provides direct guidance for envisioning alternate scenarios such that downside consequences of particular claims are obviated or mitigated, while upside consequences are enhanced or maintained. We also used this claims analysis more abstractly to help us orient to and identify relevant, nonpredecessor artifacts whose techniques and rationale could be adduced to MoleHill, and established human practices or activities, perhaps quite unlike those in our observed scenarios, but which we could try to support in MoleHill.

As a general response to the issue that programmers might not be directing sufficient effort toward design analysis, we explored theories and methods pertaining to reflective activity and design approaches promoting such activity. Our object was to use these ideas to elaborate the design of the Guru and its envisioned consequences for programmers with respect to the claims analysis in box 7.6. We studied LISP-CRITIC (Fischer et al. 1990), an experimental critiquing facility to which programmers may submit code fragments to get suggestions about how to make their code easier to read and maintain or more machine efficient. This system does not place any constraints on how programmers create the code submitted for critique, or on whether or how they use its suggestions. In our analysis, the usability rationale for LISP-CRITIC

Box 7.6
Part of the usability rationale for the UpperCasePane scenario in box 7.5.

An extensive library of classes and methods
+ encourages programmers to reuse standard decompositions in designing new functionality
− programmers must familiarize themselves with the existence and functional roles of many components
− programmers may search the library ineffectively
− programmers may make nonoptimal choices among candidate classes and methods

Descriptive class and method names
+ cause programmers to rely on names in searching for functionality and planning reuse
− may also cause false alarms (by suggesting spurious connections)

Navigating the class hierarchy
+ causes unintentional learning about existing functionality
− may also cause confusion and frustration (since the class hierarchy is so large)

Powerful system tools
+ support browsing, opportunistic problem solving, and a rapid prototyping approach to code development
− may also cause programmers to direct insufficient time and effort to code design

---

hinges on the possibility that a highly specific critique, delivered at the programmer's request and in the context of a current programming situation, can encourage programmers to reflect more on their work without undermining their preferred work style:

Situated Critique claim: A situated critique on specific code design problems—at the programmer's request—
+ causes programmers to reflect more on their code without hampering opportunistic code development
− may also cause programmers to reflect on their work too narrowly (may improve a particular code fragment, but fail to teach a more general design lesson)

We also investigated the theory and technique of reflective practicum (Schön 1987) in which a teacher models expert performance for a student, while commenting on the process of producing such a performance

Box 7.7
A MoleHill Guru scenario, contrasting "copy down" and "reference to super"

- As the programmer completes a tutorial project, he or she is prompted as to the availability of a Smalltalk Guru postmortem for this project.
- The programmer selects the post mortem and the Smalltalk Guru appears and explains that although the solution of copying down the superclass's the characterInput: method is correct, there is another approach in which the method code is maintained only with the superclass (in this case, TextPane). The Guru demonstrates how subclasses can specialize this functionality with a message send to the special variable "super," directing the Smalltalk interpreter to begin searching for the method code in the super class. (The programmer whispers, "So that's how 'super' gets used!)
- At the end of the project-specific postmortem, the programmer is offered more general Guru assistance (for example, a discussion of inheritance), but decides to go on to the next project.

---

and coaching the student on how to move toward achieving such a performance:

Annotated Demonstration claim: The coach's self-consciously annotated demonstration of expert performance
+ causes the student to integrate actions and concepts in a paradigmatic model
− may also cause the student to feel coerced (due to the power imbalance between teacher and student)

A reflective practicum scenario bears on the goal of helping programmers integrate their understanding of inheritance and the use of super in Smalltalk with their strategies for building code. We wished to facilitate the upside consequences of the Annotated Demonstration claim with a kind of software coach; we conjectured that this would mitigate the downside consequence of the claim, since the coach would only be a software tool run by the programmer. Similarly, we wanted to facilitate the upside consequences of the Situated Critique claim and conjectured that an emphasis on architectural issues, like inheritance, might address the downside consequence of the claim. These lines of design reasoning culminated in the Guru scenario in box 7.7.

This scenario describes a design response to the issues in the System Tools claim in box 7.6. Just as the programmer finishes the project, the

Guru offers suggestions about how to achieve a more modular code design, exploiting Smalltalk's inheritance mechanism via the special variable super. The Guru project post mortem encourages reflection on code design, leveraging the inclination people often have for evaluating their own activity, but it does not constrain fluid and opportunistic programming activity prior to the post mortem.

Guru claim: A situated critique on strategic code design problems, with a narrated demonstration of the correct solution—both at the programmer's request—

+ causes programmers to integrate actions and concepts, and to reflect on code design without hampering opportunistic code development

− may also cause programmers to reflect on their work too narrowly (may only encourage use of inheritance via super)

The Guru claim articulates a hypothesis as to the causal dynamics of the scenario and (of course) documents a potential remaining downside consequence (we might have underestimated how difficult it would be to encourage programmers to reflect broadly on an episode of their work). The claim indicates how our solution incorporated each of the several lines of design reasoning we developed: principled emulation of the design technique of LISP-CRITIC, hill climbing from our empirical analysis of Smalltalk tutorial scenarios, and activity modeling of reflective practicum (recall figure 7.1). As depicted in figure 7.4, the design reasoning for the MoleHill Guru integrated these diverse sources of issues and ideas: providing critique within a current problem context, providing narrated demonstration of target skills to better link concepts and actions, and allowing user control of critique initiation and user discretion as to consequent actions.

Developing scenarios through the coordinated use of direct empirical observation and abstractions from principled emulation and activity modeling has the additional benefit of continually emphasizing to the designer the continuities among various design projects. System design is highly creative, but few systems are completely novel. Nevertheless, it is easy in the context of design work to focus too singularly on the project at hand and lose the benefit of whatever might have been done and learned before.

When a scenario, a claims analysis, and a system can be seen as instances of types, one is in a position to generalize whatever is learned

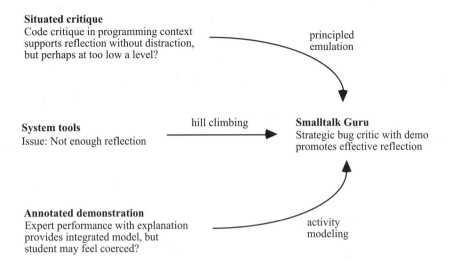

Situated critique
Code critique in programming context
supports reflection without distraction,
but perhaps at too low a level?

principled
emulation

hill climbing

System tools
Issue: Not enough reflection

Smalltalk Guru
Strategic bug critic with demo
promotes effective reflection

Annotated demonstration
Expert performance with explanation
provides integrated model, but
student may feel coerced?

activity
modeling

Figure 7.4
Design reasoning for the MoleHill Guru

about that particular scenario to the type. Our deliberate development of the Guru scenario helped us to appreciate that the Guru was a sort of bug critic (Brown, Burton, and deKleer 1982), critiquing strategic-level programming bugs through demonstration of programming process. This helped us to elaborate the design and the design rationale for the Guru, but it also created the possibility that things we learn about the Guru can be *mapped back* to LISP-CRITIC, and more generally to bug critics. Similarly, drawing on patterns of human activity, like reflective practicum, in generating scenarios to envision a system in design, can also guide us in attributing things we learn about given scenarios of use for given systems to a more general analysis of human activity. In chapter 8 we return to the topic of building knowledge abstractions out of specific design experience.

Genre Specialization in the MoleHill Goalposter

The Guru project was only one facet of MoleHill. A more ambitious objective was to build an intelligent tutoring system that would provide advice and tool support to programmers as they worked on instructional projects. The design of the MoleHill Goalposter is a larger-scale example that incorporates principled emulation and activity modeling, as well as hill climbing (Singley and Carroll 1996). We wanted to make systematic use of prior work in the design genre of intelligent tutoring systems and in studies of pedagogy.

Many tutoring systems have been developed, and a rationale for the genre has emerged (Anderson et al. 1989). We wanted to take advantage of this rationale as a point of departure for our own work. We conjectured that much of the instructional leverage for tutoring systems as a genre stems from accurate and complete task analysis of the domain and successful communication of that analysis to the learner. This is especially true for relatively strategic aspects of a skill: goals and plans.

Goal Reification claim: Reifying a learner's goals and plans
+ promotes an abstract understanding of task structure, which leads to efficient action and broad transfer
– the goal and plan language may be unfamiliar, abstract, and therefore difficult to comprehend

The upside of this claim is drawn from Anderson's cognitive principles of intelligent tutoring (Anderson et al. 1989) and is supported by a myriad of studies of problem solving and instruction. For example, Singley (1990) showed that having learners post goals to a goal blackboard improved measures of both learning and transfer. However, the usefulness of this principle is limited by the extent to which goals and plans can be transparently represented to the learner. Goals and plans are abstract mental entities that learners may not be used to discussing explicitly. And even if goals and plans can be transparently discussed, there still could be difficulties in effectively rendering them as a sequence of operations in a problem situation.

Goal reification is characteristic of tutoring systems generally; it is not just a property of a particular system or instructional setting. We surveyed tutoring systems that instantiate the claim in instructional settings similar to our own in order to understand better how the claim can be embodied in designs. We judged that the two most closely related predecessor artifacts of this type are the tutoring system Bridge (Bonar 1988) and the bug critic Proust (Johnson 1985), both addressed to Pascal programming. In Bridge, learners first code their programming algorithms with planning icons. This makes the planning level very salient to the learners, but it adds substantial complexity. It is possible that learning the planning language is at least as difficult as mastering the Pascal domain itself.

Planning Language claim: Having learners first generate a solution in terms of an abstract planning language and then translate it into code
+ promotes the learning of the plans and provides a holistic view of how plans organize code
− the planning language is an additional language to learn
− learners only make mappings from plans to code and never from code to plans

In Proust, planning structures are not generated or manipulated by learners. Instead, the system performs a plan analysis on the learner's code in the background and then provides error messages and suggested remedies couched in plan-oriented language:

Plan-based Error Messages claim: System-generated error messages couched in terms of goals and plans
+ bring the appropriate planning abstractions to bear when they are needed
+ spare the learner the burden of generating explicit goal and plan descriptions
− learners may develop superficial understandings when errors are not made
− goal-plan dialogues are restricted to errors and are not under learner control

In Proust, learners are not burdened by having to use an explicit planning language. However, the plan analysis is also less directly available to them. Learners get goal and plan information only when they make errors, and then only on goals and plans pertaining to that error. They never receive an overall analysis of the problem structure within which to understand particular plans. From our analysis of the tutoring system genre and of Bridge and Proust, we decided to pursue goal reification by providing learners with a readily available holistic analysis of problem structure without requiring them to program in an explicit planning language.

Every domain is unique. To ensure that our design solution fit the particular demands of the Smalltalk domain, we observed four persons of varying levels of expertise undertake an introductory yet representative project using the standard Smalltalk environment. Our specific goal was to understand better the processes of planning and goal management in Smalltalk so that we could support them with an intelligent tutoring system, without sacrificing important strengths of the Smalltalk environment.

We studied the UpperCasePane project, described in box 7.5, in which a programmer creates a window that transforms and displays all of its keyboard input in uppercase. The participants performed this task on their own with no help from us. They were asked to give verbal protocols as they worked, saying what they were doing and thinking as they carried out the task, and they were videotaped. From these observations, we sought to understand how particular features of the Smalltalk environment influenced their behaviors and experiences and to imagine how various problematic aspects of those features might be addressed in the design of the Goalposter. (For a fuller description of these protocols, see Singley, Carroll, and Alpert 1991.)

Many of our observations concerned problems associated with goal management. Smalltalk provides a rich set of tools to help manage the complexity of the language, but these tools also comprise a burden for learners, making the Smalltalk mountain that much harder to climb (recall claims in boxes 6.2, 6.6, and 7.2). For example, Anderson and Jeffries (1988) analyzed problems that plague beginning LISP programmers, concluding that many errors could be attributed to losses of information from working memory. One might expect that such problems would be even worse in Smalltalk: the flexibility of the environment encourages task switching and incremental development, which exacerbate memory management. Indeed, our protocols contained striking examples of programmers' getting confused, losing their place, and forgetting to perform stated objectives. For example, early in the project, one participant switched among three tasks, searching for the character input functionality, searching for the uppercase transformation functionality, and generating test code. Each time, she had to spend time reestablishing the local goal context and reinstating her understanding of the state of her progress. Our analysis of goal management in Smalltalk is summarized by the following claim (recall box 7.6):

System Tools claim: Smalltalk's powerful system tools
+ support task switching, opportunistic problem solving, and a rapid prototyping approach to code development
− programmers may lose their place or waste time reestablishing context
− programmers may direct insufficient time and effort to code design

Learning Smalltalk involves becoming familiar with a large set of existing classes, and methods, and their inheritance relationships. Beginning programmers often carry out extended searches for the right components to reuse. These searches can be biased by the alphabetical display of classes and methods in the browser. Those at the top of a lengthy list tend to get more consideration than those at the bottom. For example, one of our learners began to search the more than one hundred TextPane methods from the top down, and soon was modifying, testing, and ultimately rejecting the first few methods on that list that seemed relevant from their names alone. She finally did find the method she needed, buried in the middle of the list, but only after pursuing many false leads. Our analysis of browsing in Smalltalk environment is summarized by the following claim (recall box 7.6):

Class Library claim: Smalltalk's extensive library of classes and methods
+ encourages programmers to reuse standard decompositions in designing new functionality
− programmers must familiarize themselves with the existence and functional roles of many components
− programmers may search the library ineffectively
− programmers may make nonoptimal choices among candidate classes and methods

We decided the Goalposter should support memory management in task switching by providing some kind of external record of tasks attempted, tasks completed, and their relation to the current task. We also decided to provide an enhanced browsing environment for the Goalposter to help learners find and evaluate candidate classes and methods.

One-on-one human coaching is a highly effective instructional paradigm (Bloom 1984). We asked two additional participants to work on the uppercase text pane project with a Smalltalk expert, who had also designed Smalltalk instructional materials, acting as a coach. The coach was instructed to intervene supportively, but to avoid being directive or revealing the solution in her advice. We wanted to observe the coach's behavior as a possible model for Goalposter dialogue. This is essentially a knowledge engineering situation, in which we are trying to extract principles of operation from a highly regarded yet poorly understood model (the Smalltalk coach).

The coach reinstated learner goals whenever learners began to flounder. For example, one person began the project by spending a protracted period scanning Window classes in the Class Hierarchy Browser. He finally chanced on the characterInput: method in the TextPane class. By this time, however, he was so completely engrossed in the vagaries of the Window subhierarchy that he had completely forgotten that the project included transformation of keyboard input to uppercase. He began to suggest subgoals to himself, saying, "Now what can I do with this method? Well, I could encode characters, or count them . . ." At this point, the coach intervened: "What do you have to do for this project?" The programmer was surprised; "Oh, I guess I forgot." The coach reinstated the goal of the uppercase transformation, and the subject was on his way again. This episode is consistent with other observations of human tutoring (McKendree 1990) and gave us convergent rationale for the idea of the posting goals:

Reinstating Goals claim: The coach's reinstating of goals for learners
+ facilitates the resolution of problem-solving impasses
− this may rob learners of the opportunity of managing their own goals
− the coach's intervention may be disruptive to ongoing problem solving and memory

The danger in posting goals is that if a coach is too helpful, the learner may not become self-sufficient at generating and maintaining goals. Moreover, the coach's interventions could interrupt the learner's self-initiated efforts (Carroll and Aaronson 1988).

We found it even more interesting that the coach provided feedback even when learners were ostensibly on track. The participants seemed to appreciate this and looked to the coach for confirmatory feedback on hypotheses and goals. When searching for the class that handles character input, one participant asked, "Will it be a class under ApplicationWindow?" He continued to seek confirmation as he selected and ultimately rejected candidate classes. The coach spent a significant amount of her time reassuring the subject by saying, "Yes, that's right." We concluded that such feedback can encourage learners to pursue courses of action and more generally build confidence:

Confirmatory Feedback claim: The coach's confirmation that learners are pursuing legitimate goals
+ provides confidence and allows learners to focus attention on the chosen course of action
– this may rob learners of the opportunity of evaluating their own goals

The downside of the claim is similar to one from the Reinstating Goals claim. Whenever a system provides support there is a danger that support, can become a crutch.

Envisioning and Refining the Goalposter

The defining feature of the Goalposter is that the system creates and posts a goal analysis as the learner carries out a tutorial project. For example, as the learner browses the class hierarchy, a plan parser automatically updates the contents of a goal blackboard to reflect the system's current interpretation of the learner's actions. The Goalposter is useful after a project is finished because it saves goal traces for later inspection. Our intention is that goal traces could be annotated and saved to support analogical problem solving outside the context of the tutor:

System-Generated Goals claim: Having the system generate goal structures throughout the course of problem solving
+ promotes abstract understandings without requiring learners to generate solutions in an abstract language
– recognizing goals may evoke poorer retention than generating goals
– learners must draw correspondences between their own behavior and the display to get help

This claim addresses downsides of Bridge, Proust, and tutoring systems in general with respect to the presentation and timing of goal-oriented help. MoleHill learners carry out their programming activities in Smalltalk itself, not in a special planning language; they receive feedback on goals concurrent with their own planning and acting, not at some later point. However, learners must attend to posted goals and must make the correspondence between the posted structures and their own behavior. Also,

Box 7.8
Beginning of "Creating UpperCasePane" as a Goalposter scenario

---

- A beginning Smalltalk programmer is trying to create an uppercase textpane.
- The learner searches for existing relevant functionality, examining the methods and variables of the Character class and then the TextPane class. A goal hierarchy analysis of the learner's activity is built by the Goalposter in a window adjacent to Class Hierarchy Browser.
- While reading the code for TextPane's characterInput: method, the learner becomes momentarily confused. The learner refers to the Goalposter window for guidance in reconstructing the current state of the project. The learner sees two subgoals pertaining to the goal of finding relevant classes and methods.
- The learner considers whether all relevant classes and methods have been identified, and, after deciding that they have been identified, considers the next project objective.

---

generating information often leads to better memory than mere recognition (Carroll 1990a). Box 7.8 presents a Goalposter scenario, derived from the original UpperCasePane scenario of box 7.5. Figure 7.5 presents a MoleHill screen image of the point in the scenario where the learner has just selected the characterInput: method defined in the Window class.

We wanted the Goalposter to incorporate techniques identified in human coaching, for example, providing confirmatory feedback and reinstating goals. In box 7.8, the learner rapidly converges on the relevant functionality because the system provides concurrent feedback on the relevance of classes and methods as they are browsed. This allows more systematic progress, responding to the downsides of the Class Library claim. However, providing feedback on the relevance of browsing to the current task may discourage open-ended exploration, and thereby deprive the learner of the benefits of exploration and error: incidentally encountering material that may prove useful later and developing strategies for diagnosing and recovering from error:

Browsing Feedback claim: Providing feedback on browsing
+ supports more systematic search for appropriate components to reuse
+ provides confirmation for correct user actions
− may inhibit incidental learning and learning from errors

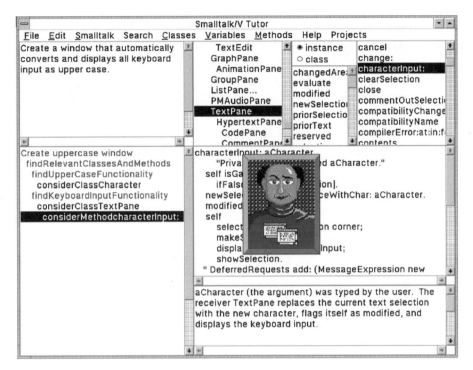

Figure 7.5
Screen image from MoleHill showing the Goalposter tool in the lower-left pane. Other panes show the Smalltalk class hierarchy browser and other tutor components, including the Guru.

The Goalposter deliberately blurs the distinction between a tutor and a task-oriented help system. It provides feedback on the correctness of goals and actions in a separate window so as to avoid interrupting the learner's work. This responds to one of the downsides of the Reinstating Goals claim, but introduces another potential downside: learners must manage their own help seeking. If the learner does not consult the Goalposter window, no guidance is provided.

Background Tracking claim: Tracking the learner's behavior automatically in a separate window

+ provides a resource for learners to reinstate goals as they work

+ minimizes the disruption of the learner's own activity

– learners must manage their own help seeking

Since learners must understand the display in order to know when and how to get help, we needed a very simple presentation. The Goalposter displays the text of an inferred goal colored either red or green. Green signifies an appropriate goal for the learner to attempt; that is, it provides confirmatory feedback. Red indicates an incorrect or irrelevant goal. The aim of this coloring scheme is to make salient the tutor's recommendation of whether the goal should be pursued. This is our response to the downsides of the Goal Reification and Planning Language claims. The presentation of individual goals in the window is telegraphic—several words at most. However, the learner can expand any of the telegraphic goals (through a menu selection) to display a fuller explanation of why the goal is worthwhile to pursue or not. Thus, the system provides both shorthand feedback on correctness and access to further help:

Color-Coded Telegraphic Display claim: A color-coded telegraphic display of goals
+ provides persistent feedback on the correctness of actions as well as access to further information
− learners must learn the display's feature language and controls

The Goalposter supports goal management during task switching. When goals are first recognized, they are posted to the display in green (if correct). They remain in green until they are satisfied, at which time their color changes to black. Hierarchical goal-subgoal relationships are shown using indentation (figure 7.5). If the learner switches to another goal, the current goal hierarchy collapses; only the top-level goal continues to be displayed (in green), followed by ellipsis. This is intended to cue the learner that the goal remains incomplete. When the goal is resumed, the structure expands and new subgoals are added. Thus, the Goalposter provides a kind of fish-eye view (Furnas 1986) of the current state of the project, with higher resolution of the currently active goal:

Fish-Eye View claim: Dynamic fish-eye views of the goal hierarchy
+ reduce the overall complexity of the display
+ focus learner attention on the goal hierarchy pertinent to current behavior
− could conceal parts of the goal hierarchy that interest the learner
− background control of display dynamics could distract, confuse, or intimidate the learner

The Fish-Eye View mechanism refines the rationale of the Background Tracking claim, while also addressing downsides of the System Tools claim, regarding problems reestablishing context during task switching, and the System-Generated Goals claim, regarding difficulties in drawing correspondences between behavior and posted goals. However, the rationale for the fish-eye view mechanism itself raises further design issues. We decided to support browsing of the goal hierarchy: learners can expand or collapse goal hierarchies by double-clicking on the telegraphic text. This addresses a downside of the Fish-Eye View claim as well as the downside of the Plan-based Error Messages claim regarding learner control.

As our work with Goalposter progressed, we integrated analysis and synthesis of usability rationale with prototyping and empirical evaluation. For example, we had originally envisioned global reordering of the goal hierarchy when learners switched tasks. We wanted to display the goal analysis of the learner's current activity at the bottom of the goal list in order to make current goals more salient:

Radical Shuffling claim: Shuffling the goal list so that the current subgoal structure appears at the bottom of the display
+ allows learners to find the analysis of the current goal easily
− this changes the position of many goals in the tree and may disrupt understanding of the display

Once we had implemented this shuffling feature and could directly evaluate its dynamics, we concluded that it was too jarring visually and required learners to reinterpret the goal hierarchy. We substituted a more local reordering, keeping the major subgoals of the solution spatially fixed with respect to one another, shuffling only the position of their subgoals. In this scheme, other cues, such as highlighting the current goal and expanding the current subgoal structure, bear more of the burden of signaling the current focus of learner activity:

Conservative Shuffling claim: Shuffling only the leaves of the tree, along with highlighting the current goal and expanding its subgoal structure,
+ allows learners to find the current goal and retain their grasp of previously posted goals
− learners may become confused about whether the Goalposter is a history list or a conceptual structure

Design Patterns and Design Models

Figure 7.6 schematizes the development of usability rationale for the Goalposter. Our approach was genre analysis of intelligent tutoring systems (the Goal Reification claim, and its specializations in Proust and Bridge), modeling of human coaching activity (the Reinstating Goals claim and the Confirmatory Feedback claim), and hill climbing from Smalltalk (the System Tools claim and the Class Library claim). We synthesized the Goalposter scenario in box 7.8, and its usability rationale, as issue-by-issue responses to these analyses. In figure 7.6 the links among claims indicate a "responds to" relation, reading from top to bottom.

The reconstruction of the design argument for the Goalposter in figure 7.6 is a simplification in that it emphasizes the primary flow of rationale and design. It is typical that rationale *overdetermines* design responses. For example, our assessment of the tutoring genre oriented us toward goal- and plan-based instruction, and in particular toward reifying these structures for learners as a general approach. Our direct empirical evaluation of Smalltalk brought to the light numerous specific problems associated with goal management in that particular domain. In this way, analysis of genre and hill climbing provided convergent rationale. Confidence about design moves can be enhanced when complementary modes of design reasoning converge in this way.

Hill climbing is always a central mode of design reasoning. The proximity of direct predecessor artifacts and situations of use to their design successors ensures at least minimal continuities in functionality, system concepts, and social practices. No doubt this is in part why evolutionary design remains the dominant paradigm in design. But the weakness of hill climbing also stems from its being bound to current situations of use. Because hill climbing takes the current state of technology and practice for granted, it is susceptible to local optimizations that may perpetuate flaws in current technology and practice. Principled emulation, and especially genre specialization, complement hill climbing quite well. It provides a broader framework for understanding a particular artifact and its use and for more globally evaluating design moves. However, the generality of principled emulation can encourage analogies that turn out to be problematic in detail. In this regard, hill climbing can help by keeping the design process grounded in current practices and contexts of use.

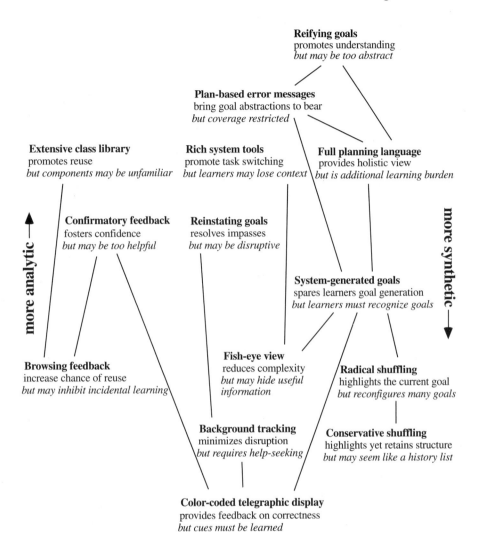

Figure 7.6
Claims map for the Goalposter

Different modes of design reasoning may be differentially susceptible to biases. For example, hill climbing seems intrinsically biased to critique and melioration: Why would one try hill climbing from the current Smalltalk environment, unless one suspected that the current environment ought to be improved and could be? Conversely, activity modeling and principled emulation seem intrinsically biased to praise and imitation: Why would one select human coaching or tutoring systems as model situations unless one already believed them to be paradigmatic in some sense? Engaging multiple design modes within a project can help to control these biases and get the most out of each mode.

Principled emulation and activity modeling allow us to make more deliberate and explicit use of survival forms, design elements, and patterns used before and with success. The usability rationale of effective human practices and significant artifacts and classes of artifacts provides guidance for generalizing and synthesizing design arguments. It renders design knowledge comprehensible and directly applicable by putting it in a common vocabulary with the analysis employed for hill climbing from direct predecessor artifacts and their use.

This is a big step toward design-based science. It moves us from a scenario-based design method justified locally and heuristically to one justified as supporting a general framework for integrating grounded analysis and design. It is a step toward a usefully abstract codification of design knowledge—general patterns and models anchored in specific designs and situations of use. But it raises many further questions. One of these is the question of where scenario-based design abstractions come from. The next chapter turns to how the task-artifact framework can provide a means of developing knowledge about artifact genres and paradigmatic activities based on experiences designing and evaluating new technology.

8

Evaluation and Theory Building

If there is a central lesson learned from two decades of effort focused on human-computer interaction, it is that we will always have to do lots of evaluation work to produce information tools and environments suitable for human use (Monk 1993; Whiteside, Bennett, and Holtzblatt 1988). A typical usability evaluation for the kinds of modest-sized tools and applications discussed as examples in this book might involve observing ten to one hundred hours of human-computer interaction and spending five to fifteen times that much analyzing data. The work will usually reveal some important usability problems and may suggest directions in which to alter a design to improve its usability. But such work requires skilled usability engineers; it is very expensive.

Inspection methods have become popular as supplements, and even alternatives, for direct usability testing (Nielsen and Mack 1994). A key motivation for this trend is that inspection costs less time and effort than direct testing (Bias and Mayhew 1994). But a complementary way to improve the cost-benefit of evaluation work is to focus on increasing the value derived from usability studies. Typically, when user testing data have been interpreted and the design changes implemented, the data are discarded. They do become part of the expertise of the usability engineers who collected and analyzed them, but just as personal memory. Usability evaluation data can become more valuable if they can be put to further uses in design and development.

This chapter develops a framework for integrating theory development with usability evaluation. It may at first seem odd to see *theory* and *evaluation* linked so directly. But theory, in the sense of design-based science, is always manifest in designed artifacts and their use (Carroll and

Campbell 1989). Usability evaluation work necessarily evaluates the theories and models embodied in designed artifacts and their use, though typically it is not articulated in such a way as to make this evident or useful.

Here then is the opportunity to make evaluation work more valuable by integrating empirical testing with claims analysis. We want to define an evaluation-driven design process in which goal-oriented analysis and empirically oriented testing evolve together. On the one hand, we want to use claims analysis to guide the selection and interpretation of testing scenarios. And on the other hand, we want to adduce the results of evaluation testing to the development of better claims analyses of the testing scenarios, and to the development of better claim abstractions.

Evaluation Goals and Methods

Several of the most fundamental concepts pertaining to evaluation originate with Scriven (1967), who introduced the terms *formative* and *summative* to distinguish the two basic roles that evaluation work can play in the development process. Formative evaluation seeks to identify aspects of a design that can be improved, priorities for redesign and refinement, and concrete guidance as to how that redesign and refinement should be executed. A typical example is gathering "think-aloud" protocols as people work through a set of tasks; the commentary is tightly coupled to specific design features, facilitating the identification of problems and reasoning about design solutions. Summative evaluation work seeks to gauge a design product, to position it on various measurement scales with respect to other design products—for example, measuring performance time and error rate for standard tasks.

Scriven also distinguished between two basic approaches to evaluation: *intrinsic* and *payoff*. He characterized the difference with an example: "If you want to evaluate a tool, say an axe, you might study the design of the bit, the weight distribution, the steel alloy used, the grade of hickory in the handle, etc., or you might just study the kind and speed of the cuts it makes in the hands of a good axeman." Direct empirical testing—for example, thinking-aloud commentaries and performance time/error rate measures—is payoff evaluation. Claims analysis and heuristic evaluation

	formative	summative
payoff	think-aloud commentary	time on task and error rate
intrinsic	critical features and rationale	comprehensive feature analysis

Figure 8.1
Basic evaluation space (Scriven 1967)

are both intrinsic evaluation. Scriven's evaluation space is depicted in figure 8.1.

Payoff evaluation produces "solid" empirical facts, but often these facts are difficult to interpret. Thus, one might discover high error rates or performance times longer than those of an alternative design, even in the hands of an expert, but one has little basis for attributing shortcomings or strengths to specific aspects of the design. More generally, it is difficult to determine whether the designers unsuccessfully pursued worthwhile objectives or successfully pursued inappropriate objectives. This is a serious limitation with respect to the formative evaluation role: "We cannot institute a remedial program—our only recourse is to start all over" (Scriven 1967, p. 60).

Conversely, intrinsic evaluation produces many interpretations but no solid facts. It enumerates features and rationale, articulates positions on apparent trade-offs among features, and assigns value judgments. It seeks, in effect, to reconstruct and assess the theory of use that is implicit in the artifact. Intrinsic evaluation struggles with the distinction between goals a designer might have articulated but not achieved and those that are implicit in the design, even though perhaps not articulated by the designers. It struggles with the problem that some interpretations are not easily "testable," in the sense of a payoff evaluation. As Scriven (1967) summarized this: "One of the charms of the pay-off evaluation is the lack of charm, indeed messiness, of a thorough intrinsic evaluation" (p. 54).

Scriven proposed a compromise, or melding, of intrinsic and payoff evaluation in his notion of mediated evaluation. He suggested focusing on explicit goal formulation in the earliest stages of design, intrinsic evaluation and modification of goals throughout the design process, and the embodiment of the goal analysis in payoff evaluation materials (Scriven 1967). Early and continuing intrinsic evaluation keeps the design goals in view for the designers; directing the intrinsic evaluation toward payoff evaluation encourages formulating design goals as testable issues; designing payoff evaluation to reflect intrinsic evaluation provides conceptual guidance for credit and blame attributions and thereby for redesign work. (In usability engineering, mediated evaluation is sometimes called usability specification; Carroll and Rosson 1985.)

The task-artifact cycle (figure 6.1) is highly compatible with Scriven's notion of mediated evaluation. Claims analysis is an intrinsic evaluation in which features are assessed with respect to their potential human impacts within given interaction scenarios. As described in chapters 4 through 7, this intrinsic evaluation can help to make design goals explicit and keep them in view as design work progresses. Moreover, the level of detail in claims analysis is precisely appropriate for designing and interpreting payoff evaluation. For example, the MiTTS claim that exploring a paradigmatic application provides a software model for the design of new functionality (box 6.12) is both testable and immediately relevant to redesign. It provides specific guidance for designing experiments to assess the use of a software model, for analyzing think-aloud protocols, for collecting and categorizing examples of programming work, and so forth. For the purposes of formative evaluation, the claim provides a specific hypothesis as to what design features might be relevant and might be altered to achieve different usability outcomes.

But the task-artifact cycle also suggests extension of Scriven's concept of mediated evaluation in which the results of payoff evaluation are directed back to the initial intrinsic evaluation, as depicted in figure 6.1. An initial description of user tasks, as scenarios and claims, is developed into an envisionment, a prototype, a system, amenable to use, and therefore to payoff evaluation. The scenario description and claims analysis guide the design and interpretation of this payoff evaluation, but the results of the payoff evaluation guide a reassessment of the original scenarios and claims, and ultimately perhaps, redesign of the system itself. This feedback loop is not explicit in Scriven's characterization of mediated evaluation.

The MiTTS project incorporated many examples of mediated evaluation. Chapter 6 described two versions of the "Starting up Smalltalk" scenario. In one of these (box 6.5) a programmer interacts with a set of Smalltalk demos, and in the other (box 6.7), with a blackjack card game. Our observations of Smalltalk programmers identified the problems described in the demos scenario. This initial payoff evaluation was elaborated by developing a usability rationale for the scenario in box 6.6—a mediated evaluation incorporating our raw empirical observations and our hypotheses about how features in the scenario may have caused the learner consequences we observed. This claims analysis suggested that the demos allow learners to be active, but do not afford stimulating or challenging learner activity or provide paradigmatic learning models. On balance, we were led to regard the demos as a problematic feature with respect to learning. Our redesign of Smalltalk (that is, our design of MiTTS) involved providing learners with situations in which they could do more and learn more, using and analyzing a paradigmatic example application with the View Matcher.

Claims analysis of the "Blackjack card game" scenario in box 6.8 guided our subsequent payoff evaluation of MiTTS. We found that for some learners, blackjack was not as familiar a card game as we had assumed and added a summary of the rules to our instructional materials (Rosson, Carroll, and Bellamy 1990). This also helped to develop our usability rationale; it indicated another downside clause: "the game may introduce learning burdens of its own if it is not sufficiently familiar to the learner." We verified that the blackjack application did provide a good learning-by-doing model for programmers. Although they sometimes just played several rounds of blackjack, this experience demonstrably helped to ground their understanding of the application functionality when they subsequently tried to determine how the software worked.

In this development cycle, initial payoff evaluation of Smalltalk learning scenarios—critical incidents (Flanagan 1954), elaborated by intrinsic evaluation in terms of claims—articulated the usability specifications that guided the development of MiTTS and the View Matcher. Usability rationale provided a framework for interpreting payoff evaluation data (mapping credit/blame attributions from payoff evaluation data to features of the Smalltalk environment) and was itself continuously refined and elaborated by payoff evaluation data.

Evaluating and Developing Design Genres

MiTTS was developed over a period of several years through an iterative process of evaluation and redesign (Carroll and Rosson 1995). Although the instructional material and software tools comprising MiTTS are fairly modest, the total investment in evaluation work was considerable—over two hundred hours of observations. We had conceived of MiTTS from the start as a theory-based design project—an application of the minimalist design theory (Carroll 1990a 1998). For example, our prior work with the minimalist theory had emphasized the importance for learners of realistic instructional tasks and support for error diagnosis and recovery. We expected that MiTTS would incorporate these principles, and perhaps even implement them with techniques derived from developments in the earlier work (for example, error blocking). But we also wanted to use MiTTS as an opportunity to extend the concept of mediated evaluation.

Chapter 7 developed the notion of a design genre as an abstraction over artifacts. The two View Matchers are instances of a kind of browsing tool that coordinates multiple views of a paradigmatic case, LISP-CRITIC and the Guru are instances of a kind of help system that provides critique of user performance, and Proust, Bridge, and the Goalposter are instances of a kind of intelligent tutoring system that reifies learner goals. Such relationships are in fact common. The Smalltalk demo scenario and the blackjack card game scenario are both specializations of a kind of scenario in which a learner is initially presented with a simplified and familiar task environment. Papert (1980) called such an environment a microworld. Box 8.1 illustrates the relationship between Papert's microworld situation and the two Smalltalk situations (the Demos claim is derived from box 6.6, the Blackjack Card Game claim from box 6.8).

The microworld concept is the linchpin of Papert's (1980) prescriptive design model for education. Its foundation is a Piagetian analysis of learning that asserts that a key achievement in mastering a complex and

Box 8.1
The Demos claim and the Blackjack Card Game claim are both specializations
of the Microworld claim

Demos claim

Running the system demos, browsing and studying demo code in the Class
Hierarchy Browser
+ captures the interest of programmers
+ motivates programmers to learn by doing
+ establishes basic Smalltalk programming skills
+ provides model applications for programmers to analyze and extend
+ may reduce time spent on instantiating and analyzing objects (e.g., in a
workspace)
− noninteractive demos offer little for the programmer to do
− programmers may have difficulty finding the demo code
− the demos are not paradigmatic Smalltalk applications

Blackjack Card Game claim

Playing and analyzing a paradigmatic interactive application (the blackjack
game)
+ captures the interest of programmers
+ motivates programmers to learn by doing
+ establishes basic Smalltalk programming skills
+ provides model applications for programmers to analyze and extend
− may encourage context-specific learning
− people may spend too much time using the application and not enough
time learning about it
− the game may introduce learning burdens of its own if it is not
sufficiently familiar to the learner

Microworld claim

Working in a simplified, familiar task environment (a microworld)
+ motivates learning by doing
+ provides a framework for analyzing and extending learning experiences.

abstract domain is the learner's construction of a transitional system—an intuitive understanding that effectively guides concrete interactions with the world. Papert urges that learners (in his case, children learning physics and mathematics) be provided with microworlds simple enough to be grasped quickly in a transitional system, but rich and open-ended enough to encourage active investigations—which ultimately will stimulate them to move beyond a transitional understanding to a mature understanding of the abstract structure (partially) instantiated in the microworld.

The Smalltalk demos and the blackjack game in MiTTS are both microworlds for learning Smalltalk. Both are simplified views of Smalltalk that encourage learner activity. Both allow learners to construct a transitional understanding of Smalltalk to help them begin developing a more complete and more abstract understanding. But the demos and the blackjack game are more specific and more concrete than Papert's microworld concept. This is manifest in various qualifications on the general microworld claim. Programmers have to find the demo code; they may not be challenged or stimulated enough by merely watching the demos; they may be distracted from their learning goals by playing the blackjack game; they may have to do additional learning about the game itself.

How should one think about these qualifications? Are they merely the peculiarities of Smalltalk or of MiTTS? Indeed, it seems that these qualifications—for the most part, downsides of the claims—are themselves quite directly generalizable and enrich the "theory" of microworlds. For example, the utility of the Smalltalk demos as learning tools is limited by the fact that programmers must find the demo code. But in fact *any time* a microworld is employed in teaching and learning, there will be set-up tasks, Someone will have to prepare the apparatus, start up the program, or otherwise initialize the microworld. And in many cases, there will need to be coaching of some sort (most likely by a teacher) to ensure successful use of a microworld. These factors may be ancillary to Papert's concept, but they are critical to making any practical use of the concept.

As is frequently the case with theory-level discussions, Papert's microworld concept is underspecified with respect to domain boundary conditions and potential downsides. He does not emphasize the possibility that a microworld could be insufficiently familiar (that the learner might have to learn something about the microworld in order to use it effectively) or the likelihood that a microworld may need to be tuned to ensure that it adequately challenges and stimulates learners, and yet is both tractable to manage and not so absorbing that it becomes an end in itself. This balance is merely assumed in his definition of microworld. And yet, from a practical perspective, achieving this balance cannot be assumed; it was precisely this design issue that motivated the MiTTS project. Thus, although it is useful to seek guidance from the microworlds concept in developing and interpreting the Smalltalk demos and the blackjack game in MiTTS as examples of the concept, it is also useful to try to generalize and map back features of the examples to develop and enrich the original concept.

We adduced the results of our payoff evaluations of Smalltalk and MiTTS to *both* the particular artifacts and situations and the genre level. We found that programmers sometimes got too little out of the demos and concluded *both* that MiTTS should afford more significant learner activity through more representative tasks *and* that microworlds in general must support significant learner activity in the context of realistic tasks. We found that programmers sometimes needed to learn more about the blackjack domain, which we had presumed was familiar, and that they sometimes were distracted from their learning goals by the more accessible, but perhaps less edifying, goals of the blackjack domain. Again, we concluded *both* that MiTTS should provide information about the "familiar" blackjack domain and limit the allure of the game itself *and* that microworlds in general should support, and not just assume, domain familiarity and address goal management problems. This two-leveled form of analysis is schematized in figure 8.2.

The microworlds example illustrates what might be called routine theory development. The microworlds theory was not invented or rejected; it was enriched. This relatively simple architecture of merely passing clauses from the level of specific design examples and situations of use "up" to the theory level may seem too simplistic. It is, at least, simple. No one has a better theory of theories than that they are sets of propositions systematically linked to empirical conditions in which they are held to apply. A benefit of the approach illustrated here is that the

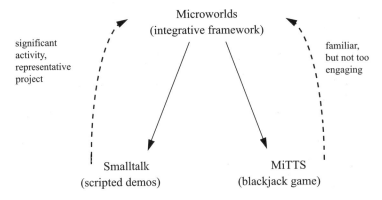

Figure 8.2
The Smalltalk demos and the blackjack game in MiTTS are specializations of the microworld concept. This relationship facilitates theory-based design and evaluation (solid arrows). Payoff evaluation of the specializations can also be generalized and mapped back to develop and enrich the underlying concept (dashed arrows).

propositions that constitute theories end up explicitly linked to their own empirical foundations—indeed, linked to the very situations that were created to instantiate them. If subsequently the weight of evidence swings another way, and the supporting linkages are weakened or removed, it is relatively easy to recognize how a theory needs to be changed—at least what the minimal changes need to be. This is not generally an easy matter when the linkages between a theory and its backing are, as is typical, less explicit.

This is a further refinement of Scriven's evaluation framework. By couching the intrinsic evaluation at more than one level, we get more constrained guidance from intrinsic evaluation for planning and interpreting payoff evaluation, as well as more value from payoff evaluation effort and results in terms of developing particular usability rationale (for example, of MiTTS) and general theories of activity situations (for example, of microworlds). Articulating the notion of design genre is also a refinement of the cumulative design techniques of principled emulation and activity modeling, discussed in chapter 7. Instead of just hopefully reasoning from possibly relevant nonpredecessor artifacts and activities (figure 7.1), we make explicit the underlying abstraction that is the basis for the possible relevance.

Attributions to Multiple Theories

The base case for evaluation and for theory development is the case in which only a single abstraction is involved. But things are typically more complex than this. The blackjack game is a microworld in Papert's sense, but it is also a game. We evaluated it as a microworld—as an environment for learning—but we could have evaluated it as a game. In the former evaluation, it was a potential problem that the blackjack game itself might captivate learners and distract them from the larger goal of learning about Smalltalk. However, from the latter perspective, it would not be a problem for blackjack to have been irresistibly fascinating. That is what games are supposed to be like. When one thinks about the role of models or theories in design, one often thinks about *one* theory or model guiding a design. But in fact it is typical for designs to be eclectic, incorporating a diversity of ideas and foundations. The naive conception of theory-based design is in part attributable to the lack of an adequate framework for describing eclectic theoretical foundations.

We have already seen, for example, in figure 7.6, how the task-artifact cycle provides a simple and flexible framework for describing eclectic lines of reasoning in design. And in this chapter, we have developed a mechanism for integrating theory development and design evaluation. What we want to do now is to marry the two. The example, again, is the MiTTS project and its relation to two streams of instructional theory.

Recall that MiTTS presents the analysis of the blackjack game model first. The basic application functionality (the model) is initially presented without any graphical user interface (or view). The learner explores and analyzes the model classes and methods, and only later is given access to the model-plus-view aggregate (see figure 5.3). This design approach was analyzed in discussion of box 6.12; the relevant claim is repeated below:

Model-first claim: Working with the application model first (without its graphical user interface)

+ simplifies early attempts to understand object-oriented design

+ provides a foundation for subsequent work with the model-plus-interface aggregate

+ highlights the important distinction between application models and their user interfaces

– may disappoint programmers who are eager to learn about graphical applications (the limited tasks may not be experienced as sufficiently meaningful)

– may encourage a programming style that proliferates objects and message sends

Both the upside and downside consequences hypothesized in this claim were evident in our payoff evaluation work with MiTTS. For example, one subject commented, "That sure doesn't look like a graphical interface; I thought that was what Smalltalk was all about!" The subject was disappointed but persevered. Subsequently, in the tutorial, he was happy to see the graphical view of the application: "This is what I suspect I really need to know," and later, "Yeah! The card hands look a lot better than that other thing did." Nevertheless, he was able to use his understanding of the model to make sense of the model-view aggregate (which learners often do not in early stages of Smalltalk learning): "The model objects are doing the work, like what we saw in that little cryptic sort of mathematical-looking line"; and he seemed to grasp the important model-view distinction, "model over here, and interface over here."

Although the Model-first claim is specific to MiTTS and the Smalltalk programming domain, it can be seen as a specialization of more general claims. All instruction must structure and sequence its content, and Model-first describes one approach and its rationale: present the model first to provide a simpler initial learning objective and a foundation for subsequently achieving a more complex objective—understanding the model-view aggregate. From this standpoint, the Model-first claim specializes the Decomposition claim of the systems approach to instructional design (see Gagné and Briggs 1979; Gagné, Wagner, and Briggs 1988). Box 8.2 presents the systems approach model in the form of a design rationale (see also Box 6.10).

The systems approach specifies little about the nature of components into which a complex learning objective is to be decomposed; it merely specifies that training each component in turn must add up in the end to the original target objective. We found further constraint for the component objectives of MiTTS in the minimalist model (Carroll 1990a, 1998): the constraint that learners should always be working on realistic tasks. Box 8.3 summarizes the minimalist model for instructional design as a

Box 8.2
Systems approach model as a design rationale

Clearly specifying the immediate learning objective and the performance criteria to be used in assessing success
+ helps the learner orient to the instructional situation and recognize when criteria have been met
– learners may focus too narrowly on meeting performance criteria (as opposed to learning), and may be unwarrantedly demotivated by failures to meet criteria

Decomposing target objectives into component-enabling objectives and training each of these in turn
+ allows complex target objectives to be systematically built up from parts
– learners may become impatient and may reject activities that seem trivial or irrelevant
– following steps may not facilitate retrieval and performance in real task settings

Keeping directive instructions and learner practice in lockstep contiguity
+ allows the learner to know exactly what to do and when
– does not promote reflection or analysis (the learner may focus too narrowly on each small task)
– learners must relinquish control

Repetitive practice
+ clarifies correct discriminations and smoothes performance
– complex tasks are not merely scripts

Making a pleasant, familiar experience contingent on a target performance
+ reinforces the target performance
– can undermine the intrinsic motivation for achievement

body of rationale intended to describe any example of the minimalist approach. The Model-first claim specializes the first claim in this rationale, the Realistic Task claim: Developing and exercising model objects is a realistic task, and an important one for Smalltalk programming (indeed, Smalltalk developers often first implement the model and only then its views; Goldberg 1990). MiTTS presents the model-only task as a framework for integrating subsequent learning about graphical applications.

Focusing eclectically on relationships between genre-level rationale and usability rationale for particular artifacts and their use enhances mediated evaluation. It provides a richer foundation for intrinsic evaluation. The Decomposition claim warns that a learner may reject a learning objective

Box 8.3
Minimalist model as a design rationale

Working on a realistic task
+ provides the learner with a framework for integrating and applying learning experiences
– realistic tasks may be too difficult (instructional objectives may need to be inferred
– there may be too many kinds of task settings to support

Working on a familiar task
+ orients and motivates learners by engaging prior knowledge
– may encourage context-specific learning
– may engage inappropriate prior knowledge

Incorporating planning and acting throughout the learning experience
+ helps orient the learner to applying knowledge
+ supports skill transfer
– increases task complexity

Retrieval, elaboration, and inference making
+ engage and sustain learners' attention
+ make skills more robust and accessible
– learners might not have access to enough information to reason successfully
– learners may be anxious about bearing such responsibilities

Diagnosing and recovering from errors
+ focuses and motivates learners
+ helps sharpen a concept of correct performance
– errors can be frustrating and disrupt task goals

---

that seems trivial or irrelevant and that merely following steps may not provide good learning transfer. The Realistic Task claim warns that there may be too many kinds of realistic task settings to support and that realistic tasks can be too difficult for learners. All of these considerations bear on the selection, design, and presentation of the blackjack project in MiTTS; a broader consideration may be a better consideration.

Making the genre-level rationale explicit allows payoff evaluation data to be adduced to design models as well as to particular designs. In evaluating MiTTS, we found that learners were sometimes initially disappointed with the model-only project; this suggests a boundary condition for the realistic task claim, an additional downside clause at least as strong as "but for Smalltalk programming, realistic but limited tasks

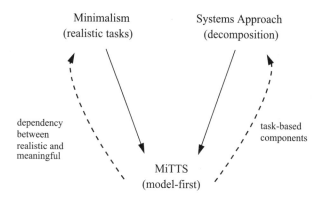

Figure 8.3
The Model-First claim specializes both the realistic task claim and the decomposition claim (solid arrows). Payoff evaluation of MiTTS can be generalized and mapped back to develop the design models (dashed arrows)

may not be experienced as sufficiently meaningful," and perhaps as general as "but for complex skill domains, realistic but limited tasks may not be experienced as meaningful." We also found that learners were able to apply their initial understanding of the blackjack model in analyzing the model-view aggregate, suggesting an elaboration of one of the downsides of the decomposition claim, weakening it under specific circumstances: "But this organization may not facilitate retrieval and application in task settings, unless the original decomposition of learning objectives was based on task components." This reasoning is depicted in figure 8.3.

Another feature of MiTTS was the use of sparse procedures: instruction was presented in terms of programming goals, and learners were allowed to identify the actions to achieve these goals on their own. The relevant claim from box 6.12 is repeated below:

Sparse Procedures claim: Emphasis on programming goals (sparse procedures) in favor of step-by-step instructions

+ engages learners' attention

+ requires programmers to infer or retrieve connections between goals and methods (thus, strengthening connections between their goals and the actions needed to accomplish these goals)

− programmers might not have access to enough information to reason successfully

- programmers may feel anxious about generating the action plans by themselves
- the learner-generated procedures may not be optimal

Both the upside and downside consequences hypothesized in this claim were evident in our payoff evaluation work with MiTTS. For example, in one episode, we observed two learners setting up objects to use in analyzing the hitMe method. They read an instruction that said "As in Topic 1, create a new instance of BlackJack named Game1 and deal a new set of hands." This is a sparse procedure; it does not specify *how* to create an instance of the BlackJack class or *how* to deal.

The learners flipped back through the manual to topic 1 and searched for relevant details. They quickly retrieved the full procedure for creating a new instance and carried it out. In the course of doing this, however, they seemed to lose track of the "deal" clause and failed to deal new hands. In consequence, they encountered nil values for some objects as they continued working on the project. They recognized that something was wrong and began trying to diagnose the problem by taking stock of the objects they had and the messages each had received. After several minutes, they concluded (without ever rereading the instructions) that a deal message had to be sent to the blackjack game. They did this and were able to continue.

The Sparse Procedures claim can be seen as specialization of both the systems approach and the minimalist models. It specializes the systems claim that lockstep instructions and practice keep learners oriented by articulating instruction at a goal level (figure 8.2): sparse procedures provide guidance as to what to do and when, but promote reflection, analysis, and learner control by requiring the learner to make sense of goals in terms of actions. In the episode, the learners lost track of the deal goal in a sparse procedure. This suggests an elaboration of the lockstep claim: in cases where the steps in a procedure are themselves complex and open-ended (for example, goals whose actions must be discovered), the succession of steps has to be verified. Learners need protection from accidentally skipping a step. As an elaboration of the lockstep claim, this suggests the design strategy of increasing directiveness and articulation. For example, the MiTTS manual could explicitly remind the learner about how instances are created or split out the deal clause on a separate line of the manual, or both.

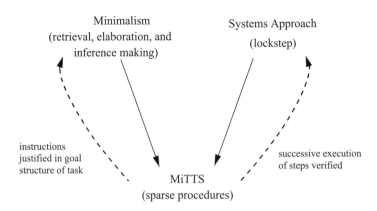

Figure 8.4
The Sparse Procedures claim specializes both the retrieval, elaboration, and inference-making claim and the lockstep claim (solid arrows). Payoff evaluation of MiTTS can be generalized and mapped back to develop the design models (dashed arrows)

The Sparse Procedures claim also specializes the minimalist claim that retrieval, elaboration, and inference making focus attention and effort by binding these activities to the context of following procedures (figure 8.3). For cases in which one needs to get a procedure just right, sheer discovery may not be efficient or pleasant. Viewing the sparse procedures claim as a specialization of the minimalist model suggests a refinement of the retrieval, elaboration, and inference-making claim: instructions need to be justified in the task's goal structure *as understood by the learner.* In this interpretation, the deal goal was temporarily lost because at the point when it was encountered, the learners did not adequately appreciate its role in the task's goal structure. Learners must understand instructions as meaningful components of a task. This, in turn, suggests the design strategy of integrating the creation and deal components into a single instruction: "Deal a new game." The relation of the genre-level and artifact-level rationale in this example of design evaluation is schematized in figure 8.4.

This is a simple but interesting example. Seeing the observed episode as pertinent to the two instructional design models suggested general implications for developing the models themselves. But seeing the evaluation data through the lenses of these two models also suggested specific, and quite different, formative design implications. Reasoning from the systems approach entrains the recommendation to add control information; reasoning from the minimalist model entrains the recommendation to collapse details that could be ineffective. In the event, we decided to pursue the minimalist course. The learners were, after all, able to resolve the problem initiated by the sparse procedure, and the process of solving the deal problem seemed to be engaging to them. However, our decision also depended on a more global concern with providing a consistent instructional orientation for the learner. MiTTS was most essentially a minimalist artifact. One goal of the evaluation was to look for justifications for making design moves *away* from minimalism. But we assumed that unless we found justification to do otherwise, we would implement design changes suggested by minimalism.

Remote and Distributed Causes

The previous section considered what might be called vertical abstraction: given usage episodes were interpreted as instantiating one or more abstract patterns. A complementary abstraction might be called horizontal: particular episodes of use can often be interpreted as elements of a pattern distributed across episodes. For example, a series of sparse procedures in an instructional curriculum might together cause effects in the behavior and experience of learners that a single sparse procedure could not cause. We called such patterns *threads*. Threads are often discovered in usability testing when one is unable to explain adequately an observed consequence on the basis of singular and proximal features.

A good example comes from an evaluation we made of a refined, commercially developed interactive tutorial for Smalltalk (Carroll et al. 1993; see also Carroll, Rosson, and Singley 1993). After over twelve hours of learning experience and a couple of further hours working on programming projects, we observed an episode in which a programmer was unable to make instances of a new class he was developing. His OverFlowStack was a subclass of the system-provided class OrderedCollection; in an OverFlowStack, items can be added up only to a specified stack limit; after that, old items are discarded as new ones are added. The programmer successfully defined the instance variable `stackLimit` in the OverFlowStack class definition, but he was unable to initialize the variable or create a class method that would make OverFlowStack instances. He never even operated the class-method radio button (visible in the upper center of the Class Hierarchy Browser in figure 5.1) to switch to class method mode. He incorrectly created an *instance* method newOverFlowStack, in which he initialized the limit variable, but he found he could not send this instance message to the OverFlowStack class to create an initialized stack. It seemed that he did not understand the class-instance distinction and perhaps was conflating initialization with instance creation.

To understand this problem, we studied videotapes of an exercise entitled "Class Methods" in which the learner had originally learned about and practiced class method installation, specializing the class Array's new: method for its subclass MonitoredArray. We observed no major problems: the programmer seemed to follow the instructions quite well; he even raised a thoughtful question as he began to install several instance methods, asking, "Why are these instance methods versus just regular class methods?" Throughout the section, the learner did express uncertainty about his understanding of the class-instance distinction, as is common for students working with new and difficult concepts: "I don't know the difference between a class object and an instance of a class—hmm—maybe subclasses are instances of classes, with additional information."

The programmer did experience a clear problem in the MonitoredArray episode, although it seemed to be conceptually unrelated to class methods. He selected an entire text block of three methods in the tutorial script (instead of selecting them one at a time) and pasted the block into the MonitoredArray class definition (instead of into a new-method template). He was unable to recover from this error, and it might well have disrupted his understanding of what he had done and learned in the exercise. We identified several potential formative evaluation implications from this episode. We considered adding an explicit suggestion to check the state of the class-instance radio button, distinguishing the three methods more clearly in the tutorial script by breaking out three individual steps and adding horizontal lines between the three blocks of code, adding a reminder to paste the methods into new-method templates, and including more discussion of class methods and the class-instance distinction.

This is a typical anecdote of formative payoff evaluation: a problem was traced to the most likely cause, and a reasonable set of redesign suggestions was raised. However, we were not convinced of the sufficiency of the analysis. The critical cut-and-paste error seemed only incidental to the class methods problem, and the tutorial text describing class methods and their interface controls seemed fairly clear. We decided to examine every point in the person's prior experience where class methods and the class-instance distinction arose. In many of these, the class-instance distinction was mentioned in the service of some other focal topic (such as comparing Smalltalk and Pascal implementations of the same algorithm). Within these episodes we found a variety of experiences that might have contributed to the class method problem in the OverFlowStack project.

From the first chapter, the tutorial relied heavily on the Smalltalk-as-Pascal analogy, highlighting contrasts and similarities to engage prior knowledge. For example, the tutorial emphasized that assignment statements are virtually identical in the two languages. This is true, but the examples used to make the point employed nonstandard instance creation (classes like String and Integer can be instantiated without invoking class methods). Such examples could present an obstacle to subsequent understanding of more typical instance creation. In this same early section, the tutorial discussed storage allocation and de-allocation, citing the analogy between Pascal expressions like `new(p)` and `dispose(p)` and Smalltalk expressions like `p := Array new: 5` (in this expression new: is a class message being sent to the class Array). The point the tutorial makes is that in Smalltalk, there is no need to deallocate variables explicitly (because of garbage collection); the learner indicated his appreciation of this feature. However, this is the first time in the tutorial that a class method appears and one of the first occurrences of the term *object*. In just eight lines of text, the tutorial conflates class instantiation with memory allocation and implies that *variable* is a synonym for *object*.

The programmer took these incidental points quite seriously. He studied some example code, concluding, "One needs to predeclare objects but not their type" (observing that the temporary variables of a method must be declared, but that their values are dynamically bound as the code runs). He also demonstrated his ability to apply the instantiation-as-allocation analogy: "Arrays are allocated with the new option."

After several pages of Pascal comparisons, the tutorial introduces a second key analogy: "Occupational abstractions like doctor, lawyer, programmer, etc., are *classes* of which we individuals are *instances.* To become a lawyer, we learn legal *methods.* Communications between individuals are comparable to Smalltalk *messages,* their content equivalent to Smalltalk *selectors.*" (p. 12; page numbers are for the Smalltalk/V PM tutorial manual; Digitalk 1990). Again, the learner read through this example more carefully than its designers might have intended. He seemed to have no difficulty with the material, concluding merely that "classes are like types." However, on reflection, it seemed to us that this analogy has several holes in it; for example, it turns inheritance on its head, saying that one becomes an instance by learning behaviors, instead of that behaviors are made available by class relations. Offering the classes-as-occupations analogy also works against an understanding of classes as objects that receive messages to create new instances. By casting classes as simply groupings of instances, it leaves no logical possibility for class behaviors, such as the creation of new instances.

The final portion of the tutorial's first chapter was a more straightforward and formal presentation. The term *object* was used synonymously with *instance of a class.* The notion of polymorphism was introduced with a clear classes-as-data types analogy: "Each of the elementary data types knows how to perform generally required behaviors such as print, duplicate and comparison operations" (p. 14). The learner acknowledged this and embellished his earlier conclusion: "Objects are not just types, but also operations on it." In the second chapter, the tutorial introduces the traditional "Hello World" programming project. It refers to this as the "big picture in a nutshell" (p. 41), perhaps to dissuade learners from studying it in detail. The text previews the exercise to orient and motivate learners, making passing reference to many of the fundamental constructs of Smalltalk (class, method, object, global variable, image, p. 42). However, the learner spent several minutes trying to make sense of this terse description: "Is global variable an instance of an object? Why is 'String' capitalized? Is it a class? Are Strings objects?"

The third chapter of the tutorial took a second pass at Smalltalk syntax and revisited the Pascal analogy, noting that objects, "the basic building blocks of the Smalltalk language . . . are analogous to pieces of data in other languages" (p. 45). This caused the learner to revise his understanding: "Before I thought that an object is an instance of a class plus methods, now 'pieces of data.'" We worried that reverting to the Pascal analogy might have undermined the programmer's differentiation of objects from data types.

Chapter 5 of the tutorial introduced classes in more detail but focused on classes as abstractions of objects—"A *class* defines the behavior of similar objects" (p. 67)—rather than emphasizing that objects are instances of classes. No class methods were discussed, permitting the misunderstanding that classes are merely groupings of objects. As elsewhere, the examples were standard procedural data types (e.g., numbers, strings), reinforcing the classes-as-data types analogy. Chapter 5 included a (very brief) section entitled, "Creating new objects and the special object 'nil.'" It presented five simple examples of instance creation, two of which were atypical (Date today and Time now), emphasizing that instance variables are initialized to the object nil. The terms *class message* and *class method* were not used in discussing these instantiation examples; rather, the examples were motivated by noting that "classes are also objects, and so can be used in message expressions" (p. 70). This highlights the paradoxical role of classes as both objects and object creators, and violates the tutorial's own convention of using *object* and *instance* as synonyms.

None of these episodes are more than quirky from an expert perspective (for fuller discussion, see Carroll et al. 1993). Smalltalk experts routinely interchange "instance" and "object" (as the tutorial tended to do), while recognizing that classes are objects too. Experts can think of classes as instance generators, but at the same time recognize that they are also themselves instances (of MetaClass). The tutorial could have shielded the learner from this terminological imprecision or clearly exposed it, but it did neither. Experts also would have no trouble with the multiple analogies: the allocation analogy clarifies some aspects of instance creation and the distinction between creation and initialization; the occupation analogy embodies some aspects of the class-instance and perhaps the class-subclass distinctions. The tutorial could have offered only a single guiding analogy or specific support for integrating the multiple analogies, but it did neither.

We concluded that the causes of the OverFlowStack incident were remote from the MonitoredArray exercise—that they were in fact distrib-

time

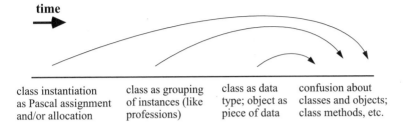

| class instantiation as Pascal assignment and/or allocation | class as grouping of instances (like professions) | class as data type; object as piece of data | confusion about classes and objects; class methods, etc. |

Figure 8.5
Class-instance thread: Multiple analogies and in-line definitions used to introduce the concepts of class and object were not problematic individually, but cumulated to produce confusion.

uted over nearly sixteen hours of learner-system interaction. The episodes of this thread were individually unremarkable; for the most part, the learner was attentive and successful in following the step-by-step tutorial instructions. None would be considered a critical incident in its own right (Flanagan 1954). But *together* they added up to a history of experiences that explains the learner's confusion about classes and objects, and in particular his difficulty regarding class methods for OverFlowStack. This analysis is depicted in figure 8.5.

Thread-Level Claims

The class-object thread is not an exotic kind of usability pattern. Most formative evaluation work brings to the light distributed patterns of this sort. However, most writing on evaluation focuses on strictly local relationships and leaves it to the creativity of practitioners to extend the simple case. In this sense, horizontal abstractions are treated much like vertical abstractions: they are ignored. But it would seem that here again is an opportunity to increase the value of payoff evaluation work.

We can extend claims analysis to describe the causal themes that constitute threads. In the simple case, claims analysis describes the usability rationale for a single episode of use. In the thread case, it describes the rationale for a set of thematically linked episodes. This can occur in several ways. Similar features may be involved throughout a set of distinct usage scenarios, triggering erroneous remindings (Ross and Moran 1983). For example, the many analogies and in-line definitions included in the Smalltalk tutorial were useful episode by episode but were mutually incompatible. Patterns of features can become more salient to people than the individual features comprising the patterns. For example, the frequent and extensive code examples in the tutorial conveyed to learners that these examples should be carefully studied, even though this was a distraction from key tutorial points. And consequences that obtain in given episodes can play a causal role in biasing behavior and sense making in subsequent episodes. For example, our learner had incidentally encountered and misused the class-instance radio button control, which may have contributed to his difficulties in the OverFlowStack project.

Claims analysis can help structure the search for threads by calling our attention to patterns of features and usage consequences. Recall that the learner had a problem in the MonitoredArray exercise with cut-and-paste for the texts of three methods. Our claims analysis for this episode included the following:

Cut-and-Paste claim: Cut-and-paste example methods from the tutorial script
+ provide a procedural template for generating new methods
+ minimize the chance of typing slips
− does not promote analysis

Direct cut-and-paste manipulation of the code examples is a good technique for generating code (Lange and Moher 1989) and minimizes the chance of distracting slips that might occur were the learner to type the code. However, these relatively mechanical manipulations of the code texts do not promote reflection or analysis of the code or of the actions being taken on the code.

The artifact feature of the Cut and Paste claim is very similar to that of a claim associated with an exercise appearing seven pages earlier in the tutorial. In this exercise, the learner evaluated a *single* Smalltalk expression to file in the code for several methods (a standard technique for updating the Smalltalk class hierarchy).

Filing-in claim: Filing-in a set of example methods in a single operation
+ provides a procedural template for change management
+ minimizes the chance of typing slips
− does not promote analysis

Based on the similarity of these features, we conjectured that the cut-and-paste problem in the MonitoredArray episode was not merely a cut-and-paste slip or indeed a purely local incident, but was in fact part of a "code installation" thread:

Code Installation claim: Presenting file-in and cut-and-paste to install example code
+ allows each method to be used in cases for which it is best suited
+ exposes the learner to a greater variety of techniques
− invites confusions between the techniques

This thread-level claim specifies how the two individual episodes are causally related: cut-and-paste requires each method to be separately handled; filing-in allows a set of methods to be handled together. Thinking of the cut-and-paste problem as a singular incident might lead to a design move of printing bold lines to separate the different methods, perhaps defeating the tendency to select the entire block. Thinking of the cut-and-paste problem as part of a thread would support a more comprehensive design analysis. Perhaps only one code installation method should be initially taught, or perhaps the two methods should be explicitly contrasted so that the distinction between them, and not merely the similarity, becomes salient to a learner.

Box 8.4 presents a claims analysis of the class-objects thread. The Data Types claim pertains to the pervasive Pascal analogy and the recurring use of example classes like Integer and Array. The analogy is potentially useful for procedural programmers learning Smalltalk, but projects a limited view of Smalltalk classes that obstructs concepts like class method. The data types analogy also combines awkwardly with the occupational analogy (Multiple Analogies claim). Neither seems to constrain or clarify the other; it is not obvious how to integrate them.

The tutorial augmented the early (and long-lived) misconceptions introduced by these analogies by treating in-line references to critical terms too casually, as stated in the Divergent Definitions claim. The tutorial created an ad hoc salad of fundamental terminology that was never nailed down: object, class, variable, instance, individual, collections of individuals, instance of a class, data type, class of object, piece of data. For a learner, such terminological imprecision can be devastating. A simple

Box 8.4
Claims analysis of the class-instance thread

Data Types claim: Recurring analogies to Pascal data types
+ make Smalltalk seem more familiar
+ guide the use of prior programming knowledge
− may lead to a view of classes and objects as data structures

Multiple Analogies claim: Emphasizing the Pascal analogy of assignment expressions, data types, and explicit allocation followed by the occupational analogy of job roles
+ stimulates the learner to create an integrative understanding
− could provide too much incompatible material to help the learner build an understanding of the classes and instances and the distinction between them

Divergent Definitions claim: Providing an assortment of in-line definitions emphasizing different perspectives on the key concepts of class, instance, and object
+ stimulates the learner to create an integrative understanding
− earlier definitions may interfere with subsequent definitions

Code Examples claim: Presenting many complete code examples throughout the tutorial
+ provides varied experiences in reading code
+ allows using the book decoupled from the environment
− could confuse the learner as to how thoroughly any given code example is intended to be studied

Instructional Prerequisites claim: Delaying discussion of the key concept of class method and its Class Hierarchy Browser controls (the class-instance radio buttons) until logically prerequisite material has been presented
+ makes possible a coherent, task-oriented exercise
− leaves learners to build their own, possibly erroneous, understandings from the happenstance of their experience, perhaps to build misunderstandings that interfere with subsequent instruction

approach would be to fix on particular usages. The tutorial's idea of equating *object* and *instance* is fine, but then care should be taken not to say that classes are objects.

The Code Examples claim refers to the huge amount of code presented by the tutorial. Reproducing all the code examples in the tutorial provides a resource but seemed on balance to be a bad idea. It makes it possible to use the manual without the interactive environment, but nobody would seriously do Smalltalk programming with paper and pencil. Sometimes the code was meant merely to be glanced at (for example, to see that the same algorithm that takes thirty lines of Pascal can take five lines of Smalltalk); sometimes it was meant to be filed-in or cut-and-pasted, and sometimes just executed. Conflating these different purposes leaves it unclear what to do. Our learner often studied code he was meant merely to scan. This prolonged some exercises unnecessarily and often led to unanswered questions that left him confused and unconfident.

The Instructional Prerequisites claim refers to the positioning of the topic of class methods in the tutorial. It is impossible to present complete code examples that exclude instance creation. When elements of the topic arose anyway, as in the early class-instance radio button episode, the tutorial finessed it, setting the stage for further problems. The tutorial's reasonably good presentation of class methods in the MonitoredArray exercise was encountered by the learner in the context of these prior confusions.

Thread-level claims integrate usability rationale over sequences of related scenarios. Analyses of particular episodes have the virtue of being firmly grounded in real use; thread-level analyses have the virtue of synthesizing the larger issues that pervade many individual episodes. At their best, threads provide a view of the forest anchored in the trees. They can help make salient patterns that might be missed on a strictly episode-by-episode analysis. In the past two chapters, we have explored the reuse of scenario and claim abstractions in guiding design and evaluation, but these have been vertical abstractions, such as microworlds, minimalism, and the systems approach earlier in this chapter. Threads can also be used in this way.

We carried out an evaluation of MiTTS that mirrored the procedures of our evaluation of the commercial Smalltalk tutorial (Koenemann-

Belliveau et al. 1994). We specifically focused on reusing the thread-level analysis of the Smalltalk tutorial. We wanted to investigate the question of whether the thread-level analysis was robust and general enough to provide guidance for an evaluation of a related but different usage situation. MiTTS, we have pointed outs, is different from the commercial tutorial. It does not emphasize standard Pascal data types in describing objects; it does not use Pascal or occupational analogies in describing objects; it does use short in-line definitions but attempts to limit and focus terminology; it incorporates a Bittitalk browser tool to shield learners from detailed code examples; it introduces the class-instance distinction early and uses it routinely throughout.

Perhaps not surprisingly, MiTTS learners are more successful in general in getting started with Smalltalk, and in particular in understanding and using the class-instance distinction. In this study, after having decided where to place the OverFlowStack class in the hierarchy, the MiTTS programmer identified creation of a class method as his first concern. He made several errors in positioning the class (he initially considered making it an instance method, and then considered placing it in the super-class) and employed a cumbersome copyedit approach to creating the method's code. But he was able to recover from these errors on his own and successfully completed the project.

There is not much of a formative payoff evaluation result here. The errors were merely incipient: the learner never actually created any wrong code. On the other hand, we had spent sixteen hours carefully observing his behavior and experience, and far more time transcribing videotapes and studying usage protocols. We wanted to learn something from all that work—to get some value out of the payoff evaluation effort. Using the thread-level claims of box 8.4, we reviewed our notes and transcripts for indications that the issues we had identified in the evaluation of the commercial tutorial could bring to the light problems we might otherwise have overlooked in the evaluation of MiTTS.

MiTTS does not rely on Pascal data types, a Pascal analogy, or other domain-level analogies. The continuing blackjack example projects a simulation-model analogy in which the objects comprising the game can be anthropomorphized as their real-world counterparts. This analogy, unlike the Pascal and occupations analogies, is so central to object-oriented programming and design that it may be wrong even to see it as an analogy. However, the simulation-model view of object-oriented code does tend to focus attention on the instance level by finessing concerns about where the simulation objects come from. We were, of course, already oriented to potential problems with the class-instance distinction.

In designing MiTTS, we had relied on brief, in-line definitions, often supplemented with pointers to a glossary. In form, this is similar to the commercial tutorial. We had taken care to keep terminology consistent. But our prior analysis of the Divergent Definitions claim encouraged us to examine the definitional thread nevertheless. We were surprised to find several problems with definitions. Indeed, the distinctions between classes and instances and between class methods and instance methods were prominent among these. The learner was able to perform, that is, to complete the programming projects, but he continued to express confusion about the class-instance distinction. Like the commercial tutorial, we had failed to be consistent in confronting the duality of classes as instance makers and instances or simplifying it away.

We confronted the Code Examples claim very directly in MiTTS, incorporating a filtered view of the class hierarchy to focus learner attention on functional analysis, and keep them from becoming captured by low-level code details. Of course, we did observe cases in which MiTTS frustrated programmers in their hopes of finding code to study. But we were surprised to find two cases in which the MiTTS materials included explicit code expressions at relatively early points in the instruction (these expressions were used to run parts of the tutorial software). Our transcripts clearly showed that the learner *was* captured by these expressions, that he spent time trying to parse and make sense of them, and that he voiced confused interpretations. We could not find subsequent consequences, but we regarded the wasted time and potential confusion as problems in themselves. We considered replacing the expressions with menu selections or other interactive techniques.

We introduced class methods early in MiTTS. The distinction between class and instance methods is drawn in the first few pages, but very briefly. Our design concept was that it would become clear through repeated encounters rather than through an extensive introduction. As we reexamined the pattern of encounters with the class method concept, we did find evidence of confusion. However, in all cases the learner was able to detect and correct these confusions. This is essentially the outcome we were driving at, so here we did not consider design changes.

In this evaluation study, several opportunities to refine and improve the MiTTS design came to the light through the reuse of our thread-level claims analysis. Thread-level claims are not vertically generalized; rather they help to amplify the otherwise weak signals in evaluation data from distributed patterns of features.

Evaluation-Driven Design

This discussion of evaluation began by sounding the theme that labor-intensive usability testing can become more cost-effective by increasing its value (as opposed to just reducing its cost). Our approach was to integrate evaluation more closely with other system development activities, in particular with the development of usability rationale, including various generalizations of rationale.

We adapted and elaborated Scriven's evaluation framework of goals and methods, and in particular his concept of mediated evaluation—an integration of intrinsic and payoff evaluation. Usability rationale is in fact a kind of intrinsic evaluation of usage scenarios; the evaluated features and hypothesized consequences of the intrinsic evaluation are systematically bound to specific usage situations. This is a sounder approach to usability inspection than merely running through lists of general guidelines taken out of context. Moreover, it produces an intrinsic evaluation that can be developed and generalized in ways that check marks on a list of guidelines cannot. For example, we developed the feedback link by which payoff evaluation data can enrich intrinsic evaluation. We developed theoretical mechanisms to generalize the intrinsic evaluation for concrete situations to genre-level descriptions, and to instantiate genre-level rationale in particular usage situations to build usability rationale. We extended the notion of scenario to the evaluation of distributed patterns of usage episodes (threads) and showed in this context how intrinsic evaluation can be reused in guiding subsequent evaluation efforts.

All methodological endeavor aspires to be theory based, since to be theory based is to be more principled, more grounded, more extensible.

Theory-based design has come to sound quixotic, even oxymoronic. Design is in the details that theory abstracts away. But when theory is tied tightly to details, to circumstances of use and particulars of tools, then perhaps we can have our theoretical cake and eat it too. The key is to keep theory at what Mills (1959) called a middle level of abstraction. Mills criticized the tendency in the social sciences to pursue what he called "grand theory": elegantly abstract systems that neither describe nor explain the evident patterns of social life. It is precisely this problem that usability rationale *as theory* seeks to address. If it seems too hokey to pursue theory development through workaday usability evaluation, we should remind ourselves that high-falutin' theory has rarely delivered substantive guidance to design.

The approach we are developing seeks to build science *in* the extant practice—to reify the practical ontology of design so that it can be used more deliberately, interrogated, improved, and applied. Thus, we want to integrate, leverage, and systematize better what already goes on in design: reasoning from prior work (hill climbing), reasoning from technical experience (principled emulation, activity modeling), and iteratively evaluating results and assumptions. A designer does not have to identify all or any of the possible generalizations of claims and scenarios in order to make use of usability rationale and other scenario-based methods. Rather, this is an option—a way to verify and elaborate the validity of a design analysis.

This chapter and the previous one present a straightforward approach to incorporating theories about uses and circumstances of use into design and evaluation. The approach acknowledges the evolutionary task-artifact cycle (figure 3.1), but seeks to inject more explicit deliberation into the process. Usability rationale of usage episodes for a current design, of issue-oriented threads of use, of the use of predecessor artifacts, of model activities, and of genre-level situations is used to develop and specify usability goals and then to state intrinsic usability evaluation results explicitly and systematically. This body of middle-level design theory is then used to plan and interpret payoff evaluation, and in its turn is refined by these data. Evaluation data clarify particular causal relationships and guide particular design decisions, but are also generalized to the issues and genres on which they bear. This framework is depicted in figure 8.6.

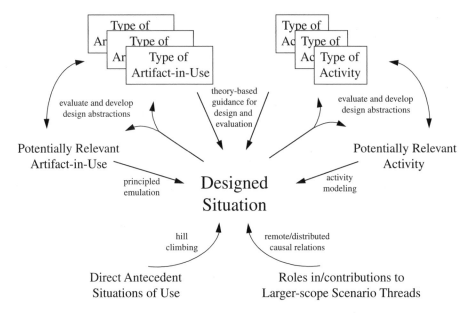

Figure 8.6
Viewing a designed situation of use in terms of scenario types and antecedents facilitates the use of abstract relationships in design reasoning and, in turn, the development of better design abstractions for subsequent reuse

Integrating evaluation with design, rationale, and theory development transforms evaluation from a discrete stage to a continuous activity in system development. This was our experience with MiTTS (Carroll and Rosson 1995). One benefit of taking a broad approach to evaluation is that we were able to shift resources to take advantage of opportunity. Sometimes it is less costly to sit down and create an intrinsic evaluation of design trade-offs than it is to schedule time in the lab and run subjects; at other times, the reverse is true. When the various components of MiTTS were stable, we collected payoff data; when they were not, we did intrinsic evaluation. We found that interleaving intrinsic and payoff evaluation, and coordinating formative and summative reasoning, promoted delaying design commitments (by making upsides *and* downsides of trade-offs salient), guided interpretation of payoff formative evaluation results (by providing an explicit proto-theory of the current design), and suggested alternative design directions (by focusing attention on scenarios in which particular usability downsides might not obtain). We found that the summative evaluation goal of positioning a system and its rationale often provokes the development of a broader scenario set (an intrinsic evaluation end).

To this point, the main argument of the book has focused on understanding and managing requirements in design. I have tried to demonstrate that scenario-based design is an appropriate orientation to the design of interactive systems in regard to the general design and technology development issues discussed in chapters 2 and 3. I pursued this by developing a specific approach to scenario-based design that addresses these general issues. This chapter extended that focus to evaluation: guiding the design and interpretation of payoff evaluation data, and at the same time recruiting and generalizing evaluation data to build better design abstractions. Between design and evaluation lies system development in the narrow sense of what a system is: software and hardware. In the next chapter we continue to pursue the argument that scenario-based design, in general, and the task-artifact framework, in particular, add value to design, development, and evaluation effort, by showing how scenarios can be used in software development.

9

Software Development

The two most challenging and important activities by far in system development are requirements engineering and usability engineering—that is, identifying, refining, and verifying what people need and then managing the development of a system or prototype to meet those needs by continually determining how it can be refined to meet them better. These two activities have been the central focus of discussion through the preceding five chapters. Requirements engineering and usability engineering are unified with a third important focus of system development: software engineering. Scenario-based approaches to software emerged nearly ten years ago as mainstream methodologies in object-oriented software engineering (Beck and Cunningham 1989; Wirfs-Brock and Wilkerson 1989) and in the past five years have become consolidated as the dominant approach (Booch, Rumbaugh and Jacobson 1998; Jacobson, Booch, and Rumbaugh 1998; Rumbaugh, Jacobson, and Booch 1998).

Object-Oriented Software

Traditionally, software design is about procedures. The software designer specifies a flow of data and control, a series of computations successively executed. The entities of software in this approach are counters, loops, tests and branches, arrays, symbols, integers, and real numbers. One of the key difficulties in the approach is learning to see real-world activities as comprising computational procedures. In contrast, object-oriented design is about modeling and simulation. The software designer describes a set of objects—modular bundles of data and behavior—that can interact in specified ways. The entities of object-oriented software are computational simulations of objects in the real-world domain: cards, decks, hands, players. Thus, instead of "iterating through an array of symbols," the software "deals a hand." Procedural software is a sequence of steps and conditions; object-oriented software is a model of the application domain (Booch 1986).

There is a significant shift underway in software technology toward the object-oriented paradigm. This is a broad issue, and many of its ramifications lie beyond the scope of this discussion. For present purposes, the shift from procedural to object-oriented software design is a shift to higher-level, domain-oriented software abstractions. Object-oriented design articulates the design of software objects at a functional level, in terms of the interactions—often called "collaborations"—among the objects. Objects are initially designed as sets of services provided to and received from other objects. Defining software objects in terms of their interfaces to other objects increases the modularity of the objects, making them more reusable and extensible. It allows and encourages software designers to think at the functional design level and defer concerns with implementation details. It makes software design interactive problem modeling.

Rosson and Gold (1989) carried out a protocol study in which experienced programmers developed initial software designs for a shopping system. They presented the requirements for the system with three sketchy scenarios: finding the least expensive brand of low-sodium oyster sauce, adding french bread to a standard weekly shopping list, and removing a pound of brie from the current shopping list. Six of the programmers were Smalltalk experts and were asked to produce designs appropriate for implementation in an object-oriented language like Smalltalk or C++. Three others were expert procedural programmers who had not worked with object-oriented languages; they were asked to produce a design appropriate for implementation in a conventional language like Pascal or C.

The Smalltalk designers all directly incorporated many items from the requirements scenarios into their solutions. For example, food items, orders, and shopping lists were included as focal software objects. These objects were not just identified and then modeled. They were actively recruited to the *process* of design reasoning. For example, one designer considered including pricing information in his standard shopping list object until he remembered that item prices frequently change. He concluded that price "belongs" with the item, not with the shopping list. Another designer used the shopping context to reason about recipes, concluding that the shopping "view" of a recipe is just the list of required ingredients.

Objects were often enhanced through this process. For example, some designers extended the standard shopping list into a more general-purpose preference object used in building shopping list instances. This abstraction was quite productive; it led the designers to provide other preference objects for brands, favorite recipes, and diet. Sometimes design objects were metaphorically anthropomorphized, that is, interpreted as communicating, intelligent agents. A designer who initially considered a shopping cart object as a collection of selected items, which could add and delete items, extended the metaphor, giving the shopping cart the behavior of delivering itself. This same designer later realized that shelved items could manage their own inventory by tallying their current instances. Another designer suggested that the shopping process could be managed by a weekly meal plan: the plan works with various recipes to determine quantities, and then with household inventory and dietary preferences to build a shopping list, which in turn works with brand preferences and current sales to produce an order.

The designers were creating behaving software models of the shopping domain, running scenarios of interaction in those models and then refactoring the models to achieve greater modularity and conceptual transparency. Rosson and Gold emphasized that the process they observed was very interactive. The focal objects that were identified early—orders and shopping lists—were returned to again and again as the programmers developed their designs. Rosson and Gold suggested that the ease with which their Smalltalk designers could identify those focal design objects was a source of task-oriented motivation to them; almost from the start, the designers could feel that they had accomplished something. The metaphorical extensions that emerged in this process were sources of novel design ideas and approaches, as well as sources of constraint beyond generic engineering criteria like efficiency. Thus, investigating questions like, "What *should* a shopping list do?" can lead to an anthro-pomorphically enhanced notion of a shopping cart, but to one that is intuitively consistent with real shopping carts in consequence might be more comprehensible to users and other designers.

Rosson and Gold (1989) called this software design process "meta-phoric extension of problem entities," which it clearly is. But their termi-nology also suggests a potential unification of the "underlying" software model with the user interface metaphor that presents system functional-ity. Explicit user interface metaphors have been pervasive in software systems for more than two decades (Carroll and Thomas 1982; Neale and Carroll 1997). For example, in the 1970s, text editors and early word processors were presented as enhanced typewriters; in the 1980s, spread-sheets were presented as electronic ledger pages. Such metaphors leverage prior knowledge about tasks and objects as cognitive scaffolding to help people learn and manage new tasks and objects. But user interface metaphors also depend crucially on the mismatch between the system and the metaphor (Carroll and Mack 1985): no one would want a spread-sheet system that really worked *just like* an accountant's ledger. Recalcu-lation, statistical analysis, and integration with other desktop applications for graphing and report generation are what make spread-sheet systems so useful. The ledger metaphor provides a starting point for creative work on the part of both designers and users to go beyond mere similarity. Both seek an appropriately enhanced ledger.

Both object-oriented software design and user interface metaphor de-sign involve a process of extending the self-evident entities of the domain model. Recently, several investigators have suggested that software design and user interface design should be coordinated—that user interface objects should map to entities in the underlying software design (Bass, Kazman, and Little 1992). In the object-oriented approach, this can be put very strongly: the software design objects and the user interface metaphors should *be* the same objects (Carroll and Rosson 1994). Thus, just as a blackjack card hand can deal itself, it should be able to display itself—and it should look something like a real card hand.

Design reasoning about software objects in a domain model is remark-ably similar to scenario-based design as we have encountered it in pre-vious chapters: known and observable tasks and objects are transformed

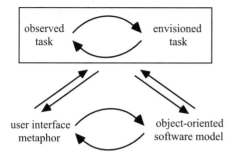

Figure 9.1
Observed and envisioned tasks provide objects for software domain models and user interface metaphors; design work with software objects and metaphors suggests extensions to the original problem entities.

through envisioned scenarios of use. But object-oriented design reasoning is also complementary to the examples of scenario-based design we have encountered before. The emphasis here is on the objects; the domain tasks serve as contexts for evoking, identifying, and refining these objects. This is an exciting complementarity that significantly expands the scope and importance of scenario-based design. Usage scenarios are ideal structures for engineering requirements and usability, that is, for identifying the required functionality of systems and evaluating the effectiveness of their realization. Shifting attention to the objects of these usage scenarios provides software domain models to implement and present that functionality.

Figure 9.1 depicts this relationship. The objects of the task-artifact cycle become the metaphors and design objects of the software system. As indicated in the figure, these relationships are reciprocal. Observed and envisioned tasks provide the objects for software domain models and user interface metaphors, but design work with software objects and metaphors also suggests extensions of the original problem entities. The box at the top of the figure is the task-artifact cycle (recall figure 6.1), a deliberated evolution of new tasks from extant tasks; observed tasks guide the envisionment of new tasks, which subsequently become the grist for further envisionment. As shown in the Rosson and Gold study, object-oriented software models and user interface metaphors also evolve mutually; the objects of a software model suggest metaphors, and these in turn suggest refactorings of the software model.

Responsibility-Driven Design

A software object is a data structure and a set of operations that the structure can perform. For example, the structure of a shopping list might include an ordered collection (of shopping items) and the length of the ordered collection. The operations might include adding an item, deleting an item, and accessing an item in a given position (possibly among other operations). In principle, one could practice object-oriented design by specifying such structures and their operations. However, as Wirfs-Brock and Wilkerson (1989) observed, such an approach will tend to undermine the modularity of objects: operations will depend on the structures for which they were defined, and therefore, relationships among objects will depend on the specific structures of the objects. Changing the structure of any one object will cause these dependencies to fail.

Wirfs-Brock and Wilkerson (1989) suggested an alternative design practice they called "responsibility-driven design." In this approach, the designer is encouraged to defer attending to the structural details of software objects. The design work focuses instead on the relationships among objects, on identifying the objects with which a given object interacts, and the actions and information for which that object is responsible within those interactions. In the Rosson and Gold (1989) study, the design reasoning that led to the conclusion that item price belonged with the item and not with the shopping list is an example of responsibility-driven design. The items and the shopping list interact within the shopping system scenarios, and need to access and manage item price information. Rosson and Gold's designers reasoned that the items themselves should be responsible for managing this information. The design conclusion was reached without any consideration about the internal structures of the shopping list or the items.

Early codifications of responsibility-driven design suggested that objects and their responsibilities could be identified directly in requirements documentation by marking all nouns as candidate design objects and all verbs as candidate responsibilities (Wirfs-Brock, Wilkerson, and Wiener 1990). The informal use of scenarios was also suggested as a method for identifying responsibilities: "Imagine how the system will be invoked, and go through a variety of scenarios using as many system capabilities as possible. Look for places where something must occur as a result of input to the system. Has this need for action been accounted for? What new responsibilities are implied by this need?"(p. 62). As illustrated by the Rosson and Gold study, these questions are often pursued by anthropomorphic reasoning, that is, by thinking of the objects of a software design as a team of intelligent agents working collaboratively.

At about this time, Jacobson (1987, 1995; see also Jacobson et al. 1992) began to promote a more comprehensive scenario-based object-oriented software engineering methodology. Jacobson was particularly interested in scaling up object-oriented methodologies for circumstances in which large software systems are specified through the course of interviews and discussions between software designers and customers. He argued that a direct way to ensure that people get the system they want is to factor the specification of the system into "use cases," simple scenarios in which users interact with systems. He emphasized that a use-case view of a system is accessible to both software designers and customers and that use cases can provide a decomposition of an overall software design into more manageable subviews. Use cases are highly compatible with responsibility-driven design: each use case provides a minimal context for identifying object responsibilities (Wirfs-Brock 1995).

Box 9.1 presents a use case in which a resident schedules a meeting using a community network (adapted from Rosson and Carroll 1996c). Like all other scenarios, use cases are deliberately incomplete: The use case in box 9.1 does not detail exactly *how* the system prompts for information, or just *what* the resident does in interacting with the system. Leaving these details open keeps the focus of discussion about the use case on designing object responsibilities, as opposed to specifying details of object implementations.

Jacobson (1995) argued that systems can be exhaustively specified by (large) sets of use cases, each describing an exhaustive set of possible contingencies and outcomes. This objective makes it very important to structure use cases to be mutually exclusive, and this, in turn, tends to make use cases correspond to individual functions. One software design benefit is that various functional abstractions can be stated in terms of use cases. For example, the Cash Withdrawal, Transfer Funds, and Deposit Funds use cases for an ATM machine are all specializations of the Card

Box 9.1
Example use case: Setting up a community meeting

Use Case: **Setting up a community meeting**

A resident can set up a community meeting in the Virtual Town Hall (VTH). The resident is prompted for various information: topic name, meeting date and time, topic description, attendee interest profile keywords. The VTH includes the resident's name as the meeting contact person. The VTH suggests an available meeting location, and the resident confirms. The resident can include attachments or pointers to documents in the Town Hall archive as background material for the meeting. The resident can send a meeting notice to potential attendees.

Transaction use case (Jacobson 1995). The software designer in effect creates a class hierarchy in which the objects defined are use cases. This is an important elaboration of object-oriented design and a very strong position regarding scenario-based software design.

But a major trade-off is lurking. Scenarios are relevant and accessible to users not because they provide elegant hierarchical analyses of individual system functions, but because they provide rich, informal, and open-ended descriptions of real practice and experience. Use cases are very incomplete with respect to the experiences of the agents who play roles in the use case, the defining goals that cause the use cases to be enacted, and the circumstances that evoke those goals. Thus, the use case in box 9.1 is mute as to the broader context of activity within which the meeting scheduling occurs; it does not suggest why the person is setting up the meeting or what the meeting may mean to that person or to the community.

Use cases also do not address the prior knowledge and current practices that bear on how the technology in the use case will be experienced and used—for example, how the person thinks about what a meeting is and the process and procedure of setting up a meeting, how the person thinks about the virtual town hall and its various capabilities (for example, storing and retrieving documents, maintaining profiles of residents, managing meeting rooms and meeting notifications), or how user errors might occur and how people might recover from those errors. Because humans do not plan, perform, or experience activities at the level of individual functions taken out of all context, specifying systems function by function will only fortuitously converge with underlying user concerns. This is one of the key weaknesses in conventional system design and one of the principal motivations for developing scenario-based design (Carroll and Rosson 1990).

Jacobson (1995) writes, "Use cases are the 'things' a developer sells to customers" (p. 310). This statement has a worrisome double entendre. Jacobson means to emphasize that customers are concerned with the functionality—what the software can do—and not with the software objects per se. But the other hearing of his statement is that by presenting attractive, albeit quite schematic, scenarios to customers—scenarios that ignore task context, activity, prior knowledge, reasoning, and experience—one may "sell" the customer use cases, yet never find out what the customer actually needs. Use cases *presume* a thorough requirements analysis but do not provide it; users and designers need to discuss requirements, not just function-oriented scripts for implementing requirements. Ultimately the software design based on the use cases will be evaluated in terms of its compatibility with people's knowledge, inferences, practices, affect, and so forth.

For these reasons, one should understand use cases as simplified views of task scenarios, simplifications that are suitable for particular roles in software design. They provide the critical link between scenarios as descriptions of use and scenarios as descriptions of software to support use. They are the software design and implementation "view" of the human-computer interaction scenarios as encountered throughout the earlier chapters of this book.

Developing Object Models from Scenarios

A scenario description of a person interacting with a system to accomplish an activity highlights a particular subset of the functionality comprising that system. From the agent's perspective, these subsets constitute a coherent and meaningful analysis of the system's functionality. A scenario-based approach to software development asserts that this "parsing" of the system's functionality can also be used—at least heuristically—to design the functionality itself. Thus, the use case in box 9.2 highlights the "setting up a community meeting" subset of the functionality of the community network system. In a scenario-based approach, one identifies and defines the software objects that enable this functional subset of the community network system. This proceeds by systematically manipulating and successively detailing the original use case. A general first step is to render the use case as an interaction script, as shown in box 9.2, making explicit just what the system and the person using it are doing through the course of the scenario narrative (Wirfs-Brock 1995).

The relationship between the original use case and the interaction script is fairly easy to grasp. And it is straightforward to create a script like that in box 9.2, given a use case narrative like that in box 9.1. However, the interaction script brings to the light many details left implicit in the original use case. It enumerates the central objects of the use case: the meeting, the form, the contact person, the location, the date, the time, the description, the attendee interest profile keywords, the Town Hall, the community archive, the document attachment, the notice. It helps designers coax out the way these objects work together to produce the functionality that enables the use case. Observe, for example, that the interaction protocol for setting the meeting location is finessed in the use case text but explicitly addressed in the interaction script.

The interaction script helps designers identify object responsibilities. For example, the meeting creates a form to gather the information it needs; the form manages dialogue with the user and returns information to the meeting; the meeting creates a notice to present and distribute the meeting information. Detailing the interaction script also can help distinguish circumstances in which the use case could "fail"—that is, fail to play out as sketched in box 9.1. For example, as enumerated in box 9.2, the Town Hall may fail to recognize the user (the community network has to have some authentication capability in order to restrict its use to bona-fide community members); there may be no suitable room available at the requested date and time; the community archive may not contain or may not return the desired attachment document; there may be no matches for the attendee interest profile among community members.

Box 9.2
Interaction script for "Setting up a community meeting" use case

---

Script: **Setting up a Community Meeting**

User Action	*System Response*
1. Initiate set up a meeting task	
	2. Create meeting; display form; include resident as contact person
3. Specify topic, date, time, description, attendee interest profile keywords	
	4. Add information to meeting; determine possible meeting locations; suggest meeting location(s) to user
5. Accept meeting location	
	6. Schedule date/time and location with Town Hall; add meeting location to meeting; prompt user for further actions
7. Request potentially relevant documents from community archive	
	8. Display view of document archive
9. Select attachment for meeting	
	10. Attach document to meeting; prompt further meeting options
11. Request send notice	
	12. Confirm notice sent

Alternatives

1. The Town Hall may not recognize the user; nonresidents cannot schedule meetings.
2. There may be no room available at the requested date and time.
3. The Town Hall may have—or at least find—no relevant documents in the archive.
4. There may be no matches among town residents for the specified attendee interest profile keywords, and hence a null to: list for the meeting notice.

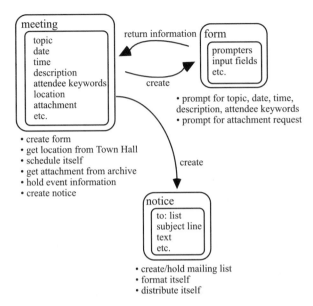

Figure 9.2
Initial object model: Responsibilities and collaborations among the meeting, the form, and the notice for the "Setting up a community meeting" use case (Rosson and Carroll 1996c)

Identifying candidate objects and responsibilities, and elaborating the use case itself support building an initial object model. Like any other design process, building an object model is not a one-shot solution process. Some of the objects identified early may be refactored into multiple objects or subsumed by other objects later in the design process. In general, many further objects will be considered as the software design process moves forward. However, it is useful to be able to produce a concrete and plausible starting point for these reconsiderations as early as possible. Figure 9.2 presents an example of an initial object model for the "setting up a community meeting" use case.

The initial object model for "setting up a community network" articulates three central objects: the meeting, the form, and the notice. It specifies the information that each object manages (for example, the form holds prompters and input fields) and the responsibilities of each object, with respect to one another (the main ones are indicated by the graphical links; for example, the prompter returns information to the meeting) and with respect to other objects not yet articulated (the meeting works with the Town Hall object; the notice sends itself to community members). Building this model brings to the light further important design distinctions—for example, the relationship between the meeting and notice differentiates the role of *being* the event (for example, holding event information, negotiating place and time with the Town Hall) from the role of *advertising* the event (formatting and distributing event information).

Interaction scripts can also help to guide user interface design (Wirfs-Brock 1995). By pulling apart the roles of the person and the system in the use case, the script indicates where and how the system will prompt and respond to the person and what sorts of user actions the system will support. The script can guide initial design and incremental detailing of the overall look and feel of the interface, the content of system prompts, selection defaulting in menus, information layout, display graphics, opportunities for help, and so forth. Finally, scripts can serve as test cases for candidate object models and user interface designs. Given a design worked out to any level of detail, the designer can walk through the steps of the interaction script in order to verify the adequacy of the design for that script, checking that each object has the information and the behaviors to respond effectively to requests it receives from other objects (Rosson and Carroll 1995a, 1995b). Thus, the initial object model in figure 9.2 could be tested for generality with another use case interaction script, such as "filling out the county survey."

A complementary approach to walking through all the object interactions that comprise an interaction script is the approach of focusing closely on the point of view of particular key objects. Beck and Cunningham (1989) devised a pencil-and-paper design tool that has proved remarkably durable. Their Class-Responsibility-Collaborator (CRC) cards record the currently identified responsibilities and collaborators for a given object. Beck and Cunningham suggested that designers focus initially on describing just one or two key objects and that they "pick up the card whose role they are assuming while 'executing' a scenario" (Beck and Cunningham 1989, p. 3). The CRC technique explicitly encourages the tendency of designers to anthropomorphize or metaphorically extend their design objects, and makes it a technique for exploring object interactions in scenario contexts. The CRC tool is nearly universal in contemporary object-oriented design practice; it is difficult to overestimate its impact on both teaching and practice in object-oriented software engineering.

We have adapted the CRC technique, making object point of view even more explicit (Carroll et al. 1994; Robertson et al. 1994). Because they are simplifications of task scenarios, use cases implicitly adopt an agent's point of view, for example, as in box 9.1. This is the right default, of course, but work like that of Beck and Cunningham (1989) and Rosson and Gold (1989) indicates that adopting the perspective of the design objects themselves can be very stimulating to designers. We write out point-of-view scenarios, transforming the original use case descriptions to emphasize how they would "appear" to particular design objects. Box 9.3 shows the "setting up a community meeting" use case from the point of view of the meeting and the contact person objects.

Point-of-view scenarios can make more salient the specific needs and responsibilities of the object whose point of view is depicted. For example, should the contact person provide a name and e-mail address to the meeting, which then passes this information to the notice, or should the contact person collaborate directly with the notice, after the notice is created by the meeting? Should the meeting get date and time information back from the form and then request a location from the Town Hall for that date and time, or should it expect the form to make this request of the Town Hall, and just return the meeting location? Seeing the "setting up a community meeting" scenario from the point of view of the contact person and the meeting can help the designer work through these decisions.

Point of view can also help to reveal "hidden objects," that is, objects that other objects depend on but are not themselves obvious in the original use case. Contact person is an example of a hidden object in the "setting up a community meeting" scenario. Indeed, perhaps *because* the original use case is presented from the meeting instigator's point of view, it is not obvious that there will also be an object that holds information about that person as a community resident. Were we to continue with the example, the Town Hall would be seen to be a complex object including buildings, for example, each of which has rooms, some of which are

Box 9.3
Point-of-view scenarios of "setting up a community meeting" for the meeting and the contact person objects

---

The Meeting's Point of View

From my point of view, I was created by the Town Hall, and the first thing I did was to open a form to gather information. The form gave me a contact person, a topic, a date, a time, a description, and a list of interest profile keywords. I asked the Town Hall for meeting rooms available at the specified date and time. I then asked the form to query the user about which of these locations would be best. I was also given a document as an attachment. When the user asked me to, I created a notice to advertise myself.

• Parts: a topic, a description, a list of interest profile keywords, etc.
• Collaborators: a contact person, a form, a document attachment, a notice, a location, a date, a time
• Responsibilities: collect meeting information, schedule self, create notice, etc.

The Contact Person's Point of View

From my point of view, I hold information about the particular resident who initiated the "set up a meeting" task. When the meeting created a notice describing itself, I provided the contact person's name and e-mail address.

• Parts: Name, e-mail address
• Collaborators: Meeting
• Responsibilities: provide name and e-mail address

---

meeting rooms, each one of which has a schedule, some of which have an open slot at the requested date and time for the meeting. Figure 9.3 is an elaboration of the object model in figure 9.2, incorporating these further objects and relationships.

As schematized in figure 9.4, the scenario-based software design process is a set of heuristic manipulations on task scenarios, each intended to help articulate the underlying objects. Use cases are a simplification of task scenarios that emphasize functional requirements, but can be more holistically use oriented than traditional command-by-command

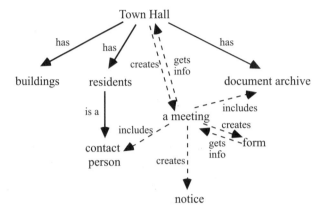

Figure 9.3
A more elaborated object domain model for the "setting up a community meeting" use case

functional requirements. Use cases can be transformed into interaction scripts and point-of-view scenarios, as well as employed directly to develop object models. Interaction scripts differentiate human and system roles to isolate specific actions and responsibilities in the use case narrative. Point-of-view scenarios emphasize the role and perspective of one particular object through the narrative of a use case. Interaction scripts can be successively detailed into user interface mock-ups and prototypes.

As depicted in figure 9.4, all of these representations can be used to elaborate and refactor the object model. For example, working out the user interface presentation for the notice may help the designer to realize that sending the archive document as an attachment could entrain versioning problems (that is, if the original document in the archive is subsequently changed, the document attachment sent with the notice may be inaccurate when it is received and read). In this way, the user interface could suggest a different underlying object model in which the meeting only maintains a pointer to the document in the archive; the pointer, and not the document, is then included in the notice, ensuring that all recipients of the notice read the most current version of the document attachment. To the converse, candidate object models can be used to refine the various scenario representations. For example, as the object model be-

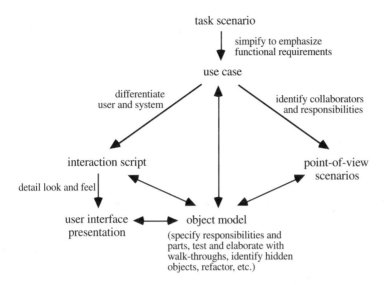

Figure 9.4
Developing a software object model from a task scenario involves a set of heuristic manipulations of the task scenario

comes more elaborated, the designer can elaborate interaction scripts and point-of-view scenarios to check that they still reflect the original narrative sense of the task scenario.

The Scenario Browser

In the early 1990s, we began to develop a design-support environment for object-oriented software. We wanted to investigate tools that could help designers adopt a seriously scenario-based approach to developing object models. The driving idea for this work was to leverage the multifarious nature of scenarios more deliberately. The approach we took was to support concurrent development of a variety of scenario-based design "views" in a hypertext browser. We wanted to make it easy for designers to interleave work on use case narratives, usability rationales, interaction scripts, point-of-view scenarios, and so forth. We wanted designers to be able to switch among these views easily, referring to one while working on another, and we wanted them to be able to share the work performed

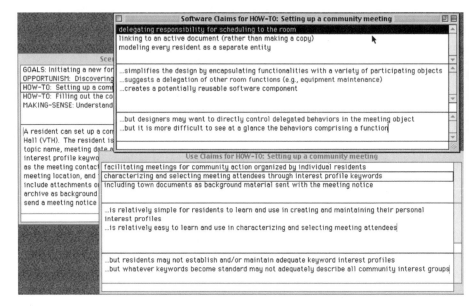

Figure 9.5
The Scenario Browser environment coordinates a set of design views. The Scenario Browser is at the left; the Usability Claims Browser for the currently selected scenario is at the lower right; the Software Claims Browser is at the upper right.

on one view directly with work subsequently performed on another. Our work has focused on a series of tool prototypes called the Scenario Browser environment (Rosson and Carroll 1992, 1995a, 1996c).

Design work with the Scenario Browser environment revolves around a set of task scenario narratives. The upper pane of the left-most window in figure 9.5 shows a list of scenarios developed for the Virtual Town Hall. The designer can create scenarios within various categories: *goal scenarios* describe people identifying task goals that are supported by the system; *opportunism scenarios* describe people exploring functions and information presented by the system; *how-to scenarios* describe people carrying out routine activities supported by the system; and *making-sense scenarios* describe people diagnosing the system, solving problems of various sorts, and understanding how the system works (we return to these categories in the next chapter). The designer selects a scenario category and specifies a (descriptive) name in order to open a text pane into which a scenario description can be entered. The scenario description is free-form; it can be any representation that the designer considers useful, although it is typical to enter narrative texts. In figure 9.5, the how-to scenario "Setting up a community meeting" is selected in the upper pane; its description, the text from box 9.1, appears in the lower pane.

In addition to managing this library of task scenario narratives, the Scenario Browser provides mechanisms for establishing links to other "views" of each scenario: a usability rationale, a software design rationale, a set of point-of-view scenarios, an object model, and a class hierarchy. The bottom window in figure 9.5 is a use claims view for the "Setting up a community meeting" scenario. Several key features for that scenario are listed in the top pane of the use claims view window; the feature "characterizing and selecting meeting attendees through interest profile keywords" is selected. The middle pane of the window displays upside consequences of the keyword profile feature that have been identified (for example, "is relatively simple for residents to learn and use in creating and maintaining their personal interest profiles"), and the lower pane displays downside consequences that have been identified (for example, "but residents may not establish and/or maintain adequate keyword interest profiles").

The upper right window in figure 9.5 shows a software claims view for the "Setting up a community meeting" scenario. Software claims are analogous to usability claims, but address features of the implementation that have consequences for the quality of the software design; they articulate the rationale for object responsibilities. The consequences pertain to the needs and concerns of designers and developers instead of to those of users. Several key software design features for the scenario are listed in the top pane of the software claims window; the feature "delegating responsibility for scheduling to the room" is selected. The middle pane displays upside consequences of the delegating-responsibility feature that have been identified; for example, the feature creates a more modular design that might be easier to maintain and whose elements might be easier to reuse in other designs (cf. "creates a potentially reusable software component"). The lower pane displays downside consequences that have been identified; for example, the feature creates a more generic and distributed design that may be more difficult to tinker with (cf. "but designers may want to directly control delegated behaviors in the meeting object"). (Software claims were originally proposed by Harrison, Roast, and Wright 1989; they are discussed in more detail in Rosson and Carroll 1995a; software design rationale more generally is discussed in Moran and Carroll 1996.)

In the use claims and software claims views, a designer can establish links from the features and consequences of particular claims to other scenarios. A given feature may have consequences in several scenarios; it may have identical or different consequences across various scenarios. Analogously, a given consequence may be identified in several scenarios; it may be associated with the same feature in various scenarios or with different features. These hypertextual links can help designers to analyze contemplated design changes, browsing usability links to assess how groups of related scenarios might be affected by changes to given features. Designers can also establish links between usability and software claims to facilitate work on potential trade-offs between ease-of-learning/use and ease-of-implementation/maintenance goals. They can also aggregate claims across scenarios to get an overall impression of kinds of issues involved in the design.

The Scenario Browser provides further tools to employ scenario analysis work directly in software design and implementation. For each scenario, the designer can open a Point-of-View (PoV) window to identify responsibilities, parts, and collaborators for currently identified design objects. The left-most window in figure 9.6 is a PoV view for the "Setting up a community meeting" scenario. The window's left pane is a list of the objects identified so far; selecting an object in the list allows the designer to enter that object's point-of-view scenario. In the figure, the meeting object is selected, and its current point-of-view scenario, parts, collaborators, and responsibilities have been recorded.

The designer can use these collaborators and responsibilities to prototype and experiment with software objects using the network view, shown in the right-most window of figure 9.6, and the Bittitalk browser, shown at the bottom of the figure. The top left pane of this browser is a Smalltalk workspace in which the designer can create objects and send messages to them. In the figure, the designer has created meeting as an instance of the class Discussion (this relationship is noted in the bottom-

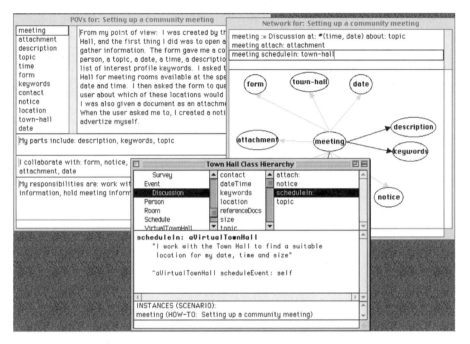

Figure 9.6
Further design views from the Scenario Browser environment. The Point-of-View Browser is at the left; the Network Browser is at the right; an application-specific Bittitalk Browser is at the bottom.

most pane of the class browser) and has just described the room scheduling collaboration between the meeting and the Town Hall, using a scheduleIn: message. Objects that are created in the workspace are displayed graphically in the bottom pane; connections among these objects are displayed as links in the graph. The current object model from the meeting's point of view is a subset of the graph shown earlier in figure 9.3.

The objects in the network view are "live" Smalltalk instances; the designer can interactively model a scenario as a set of Smalltalk objects, send messages to the objects comprising the current software model for a scenario, and add or remove objects and object attributes. Working initially and directly with live instances allows designers to develop new objects and behaviors without first having to address the more abstract task of writing complete class definitions and methods before any behavior can be observed (Gold and Rosson 1991). And while doing this, the designer can also switch among the other browsers. The network view encourages cross-scenario consistency by making it easy for designers to reuse objects that have been implemented for other scenarios. The designer can use the "other objects" menu choice in network view to display a comprehensive list of objects implemented for all scenarios. The designer can select an object, using it unchanged in the current scenario or elaborating and modifying its state and behavior as needed.

Designers can use a Bittitalk browser to refine and consolidate implementation work. The Bittitalk Browser, shown at the bottom of figure 9.6, displays a filtered view of the Smalltalk class hierarchy, limited to those classes and methods pertaining to the current design project (in this example, the Virtual Town Hall; recall the discussion of box 5.2). With this tool, the design can exploit Smalltalk's inheritance hierarchy and other abstraction mechanisms to generalize the scenario-based, instance-level prototypes to a final design. This design can be specified as class descriptions and method comments (that is, stubs), or can be fully implemented as a Smalltalk application.

The collection of tools in the Scenario Browser environment allows designers to interleave a great variety of design activities, including initial scenario sketches, textual specifications, usability and software rationale, object inventories and point-of-view scenarios, scripts and instance-level prototypes, and refined class libraries. It supports the generally observed fluid and opportunistic nature of design and development work (recall chapters 2 and 3) and supports the specific preference Smalltalk designers have for integrating design abstraction with concrete implementation and exploration (Rosson and Carroll 1996a). It encourages the model-first design strategy (discussed in chapters 5 and 6). At any point, the designer can switch to another browser and to another design activity, adding a scenario or revising a rationale while completing the software for the implemented design.

The Scenario Browser is work in progress. Directions of current interest include improving support for implementation and for history management, as well as adapting the tools for programming education. Sharing object implementations among scenarios implicitly enforces a level of consistency checking, but designers are not forced or even prompted to share implementations among scenarios, and there is no guarantee that when an implementation is reused and adapted for a particular scenario, it will continue to work correctly in the original scenario for which it was developed. The Scenario Browser encourages evolutionary development and incremental design documentation; these were some of its key objectives. But this style of design work results in a voluminous design history of requirements, implementations, and rationale, which can become unmanageable. Currently, we prune this material by hand, but tool support for managing scenario libraries would make the environment more useful.

Although our initial focus was design support, our work on the Scenario Browser has also converged with the MiTTS project. In the MiTTS work, we came to realize a significant need for instruction in object-oriented design quite apart from its role in Smalltalk programming. From this perspective, the Scenario Browser appears as a design-oriented View Matcher environment. And indeed, Beck and Cunningham (1989) originally developed CRC cards for instructional purposes. We have incorporated some of the techniques and representations of the Scenario Browser into ODE, the Object Design Exploratorium, a discovery learning environment for object-oriented design (Robertson et al. 1994), and have also used them in an example-based professional education tutorial (Rosson and Carroll 1996b).

The Specification-Implementation Gap

Chapter 2 criticized waterfall models of software development, particularly with respect to the design of interactive systems. In a design waterfall, there is a nasty gap between the specification of a system and its successful implementation. In that gap lie emergent requirements, mismatches and interdependencies between the things people want to achieve and experience and the capabilities and side effects of the software they use, and organizational hurdles for the coordination of work and activity.

One way to narrow, or at least to bridge, the specification-implementation gap is to integrate various aspects of system development. As shown in previous chapters, coordinating the analysis of work flow and usability issues for current technology and its envisioned alternatives can inject greater rationality and depth into the design process. The Scenario Browser helps designers to interleave development of task and software models. One benefit is to ensure that user interface metaphors are more than mere cover stories for the presentation of system functions. Of course, metaphors can be engaged (that is, recognized or constructed by users) by superficial aspects of user interface look-and-feel: if something looks like a trash bin, think of it as a trash bin. However, when a metaphor conveys relationships among objects in the underlying software model, it is more likely to be consistent, revealing, and useful. For example, various desktop objects share data and implement similar behaviors (like "opening"). If the underlying software design is a hodge-podge with respect to these interface objects (and conversely), that will eventually become apparent through the course of creative task interactions in which the metaphor breaks down, perhaps in ways that are uninterpretable to people using the system and disastrous for their work.

If the user interface metaphor is a systematic view of underlying software model, creative use of system's functionality is more likely to succeed, and where it does break down, the function and the user interface will break down together, more transparently suggesting how both can be debugged and further developed. This unification is enabled by the responsibility-driven approach to object-oriented software design. Creating an object domain model, a software simulation of the task entities, engages metaphoric reasoning about what various software objects "should" do and how. It places the person's task in the center of the software design process. Unlike a traditionally function-oriented software process—or indeed like a purely look-and-feel user interface specification—this ensures that the software that is created will be precisely directed toward supporting the activities and preferences of the people who will use that software.

Design reasoning about object responsibilities can also suggest possibilities for extending extant tasks and domain objects, for example, to incorporate rooms that schedule themselves. As discussed in chapter 2 and subsequently, technology characteristically alters human practices (the task-artifact cycle). Thus, designers are always in the position of designing for currently understood needs and preferences, all the time knowing that the system itself will ineluctably transform these. Techniques for analyzing the causal dynamics of use situations, such as usability rationale, are approaches to managing this uncertainty. Reasoning about object responsibilities can play a role in this as a means for suggesting potential redesigns of a task domain.

The key to integrating software design with task specification is the common design language of scenarios. Scenarios focus and integrate a variety of system development activities in requirements engineering, usability engineering, and software engineering. They make system development more coherent and more user centered, addressing in one stroke its two most significant chronic deficiencies.

10

Finding Scenarios and Making Claims

Scenarios can serve as an integrative design representation, guiding the development and application of design knowledge. Chapters 3 through 9 described and illustrated some of the roles scenarios can play in design, but for the most part the scenarios themselves were givens. This raises the methodological question: Where do scenarios and claims come from? This chapter and the next address that operational perspective; we ask *how* to do scenario-based design and analysis rather than *why*.

Where Do Scenarios Come From?

Part of the attractiveness of scenario-based design is that scenarios are so accessible. All stakeholders in a design project—customer, developer, future user—can describe and analyze them. Every observable or imaginable event of human-computer interaction is part of some scenario. Thus, the practical problem is less one of finding scenarios at all and more one of generating and identifying good scenarios or good sets of scenarios, where "good" means scenarios that raise and illuminate key issues of usability and usefulness, or that suggest and provoke new design ideas.

Scenario descriptions are fundamentally heuristic; indeed, they cannot be complete. For any nontrivial system, there is an infinity of possible usage scenarios. The incompleteness of scenario descriptions is an important property but not unique to scenarios. The only complete specification of a system is the system itself, and the only complete specification of the *use* of a system is an infinite log of its actual use, along with comprehensive cognitive and social analysis of that log (Carroll 1990b).

Practically speaking, complete descriptions of systems or of their use are unattainable.

Although scenario descriptions cannot be complete, they can provide better or poorer coverage of a system. A set of scenarios has good coverage if it includes examples of the significant uses of a system and the major types of agents, goals, actions, events, obstacles, contingencies, and outcomes that constitute these uses. Of course, this just pushes back the question to one of how to identify significant uses and major components in situations of use.

An important issue of coverage is scenario *bias* (Carroll and Rosson 1992). Designers often more easily see the touchstone scenarios that instigate and provide vision to a design project, but less easily see the error scenarios in which people misinterpret display information and subsequently reach dead-ends, that is, scenarios the system should *not* evoke ("antiscenarios" according to Johnson and Benner 1993). Usability specialists may have a complementary bias; they may see error scenarios lurking in every display and every user action. Analysts may also be biased by their theoretical commitments; for example, an analyst who believes that people need to have opportunities to reason on their own, explore system functionality, and customize interface tools may under-estimate the potential problems of users who take significant initiative and then get lost and confused.

To create scenario descriptions with good coverage and minimal bias, one should take a eclectic approach. I suggest seven methods; they are largely complementary and can be pursued together to comprise a fairly comprehensive methodology for scenario generation. All are heuristics. All can be employed to varying extents. Using the whole set of methods protects against the potential distortions of any one method.

Ethnographic Field Study

The most revelatory scenarios come from opening ourselves to the real world—from noticing what really happens in human activity. We may not be able to describe completely or understand the context of use for a complicated piece of computer equipment, but we can learn much merely by watching.

An excellent approach to gathering scenarios from the real world is ethnographic inquiry (Ackroyd and Hughes 1992; Fetterman 1989). The ethnographer seeks to enter the world of another person or persons, imposing no expectations and making no assumptions. The observer tries to make sense of what goes on and identify important categories and distinctions in the world as found. The observer builds an ontology of the agents, goals, actions, events, obstacles, contingencies, and outcomes from scratch. What events occur in the domain? What types of roles do people play? What goals do they pursue? What are they uncertain about? How do they work together? What actions do they take? What are common obstacles to goals and actions? What depends on what? What sorts of variations occur in actions and events, and with what consequences? What are the typical and significant outcomes that occur in the domain?

A well-known example is Suchman's (1987) study of document copier systems. Suchman observed people using a sophisticated photocopier that incorporated sensors to allow it to provide informative prompts. In one example, a person is in the midst of a fairly complex copying task and, for reasons unknown, begins the task of copying a multipage document by placing the first page in the document handler (Suchman 1987). The copier senses the page and prompts the user to press Start. The person does this, and four copies are produced. The copier now prompts the user to remove the original from the document handler. She does this and awaits further direction regarding the second page (holding it over the document handler and watching the display). However, the copier senses the copies of the first page in the output tray and prompts the user to remove them. At this point, the interaction has completely broken down: the output tray prompt does not address the person's current goal; she ignores it and places the original of the second page into the document handler, retriggering the prompt to remove originals from document handler. The person says, "'Remove the original—' Okay, I've removed the original. And put in the second copy."

This is a simple but striking scenario of interaction. It is utterly mundane in the sense that the person's goal and the actions she takes seem appropriate and reasonable, but she nonetheless encounters a significant usability obstacle. Such a scenario raises serious design issues. For example, the copier parses an interaction as complete only when its output tray sensors indicate that copies have been removed. It requires a person who wishes to copy a multipage document manually to remove the copies of each successive page as they are produced, which conflicts fundamentally with how the person conceives of her task. More generally, the interaction breaks down because the copier was designed to convey that it really does "understand" what the user is doing (Carroll and Aaronson 1988).

Suchman's scenario is an example of a very routine interaction that turns out to be surprisingly problematic. Ethnographic field studies are also good for discovering "exotic" error scenarios. Some human errors involve so much tangling of events and creative interpretation that they would be difficult to anticipate. For example, a learner we studied was creating a lease using a document processing system. She made a series of serious errors and produced an obvious and ugly editing disaster (Mack, Lewis, and Carroll 1983). Concurrent with these events, she was building an interpretation: having no technical knowledge about or prior experience with leases or other legal documents, she was able to interpret her work as constituting a lease. To our amazement, she concluded that she had in fact succeeded with the project. We might have imagined the individual events of this scenario, but we could never have anticipated the creativity of her interpretation—and it is the interpretation that makes the scenario significant.

Ethnographic description does not focus only on error; indeed, error scenarios must be weighed against and interpreted against scenarios that flow successfully. However, in practice it is far more difficult to recognize the categories and dynamics of successful interaction; when things go well, information systems and applications become invisible to the user and to the analyst (Winograd and Flores 1986; Dreyfus and Dreyfus 1988). The practical know-how of ordinary work and the organizational assumptions that comprise the social context for the work often remain implicit—tacitly understood by coworkers but never articulated as such.

Bentley et al. (1992) described the work of an air traffic control center, highlighting the importance of continual coordination. In their analysis, current paper flight strips were revealed to be a highly effective shared resource for maintaining controller vigilance and for keeping potentially critical information at hand. The fact that the strips must be requested and are held in the hands are significant factors. Without this insight, the flight strips are just the sort of information artifact that conventional "automation thinking" might suggest could be presented in a window of the computer display. (For further examples and discussion, see Blomberg 1995.)

The very notion of ethnographic analysis can be intimidating to designers facing deadlines and limited resources, and perhaps picturing images of anthropologists living for years at a time in traditional cultures. However, as Hughes et al. (1994) emphasize, ethnography is an adaptable approach. It always involves immersion in the context of use and always requires penetrating observation and analysis, but it does not necessarily take a huge amount of time or effort. In our own design practice, we often rely initially on a coarse-grained ethnography to identify efficiently the most typical and critical scenarios of a domain of human activity, and then refine this initial understanding through continuing fieldwork as our initial design is refined and developed (Carroll 1990a; Carroll and Rosson 1995; Carroll et al. 1998).

Participatory Design
Ethnographic field studies often bring to the light facts in the background of the context of use, circumstances and relationships of which the actors themselves may be unaware. But people also have needs and concerns that they are keenly aware of and about which they can be highly articulate, but may not be obvious or perhaps even apparent in field studies. One way to address this is to incorporate interviewing and discussion into ethnographic investigation. A more radical and direct approach is to involve prospective users *as designers* in setting goals and planning prototypes—that is, instead involving them only after initial prototypes exist (Greenbaum and Kyng 1991; Kuhn and Muller 1993; Schuler and Namioka 1993). Participatory design is not an alternative to ethnographic field study; the two are complementary and work well in combination.

Scenario identification and generation is certainly an arena of design activity for which prospective users are uniquely qualified; they already know the current context of use, they can articulate their domain knowledge in terms of the domain's scenarios, and they may have specific ideas for appropriate enhancements. Some of our Raison d'Etre scenarios in box 4.1 were suggested by members of the project team we studied. However, often the designer cannot merely ask for such information, and the user cannot merely give it; the two speak different "languages" and live in different "cultures," and these differences must be bridged to allow effective communication. Participatory design is therefore a process of sharing perspectives, developing mutual trust and respect for different kinds of knowledge and skill, and fundamentally, mutual learning (Kyng 1995). Users acquire better understanding of the technological possibilities and constraints for the project, while technologists learn more about defining goals, basic tasks, and contexts of use. Participatory design injects unique information into the design process, but it does this by redistributing power in design work.

Kyng (1995) argues that usage scenarios must be developed through direct collaboration. The users' knowledge of the work domain and the developers' understanding of the technology must confront one another face to face: reading the scenarios later cannot substitute for participating in their development. For many developers, it is a challenge to be able to see such intimate and equal interaction with users as part of their work and responsibility. Muller et al. (1995) emphasize techniques to "problematize" design collaboration, that is, to carry out discussion of design issues in vocabularies that do not disproportionately favor the preexisting knowledge of either designers or users. Their novel paper-and-pencil representation schemes are equally accessible to both, and thereby help to create a more level playing field for participatory design.

Laughton (1996) worked with public school teachers to design networked communication applications. This domain is in some ways even more challenging than the government and business domains investigated by Muller and Kyng: teachers are responsible for designing classroom activities and increasingly are expected to incorporate information technology into these activities, but they are provided with little support and no on-the-job time for doing this. In Laughton's method, which integrates elements of ethnography with participatory design, teachers and developers visit one another's work sites, demonstrating and discussing techniques and technologies and brainstorming about possibilities. These interactions are then analyzed in terms of the teachers' concerns, goals, motivations, and constraints. Based on these initial sessions, Laughton created scenarios envisioning activities and technology that could be developed. The scenarios were subsequently used as discussion artifacts, to verify shared understanding of design requirements already identified and propel the design process toward further articulation of requirements and envisionment of solutions. Laughton concluded that the process of collaboratively discussing and refining scenarios was effective for both eliciting the teachers' knowledge and evoking a strong sense of ownership and commitment in them.

Participatory design is not a panacea for engaging users in the development process. As Laughton (1996) emphasizes, technologists implicitly retain control over the methods of design collaboration and of the kinds of representations used; indeed, the technologists choose and then manage the participatory design process. We are continuing this line of investigation; we videotape classroom interactions and then ask the teachers to select the significant episodes and lead group discussion of them as potential requirements scenarios (Chin, Rosson, and Carroll 1997). Nevertheless, we still see evidence that the teachers feel a power imbalance; they find it difficult sometimes to value their own needs and preferences against technology constraints. After all, the explicit reason for our design collaboration is to develop new technology. On the other hand, empowering users continues to frustrate and intimidate some of our implementor colleagues: it takes time and effort, and it shifts power.

Reuse of Prior Analyses

Ethnographic field study and participatory design are paradigmatic empirical approaches. They involve constructing scenarios from direct observation, interview, discussion, and collaborative interaction. The special value of these sources for scenarios is that they may surprise us; we may see a work practice or problem, hear about a need, or discover a novel possibility. In most ways they work best if carried out with a tabula-rasa of expectations, an openness to discover the work domain as it is experienced by its actors. However, no one has the time or the resources to develop every software system from scratch, and indeed, doing so would eschew the potential benefit of whatever has been learned through the course of all the system development work that has gone before.

Much of what is called design work is really *re*design. In designing an air traffic control system, a tutoring system, or a programming environment, one takes into account, at least implicitly, the features, functions, and usage scenarios of prior systems of that particular type. Such reuse is readily apparent with regard to user interface conventions for presenting information and issuing commands. Indeed, a substantial part of user interface design expertise is knowing how to reuse prior solutions. Tasks also are reused and redesigned.

We have seen several examples of the reuse of scenarios. In direct hill climbing, the designer adapts specific antecedent situations of use; the development of the View Matcher was an example. In activity modeling, the designer adapts knowledge about a potentially relevant domain, as we did in developing the Smalltalk Guru. In principled emulation, the designer adapts knowledge about a potentially relevant artifact-in-use; the Goalposter was an example. The scenarios are grounded in prior design work instead of in direct investigation of the target usage situations or in direct collaboration with intended users.

To reuse previous design analyses we need to ask what a current usage situation resembles or instantiates. If we can see a current design project as similar to some previous project (or projects), we can consider the scenarios identified and analyzed in the previous project as candidate scenarios for the current project. This is a kind of analogical reasoning; it can be relatively mechanical or relatively creative. Chapter 5 described how the design of the MiTTS tutorial and the View Matcher were anchored in a particular touchstone scenario of interactive learning; here the analogy was fairly obvious and direct. Chapter 7 described how the Reuse View Matcher was developed from the design analysis for the MiTTS View Matcher. The analogy from learning scenarios to reuse scenarios is less obvious.

Ethnographic field study, participatory design, and direct scenario reuse share a common limitation that stems from their greatest strength: all are anchored in particular prior tasks and tools. But any design context is novel and unique in some respects, and reused scenarios could always be erroneous to that extent. Relative to field studies and participatory design, scenario reuse is an especially inexpensive way to develop a preliminary scenario analysis. Indeed, if even the most generic and routine scenarios can be more readily identified through this method, that may release some effort that can be focused on identifying relatively novel and unique scenarios through more effortful empirical methods.

Moreover, scenario reuse offers important benefits. Prior scenario analyses may have already been critiqued and refined by other designers; they may be complete and sound in ways that complement direct empirical studies; they may offer better breadth of coverage, where the empirical methods offer better depth. Reusing scenarios and scenario analyses also provides a vehicle for what was called cumulative design in chapter 7. To the extent that the scenarios of one design analysis are reusable in another, the two designs may share a common abstraction in terms of the kind of human activity and task-related artifacts involved.

Scenario Typologies
Analogical reuse of prior scenario analyses is somewhat opportunistic. Sometimes a designer sees a productive analogy, sometimes not. One way to support scenario reuse is to identify categories or types of scenarios and domains. Typologies impose structure on scenario libraries, simplifying the reuse task. The designer can evaluate whether a particular type of scenario provides a useful analogy rather than having to evaluate each scenario token. This can also help ensure better coverage in scenario representations by ensuring that designers more systematically sample the full space of scenario possibilities. For example, using a word processor would typically involve many specific instances of the routine editing category. A representative set of word processing scenarios should include instances of this category but should not consist only of instances of this category. Recognizing and naming scenario categories makes them more salient and helps to ensure that they are included and balanced in scenario analyses.

Scenario typologies can exist at different levels of abstraction. Routine editing is a kind of scenario that arises in many domains besides word processing. We generalized across a set of our scenario-based design projects in several different domains to construct a domain-independent typology (Carroll and Rosson 1992). We grouped scenarios in terms of the underlying concern of the actors in the scenario. We were guided very generally by Norman's (1986) theory of human action, but essentially just grouped scenario tokens we had empirically identified. For example, an office worker may want to edit a letter with a word processing system. But more generally, the person is concerned with performing a routine task, with following a procedure. At this more general level, editing a letter is similar to printing a letter, filling in a form, setting up a meeting, and writing a simple script.

Our typology distinguishes six categories. Initially people must orient to novel task situations, identifying and analyzing appropriate goals. Thus, a person may know something about the functional capability of a word processor—enough to have wanted to switch it on—but may wonder how the device can help in pursuing document preparation goals like writing a letter. We call this concern *orienting to appropriate goals.* People are often interested in *interacting with the environment opportunistically;* they wonder what the objects they encounter can do and explore the consequences of various possible actions—for example, choosing the menu for page layouts just to see what it does. People sometimes seek specific information, *searching under a description*—for example, looking for the "menu that allows you to see formatting characters."

The earlier example of routine editing illustrates the concern we call *following procedures.* People also have reflective concerns, one of them *seeking and using explanations:* a person may lose track of a print job and wonder why nothing has printed yet and how the print queue works. Finally, people evaluate their own actions to determine whether goals were attained, and to consider how they will act in the future—for example, devising a more streamlined way to do a simple buck slip. We call this concern *reflecting on and crafting one's own work.* Box 10.1 lists examples of the various types of user concerns from earlier sections of this book (a simplified version of this typology is incorporated into the Scenario Browser tool, as shown in figure 9.5).

The user concern typology provides a rubric for organizing our evaluation of the eighteen scenarios in figure 7.1 as reuse candidates. The typology also guides the generation of new scenarios; for example, we generated the "what do sliders do?" scenario in box 7.1 from the typology; it became a key element in the design for the Reuse View Matcher. Box 10.1 shows no examples of scenarios for reflective concerns regarding MiTTS; this gap might raise the design challenge of how to incorporate explanation-based learning into the "analyzing card-hand display" scenario (Carroll and Rosson 1991). The user concern typology supports

Box 10.1
A typology of user concerns.

Orienting to appropriate goals
Orienting to the project (box 4.2)
Starting up Smalltalk (box 6.5)

Interacting with the environment opportunistically
What is the project all about? (box 4.1)
Analyzing or trying interesting messages (box 5.1)
What do sliders do? (box 7.1)
Discovering the Swing Dance group (figure 9.5)

Searching under a description
What was Bonnie's role in September 1991? (box 4.2)
Analyzing card-hand display (box 6.1)

Following procedures
Creating a perspective on the design history (box 4.2)
Following tutorial steps (figure 5.1, box 6.9)
Hooking up a BoardGamePane (box 7.1)
Creating an UpperCasePane (box 7.5)
Setting up a community meeting (figures 9.1, 9.5)
Filling out the county survey (figure 9.5)

Seeking and using explanations
Analyzing slider scale conversion (box 7.1)
Understanding the "reply-to-interest group" function (figure 9.5)

Reflecting upon and crafting one's own work
Looking for the fast-forward button (box 4.2)
Contrasting "copy down" and "reference to super" (box 7.7)

Note: The example scenarios come from discussions of Raison d'Etre (chapter 4), MiTTS (chapters 5 and 6), the Reuse View Matcher (chapter 7), MoleHill (chapter 7), and the Virtual Town Hall (chapter 9).

tracking the impacts of design decisions for categories of work activity and interaction, a higher-level and somewhat complementary view to tracking impacts for specific scenarios. Finally, the typology is a research tool for investigating cross-domain generalizations about scenarios.

Nevertheless, we regard the typology as heuristic. We have found it useful, but are not convinced that it is well factored or couched at the most significant level of abstraction. Surely there are other levels of abstraction for which scenario typologies could be developed. We believe, for instance, that more specific, relatively domain-dependent scenario typologies could be especially useful to designers who work in particular domains, for example, educational technology for classrooms. (Chapter 3 briefly mentioned scenario typologies of Wack 1985b and Schwartz 1992 from strategic management.) Since we have not yet developed and used other typologies, we have no basis for preferring this one; we merely have some experience with it. Two interesting, and open questions for further investigation are what levels of abstraction are most significant for scenario typologies and what set of levels is most useful for organizing scenario libraries, guiding the generation of broad and well-balanced scenario representations and tracking support for categories of activity in the development process.

Theory-Based Scenarios

Design theories and theories of human activity are bound to scenarios and types of scenarios; we can both apply and develop those theories by reusing and evaluating their characteristic scenarios. For example, some of the MiTTS scenarios are specializations of minimalist instruction scenarios. The characteristic scenarios of minimalist instruction—pertaining to articulating and pursuing one's own learning goals—guided our design of MiTTS and later its evaluation. As discussed in chapter 8, such a theory-based approach allows the evaluation of a specific design to contribute to the assessment and development of the theory or theories instantiated in the design.

In time, the theory-based approach could help to create a systematic foundation of design knowledge that can be applied in the future. The design of the MoleHill tutor developed from a generic tutoring scenario in which the learner's goals and plans are represented, but also contributed to the development of the design theory of tutors, providing scenario analyses that could be reused in the future.

The inferences of theory-based scenario reuse are systematically scoped. For example, MiTTS scenarios are specifically pertinent to the design of minimalist Smalltalk tutorials, but also relevant to other programming language tutorials, other minimalist tutorials, and more generally other instructional systems. The scenarios identified and analyzed for Raison d'Etre in chapter 4 are potentially reusable by someone building a multimedia design history system, but they are also relevant to text-based design history systems, collaborative hypermedia systems for applications other than design history, systems that involve coordinating text and video, and so forth. Most generally, theories of human activity could be cast in terms of universal scenario patterns; this has already been done to some extent in the particularly important area of errors (Hollnagel 1993; Norman 1988; Reason 1990).

Making explicit use of theories of human activity and of design genres is potentially a far more powerful method for scenario generation than analogical reuse or heuristic typologies. Theories provide specific grounding for the scenarios and boundary conditions on the relevance of the scenarios. Thus, the risk of erroneous scenarios is less than it is using analogy or typologies. A limitation of the theory-based method is that the state of theory is always to some extent incomplete; thus, theory-based scenarios may not exist for a given design situation, or they may conflict (as they do in the case of MiTTS with respect to minimalist instruction and the so-called systems approach).

Technology-Based Scenarios

All the methods described so far are use oriented: they involve either observation and discussion of use or analysis of existing artifacts-in-use and their abstractions. A distinct source of scenarios is the technology embodied in the scenarios. While it is true that much design work has an evolutionary character, some of the most interesting work incorporates novel technology. For example, it is still novel for people to do routine professional work in immersive virtual environments (that is, surrounded by high-fidelity, manipulable, three-dimensional projections); it is novel to experience physical environments permeated with computing devices and sensors—for example, to wear clothing that manages temperature, adjusts lighting, reroutes communications, and so forth as the wearer moves around; it is novel to engage in multiparty, synchronous collaboration over the Internet in which participants jointly design and experiment with graphical simulations of complex physical processes.

Ethnographic field studies of predecessor situations can guide the development of these technologies and define effective applications, but they could also easily miss truly revolutionary ideas. Participatory design also can be useful; it surely would help potential users better understand and appreciate the new technology. But participatory design is limited by the facility of users to imagine truly novel situations. And of course, novelty undermines reuse. It makes analogies less valid, magnifies the risks inherent in typologies based on prior design work, and tests the boundary conditions of theories.

Therefore, just by elimination, it behooves us to generate scenarios that emphasize the special, novel affordances of new technologies. For example, in the mid-1990s we designed a "virtual school" in which middle and high school students in physically distinct classrooms could collaboratively plan, execute, write up, and discuss projects in physics and physical science (Koenemann et al. 1999). As the project began, we hypothesized a technology scenario in which a student was able to find virtual school collaborators and to carry out discussions and experiments from home, as shown in box 10.2. This was not based on specific observations, direct requests from teachers or students, or any prior instructional scenarios; rather, it was based on an obvious affordance of the network and a technology goal we set for our virtual school software.

This technology-based scenario was not merely a statement of our wishful intentions, divorced from real use and real users. It was an explicit scenario of use that we thought was technically feasible to support and might be valuable to students and to teachers. We used the scenario as a starting point and reference point for subsequent design discussions with students and teachers and for our own subsequent software development work.

A false dichotomy is often assumed to exist between technology-driven design and use-driven design. Clearly, use is the final arbiter of the success of technology. And an important thrust of scenario-based design is that

Box 10.2
Technology-based envisionment scenario

• Marissa, a tenth-grade physics student, is studying gravity and its role in planetary motion. She goes to the virtual science lab and navigates to the gravity room.

• In the gravity room she discovers two other students, Randy and David, already working with the Alternate Reality Kit (Smith 1987), which allows students to alter various physical parameters (such as the universal gravitational constant) and then observe effects in a simulation world.

• The three students, each from a different school in the county, discuss possible experiments by typing messages from their respective personal computers. Together they build and analyze several solar systems, eventually focusing on the question of how comets can disrupt otherwise stable systems.

• They capture data from their experiments and display them with several visualization tools, then write a brief report of their experiments, sending it for comments to Don, another student in Marissa's class, and Ms. Gould, Randy's physics teacher.

---

use can provide early, continuing, and highly articulate guidance throughout the processes of technology development and design. Technology-based scenarios do not undermine or devalue other sources or types of scenarios; they are complementary.

Transformations

The seventh method we use for identifying scenarios is a general brainstorming technique (DeBono 1990): transformations. The general notion is that we can take an existing set of scenarios and manipulate it to create a larger set. One very powerful manipulation is to ask, "What could go wrong?" for each action in each scenario. For example, one version of a Web-based statistics tutorial we designed allowed a main window to spawn various data visualizations. Students could flexibly coordinate the information in the main window with self-initiated, opportunistic interaction with the visualizations. However, in our initial design, when the student traversed a link to the glossary to clarify a term on the main page, the spawned visualizations were all closed—destroying the context of the glossary inquiry and more generally the context of the student's work. By asking what could go wrong with this early design during a formative evaluation walk-through, we were able to develop a better solution even before any student used the system. (Carroll and Isenhour 1999).

An important facet of our scenario typology is to support hypothetical "what could go wrong?" lines of reasoning. That is, in addition to detailing how the various user concerns of the typology can be instantiated or satisfied, we also try to anticipate and detail how each can go awry. For example, we studied an opportunistic interaction scenario for the IBM Displaywriter in which people selected options over and over, apparently expecting some sort of closure signal from the system when a complete or correct set of options had been specified (see Carroll 1990a). This example exposes a general sort of opportunism error in which people become too locally driven by displayed objects and their immediate affordances, losing track of whatever higher-level goals they were pursuing. This use of typology definitely undergenerates error scenarios; it cannot anticipate exotic or tangled errors like the phantom lease scenario. But it multiplies the potential utility of any scenarios generated by the typology.

Another scenario transformation is to exchange points of view and ask how each scenario would appear to another actor (or to various system components). Part of the Shell Oil scenario analysis of the 1970s involved elaborating point of view—for example, developing a scenario involving steep increases in taxes by oil-producing countries from the perspective of various stakeholder countries (oil-producing countries with substantial oil reserves and the ability to make use of additional oil income, countries with limited reserves and limited ability to make use of increased income, oil-consuming countries with high inflation, and so on; Wack 1985a). In the design of Raison d'Etre, we considered different views of the development team meeting scenario (box 4.3). The project manager may see the scenario in terms of building a consensus view, for example, while a team member may see it as a matter of receiving the official view. Neither point of view is right or wrong; both the manager and the team member are users. Had we identified only one point of view, this transformation would have helped ensure better coverage by evoking the other.

We considered point of view in chapter 9, incorporating viewpoints of design objects as well as of scenario agents. For example, the meeting and the contact person respond to different events in box 9.3. From the contact person's point of view, the scenario involves initiating a meeting request and filling in a form. From the meeting's point of view, the scenario is more complex, involving creation of a form, identification of potential meeting rooms, access and attachment of a document, creation of a notice, and several follow-up interactions.

A third transformation is the exchange of the tools and other task objects occurring in a given scenario with another set of tools and objects. On the one hand, this transformation can help start a critical discussion of current practices. Replacing familiar objects makes the scenario easier for users to criticize; it no longer looks just like their own practices. On the other hand, this technique is a simple way to bridge from observed scenarios to envisioned scenarios. Merely inserting the objects of some alternate technology produces a vivid level-zero design—easy to criticize but also easy to improve. In one published design case, this technique (called retooling scenarios) was effective in analyzing and redesigning a World Wide Web site (Erskine, Carter-Todd, and Burton 1997).

A fourth transformation, perhaps the weakest, is to generate the cartesian product of the agents, goals, actions, events, obstacles, contingencies, and outcomes of currently identified scenarios. This is clearly a brute force technique and can be refined. For example, Potts (1995) suggests generating a set of scenarios such that every known goal is achieved in at least one scenario, and every known obstacle occurs in at least one scenario. He suggests further that a selection of the most interesting combinations of obstacles be included in scenarios and that the goals included in the scenarios be ordered to respect known dependencies. This is a nice example of a method that takes a set of scenario elements—the list of goals and obstacles—and generates a systematic scenario description for it; of course, the completeness of the description depends on the completeness of the original set of scenario elements.

How to Make Claims

Enumerating typical and critical use scenarios characterizes the scope of an artifact's actual use or the anticipated use of an artifact still in design. The details of each scenario show how and why that scenario was supported or not supported by the artifact. The scenarios provide a working representation for exploring and altering the design. Claims analysis, as illustrated in prior chapters, provides a more general and explicit representation of the causal relationships that constitute scenarios. Claims sharpen the understanding of relationships that may only be suggested by the scenarios themselves, highlighting just *how* artifacts in use afford actions, suggest explanations, signal progress and error, and so forth. Claims are intended to make descriptions and stories about use into propositions and hypotheses about usability; they are intended to help designers and analysts keep many relationships in mind by isolating and succinctly stating those relationships.

A claims analysis is not merely a filtered view of the more complete usage picture available in the scenarios from which the claims were derived. Claims are constructed and developed and typically include information that was not explicit in the original scenarios. Claims analysis brings to the light issues, conflicts, and contradictions that are not readily apparent in a scenario. For example, earlier in this chapter we considered Suchman's (1987) important scenario of photocopier use. Kellogg (1990) subsequently developed a claims analysis of Suchman's scenario, raising issues Suchman that had not identified at all—for example, the question of why and how the user might have been led to assume the iterative copy procedure. Rather than being merely a filtered view of Suchman's ethnographic description, Kellogg's analysis transforms the description into an explicit design hypothesis that directly indicates design changes and the rationale for those changes.

How can one recognize and construct claims from scenarios? Like scenario generation, claims analysis is open-ended and creative. There is not a single "correct" claims analysis; rather, there are many more and less complete, incisive, empirically grounded, and useful analyses. In our experience, it is generally useful to revise, refine, and refactor a claims analysis to emphasize key issues, lines of reasoning and evidence, and possible design actions. This is typically an ongoing process. An analysis can fairly quickly become good enough to use, and eventually becomes relatively stable, but it is rarely final. A claims analysis is a design rationale (Moran and Carroll 1996) for a scenario-based design, and as MacLean et al. (1996) insightfully observe, design rationales are themselves designed artifacts.

We suggest again an eclectic approach involving seven different methods. These methods are somewhat more overlapping than the methods for scenario generation, and indeed, the methods for identifying claims correspond in many cases to methods for generating scenarios.

Scanning for Causes and Effects

The simplest method for constructing claims is to scan scenarios for causes and effects. This is essentially an editorial method: one summarizes what is literally there in the scenario. The method can be more finely operationalized by highlighting the agents and verb phrases in a scenario text and then successively evaluating and summarizing all apparent causal relationships.

Even this method is not utterly straightforward, however. Apparent causal consequences for agents in a scenario are not all equally valuable. For example, relationships are more plausible if they can be grounded in the social and behavioral sciences. The Overview Pitch claim in box 4.6 is to a great extent a purely textual summary of the "development team meeting" scenario in box 4.3. But the plausibility of the claim rests on a substantial foundation of social psychology, as subsequently discussed in chapter 4 in connection with its generalization, the Social Conformity claim.

Moreover, it is difficult, verging on impossible, to "just" read and summarize scenario texts. People ineluctably construct interpretations for texts and other descriptive materials they encounter, incorporating various sources of knowledge beyond the literal content (Bartlett 1932; Bransford and Johnson 1973). As one becomes more experienced at claims analysis, it becomes typical to read *through* the scenario itself directly to causal elaborations and social and behavioral rationales. Indeed, it can be productive to regard literal scenario content as grist for intrinsic formative evaluation and for brainstorming about possible causal relationships.

In general, pairing off and directly contrasting before and after scenarios (scenarios that describe an existing situation and those that describe an envisioned situation) helps to force out claims. Of course, envisionment scenarios often would have been conceived of to address specific, articulated needs, and in that case, at least some of the relevant claims are already identified. But even in this case, placing the envisioned descriptions alongside descriptions of current situations will often immediately suggest issues that can be interrogated and developed further as claims.

Participatory Analysis

Participatory analysis (Chin, Rosson, and Carroll 1997) is a refinement of participatory design in which users directly analyze current and envisioned scenarios of use. Just as the users may be able to bring detailed domain knowledge to bear on basic-level scenario generation, they may be able to bring such knowledge to bear on claims analysis. In both cases, the knowledge the users have may be so subtle and unarticulated that it can become available to the system developers *only* through direct design collaboration.

Laughton (1996) speculated that his scenario-based participatory design work might have better anticipated some design issues if he had included claims analysis, but he also questioned whether his collaborators would have been engaged by such a detailed analysis. This is a natural concern; indeed, a strong theme in approaches to participatory design is shielding user-designers from some of the technical complexity of design methods. Chin, Rosson, and Carroll (1997) showed that public school teachers could work effectively with the upside-downside trade-off schema of claims analysis. Specifically, they showed that in a participatory analysis project, teachers were as capable of contributing to a claims analysis as system developers and user interface designers. Perhaps the teachers' domain knowledge balanced out any difficulties they may have had with claims analysis per se.

Chin, Rosson, and Carroll (1997) used a design review approach to participatory analysis. A series of classroom activity scenarios were presented to the entire design team. Each scenario was presented as both a textual script and a videotape. The group then identified features and generated observed and potential consequences of the features in a brainstorming exercise. The goal of the exercise was to generate as many features and consequences as possible; evaluating, refining, and refactoring features and consequences was deferred. In this context, all the design team constituencies were motivated to engage their own special knowledge of design and the particular design context, and try to leverage one another's knowledge in generating the greatest diversity of hypotheses.

Systematic Questioning

A well-developed method for evoking background knowledge is systematic questioning (Graesser and Clark 1985). As applied to claims analysis, this involves questioning each event, action, goal, and experience described in a scenario: Why did that happen? Why didn't other things happen that might have? Why did a given actor do what he or she did, and not something else? How did that actor do what they did? Why did each person think or feel what they did, and not something else? Why did each person have that experience? What was the outcome of the scenario for each actor? This method was used for the examples described through chapter 6. It has also been applied to identifying design object responsibilities from scenarios (Robertson 1995).

Systematic questioning is not a discovery algorithm. There are many levels at which one can answer any question. Some answers are better than others for given purposes. Moreover, we are not necessarily seeking a single answer. Events do not always have unique causes. Some consequences may depend on the convergence of two or more separate causes; others may have two or more causes any of which alone is a sufficient cause. For example, we might ask why a person followed a particular prompt. One answer is that the language in the prompt was strongly directive. Another is that the prompt was highlighted; a third is that the same prompt appeared in another menu and the person had followed it before in that other context; still another answer is that the prompt was positioned above the only other prompt currently displayed—the person followed the most salient prompt.

Error scenarios are particularly good sources for claims; they unavoidably raise questions. When we see someone snarled in some misconception or unfortunate sequence of actions, we wonder why and how it happened, and how it affected the person. This can be useful to analysts, particularly in getting an analysis started. However, one has to be careful to avoid focusing too narrowly on only certain causal relations in a complex situation. In an error scenario there are still features that might have caused favorable outcomes; to make a good claims analysis, we need to identify them and ask what their consequences could have been and why those outcomes did not obtain.

The stylistic convention of grouping all the upsides and downsides pertaining to a design feature can also help generate questions. Thus, if one identifies a claim without a downside, or perhaps without an upside, one can more aggressively ask why. Not everything is a trade-off, but it is a productive heuristic to assume that there is an underlying trade-off and to try to identify it. The main objective of systematic questioning is to generate lots of candidate claims.

Questioning Stages of Action

Theories of human activity can facilitate systematic questioning by providing a general list of questions. For example, Norman (1986) described an action cycle in which individuals frame their goals, plan courses of action in support of these goals, take action, interpret the consequences of their actions, and evaluate action consequences with respect to the instigating goals. We developed the set of questions in box 10.3 as a heuristic for comprehensively interrogating the trade-offs implicit in scenarios (Carroll and Rosson 1992). For any feature in a scenario, one can pose each of these questions to identify possible consequences for actors. Thus, if one were analyzing the MiTTS tutorial scenario in box 6.11, the first two questions under "Goals" in box 10.3 would call attention to the way that the feature of exploring a blackjack game engages specific prior knowledge of card games to evoke learner goals. The questions under "Interpretation" call attention to the possibility that learners might mistake the scope of attained concepts as blackjack and not Smalltalk (cf. "what incorrect inferences are most likely most costly?").

The question list can be used like the user concern typology in box 10.1; that is, for a given artifact, one can try to instantiate one or more claims from each question in the list. Box 10.4 is an analogous list of questions to pose in analyzing the group or organizational-level causal dynamics implicit in a scenario of use (Carroll 1996). Like individuals, groups frame goals, plan courses of action in support of these goals, take actions, interpret the consequences of actions, and evaluate actions with respect to goals. Although we have much less experience with organizational-level claims analysis, we have suggested some questions within each of the five stages of organizational action. As we analyze scenarios of use, like the MiTTS tutorial scenario, we can pose these questions to illuminate the organizational consequences of various features the scenarios. For example, in the third claim in box 6.13, the clause "creates a

Box 10.3
Questions to prompt claims regarding various stages of action (Carroll and Rosson 1992)

Goals
• How does the artifact evoke goals in the user?
• How does the artifact encourage people to import preexisting goals?
• How does the artifact suggest that a particular task goal is appropriate or inappropriate? simple or difficult? basic or advanced? risky or safe?

Planning
• What distinctions must be understood in order to analyze a task goal into enabling methods?
• How are these distinctions conveyed by the artifact?
• What planning mistakes are most likely? most costly?
• How does the artifact encourage the use of background knowledge (concepts, metaphors, skills) in planning a task?

Execution
• How does the artifact make it easy or difficult to perform a task?
• What slips are most likely? most costly?
• How does the artifact indicate progress in task performance?

Interpretation
• What are the most salient features of the artifact? what do these features communicate to the user?
• What features are commonly missed, and at what cost?
• What features of the artifact change as people carry out a task? What do these changes communicate to the user?
• How does the artifact guide the user to make correct inferences?
• What incorrect inferences are most likely? most costly?
• How does the artifact encourage the use of background knowledge in making inferences?

Evaluation
• How does the artifact convey completion of a task?
• How does the artifact help people recognize, diagnose, and recover from errors?
• How does the artifact encourage elaboration and retrieval of task goals and methods?

Box 10.4
Questions to prompt organizational/group claims (Carroll 1996)

Goals
• How does the artifact evoke new goals in the organization?
• How does it differentially evoke goals across personal roles in the organization?
• How does the artifact support or conflict with various organizational goals?
• How does it support the articulation of unspecified organizational goals?

Planning
• How does it support the coordination and conflict resolution among group members?
• How does the artifact support the use of varying background knowledge in planning a task?
• How does the artifact support the integration of individual planning efforts?
• How does the artifact encourage vertical and horizontal lines of communication in planning?

Execution
• How does the artifact support or require structuring work activities (collaboration, division of labor)?
• How does the artifact limit or enlarge autonomy and scope of action for various group members?
• How does the artifact help the work group to coordinate and document progress?

Interpretation
• How does the artifact indicate progress in task performance to various group members?
• What inferences and interpretations are most likely for persons in various organizational roles? How are they facilitated? What are their consequences for the group's learning and performance?
• How does the artifact support the integration of individual interpretations?
• How does the artifact encourage responsibility taking?

Evaluation
• What kind of management structures does the artifact support, and how?
• How does the artifact enhance or undermine group morale and social equilibrium?
• How does the organization reward group members for successfully learning and using the technology?

community focus on design" is a Goal consequence; it is an answer to the question of how MiTTS evokes new goals in an organization, and supports the articulation of previously unspecified organizational goals. "Creates a background of shared design information" is an Interpretation consequence; it cites the possibility of the group's learning from its own actions. The potential for disturbing the division of labor is an Execution consequence, since it bears on the organization's structuring of its work activity. And the possible narrowing of the organization's design view is an Interpretation consequence regarding the type of inferences that members of the organization might make.

Reuse of Prior Analyses

The previous four methods involve directly extracting or generating claims from scenario descriptions. Such direct methods are very important, since many of the most critical causal relationships inherent in usage situations are relatively unique. However, not every facet of every usage situation is unique, and no development project has the resources to reinvent every wheel. Given a literature of extant claims analyses, one can supplement the direct methods with analogy. Earlier in this chapter, analogy was suggested as a method for identifying candidate scenarios from prior scenario analyses. Taking into account the causal relationships in scenarios can help ensure more apt analogies. The specific features and claims in the scenarios articulate further constraints on analogical mappings.

Our early development of and experience with claims analysis concentrated on learning situations. We analyzed the tasks of learning Hypercard and the Displaywriter (Carroll and Kellogg 1989; Carroll, Kellogg, and Rosson 1991) and Smalltalk programming (Bellamy and Carroll 1990, 1992; Carroll and Rosson 1991; Singley, Carroll, and Alpert 1991). Because of this focus, we repeatedly encountered a particular set of learning consequences. For example, in all of these projects, we identified the claims that reducing the device space available to a learner constrains hypothesis generation (keeping learners on track), that preempting errors and error consequences focuses learner attention and motivates action, that concrete objects and examples suggest goals and goal mappings (Carroll and Kellogg 1989). When we noticed that we were analyzing and managing many recurring causal relationships, we began to use our prior claims analysis work regularly in developing new designs. For example, in developing MiTTS and its View Matcher tool, we read through claims analyses for Hypercard and the Displaywriter asking ourselves, "What could this feature or consequence correspond to in our new design?"

Our development of the Reuse View Matcher (Chapter 7) was a deliberate experiment in the reuse of a claims analysis (Carroll and Rosson 1991). The scenarios and claims for the Reuse View Matcher were developed as explicit analogies to those of the original View Matcher; as depicted in figure 7.2 regarding the use of demos and examples. Indeed, the task-artifact cycle, as described in chapter 3 and subsequently, is essentially a framework for proactive analogy. The key idea is to identify explicitly predecessor activities and designs (that is, as analogical sources) and systematically recruit them to a new design. The designer incrementally edits scenarios and usability consequences to obtain more satisfactory analogues.

The outstanding strength and hazard of analogy is that it extends single, concrete exemplars. As an analytic method, it is relatively lightweight. Scenarios and claims are analogically extended by being copied into a new domain, and then revised and reworked as necessary and possible. It can be a kind of creative design exercise—for example, can you see the View Matcher as reuse programming tool? If so, can you see it as a computer-assisted design tool? And so forth. However, analogy is not systematic; an analogy may or may not be valid, consistent, or paradigmatic.

Theory-Based Claims

One can reuse claims analyses pertaining to *classes* of usage situations, as well as to particular situations. For example, the Microworld claim (box 8.1) describes a substantial class of situations in which learners initially master a simplified environment as a means to building a more complete understanding of a complex domain. If we recognize that a particular scenario we are designing or analyzing instantiates the Microworld claim, we can assimilate that particular scenario to the body of knowledge pertaining to microworlds: the claim itself, its empirical grounding (for example, in Papert's 1980 studies of children learning physics and mathematics), its theoretical grounding (for example, in Piagetian psychology), and its extensions (for example, its known relations to the Demos claim, the Blackjack Card Game claim, or the minimalist design model; see chapter 8).

Theory-based reuse can help us to generate, factor, and justify a claims analysis more quickly. Unlike a concrete example, a theory-level claims analysis is couched at an abstract level, and often includes explicit specification of its boundary conditions, that is, of the kinds of situations to which it should be applied. Theory-based claims are reused by instantiation, not by analogy. A theory-level claim, like the Microworld claim, provides a literal and grounded foundation for writing an artifact-level claim, like the MiTTS Blackjack Card Game claim, and subsequently guides the use of the claim in design rationale and mediated evaluation.

Chapter 7 discussed annotated demonstration and situated critique as other examples of theory-based claims. It discussed a set of claims pertaining to tutoring systems as a theory of the tutoring systems design genre. Chapter 8 discussed claims analyses for the minimalist instructional model and the systems approach to instruction.

Theory-based claims analysis and analogical reuse of prior analyses could be supported with a digital library of hyperlinked scenarios and claims analyses (at various levels of abstraction) and direct access to the systems to which these analyses refer (or at least to rich on-line descriptions, including screen shots and other vivid presentations). Without such a tool (we refer to the idea as a "claim browser"), carrying out cumulative claims analysis requires considerable work with design rationale documentation or a significant level of experience and skill, or both.

Transformations

A claims analysis is always a work in progress. The causal relationships in claims purport to explain a scenario or a class of scenarios. Like any other theory, a claims analysis may need to be developed in the light of further data—in this case, further scenarios. It can be useful to try to anticipate this process of development by transforming scenarios and claims. One technique is to refactor the clauses of a claims analysis linguistically. For example, the various upside and downside clauses can be randomly reordered, omitting the telltale + or − judgments. Consider the reordered Browsing History claim (box 4.6):

Browsing History claim: Browsing a video database of statements, stories, and reflections of team members
may overwhelm people with the amount of information to be browsed
accesses a variety of views
involves query categories that may not fit the person's goal
clarifies and enriches answers to queries via collateral information
provides direct and flexible access to views
conveys/builds group vision

Placing the various clauses in different proximities can sometimes help to clarify what was really intended or important in the claim. In the Browsing History claim, reordering emphasizes the importance of "conveys/builds group vision" and "accesses a variety of views," which is finessed in box 4.6, where they are listed as the first two consequences. The reordering also emphasizes the browsing downside and therefore also highlights questions about query categories.

Another linguistic refactoring is to break up complex clauses. The discussion of reusing claims cited several relatively complex relationships: that preempting errors and error consequences focuses learner attention and motivates action, that concrete objects and examples suggest goals and goal mappings. These clauses can be linguistically unpacked. Preempting errors focuses learner attention; preempting errors motivates action; preempting error consequences focuses learner attention; preempting error consequences motivates action; concrete objects suggest goals; concrete objects suggest goal mappings; examples suggest goals; examples suggest goal mappings. Not all of these simple clauses seem equally valid; for example, concrete objects may suggest goal mappings only when they are also familiar objects. Simplifying the language increases the salience of each individual proposition.

A transformation beyond mere refactoring is that of denying a causal consequence (Carroll and Rosson 1992). Thus, in considering the concrete objects claim, one might assess the transformed claim, "concrete objects do not suggest goal mappings." By producing a clearly erroneous claim, this wording makes salient a challenge to the analyst of stating precisely when and how concrete objects *can* suggest goal mappings. In the Browsing History claim, it is an upside that one might encounter interesting collateral information in the course of pursuing a specific query. However, one might also *not* encounter interesting collateral information; indeed, one might encounter distracting information, irrelevant information, unwanted information, and so forth. Our design analysis and evaluation of Raison d'Etre did not indicate that these were significant problems, so the current statement of the Browsing History claim does not incorporate these potential downsides. But we generated and considered these clauses using the denial transformation.

A third type of claim transformation derives from the "what could go wrong?" scenario transformation. Since claims articulate both the potential upsides and downsides inherent in a scenario, the claims analysis for a scenario can be assessed as an explanation for the entire set of error scenarios generated by the "what could go wrong?" transformation. Of course, one might not want to incorporate explicit downside clauses for every possible circumstance in which things go awry, but this transformation provides a technique to become aware and consider including these potential downsides. For example, in the "browsing project history" scenario (box 4.5), one thing that could go wrong is that a query could be difficult, even impossible, to express. In this case, hypothetically asking what could go wrong with the query mechanism led to the identification of a downside clause that was incorporated into the claims analysis.

A fourth type of transformation is to recast scenarios from particular points of view. This transformation can often help to generate additional scenarios. But it can also help to identify hidden consequences for actors and objects, particularly for actors and objects playing support roles in the scenario narrative. For example, one of the original goals of the Raison d'Etre project was to create case study resources for design education. However, design students are actually rather invisible stakeholders in the Browsing History claim. Reexamining the claim from their point of view would lead to the identification of additional consequences.

Managing Scenarios and Claims

Why so much emphasis on generating scenarios and claims? The answer is that generation is the hardest step and the most important step. If we can and do generate lots of candidate scenarios and claims, we will have lots of guidance in specifying, prototyping, and evaluating designs. If we cannot or do not generate adequately comprehensive scenario descriptions, or if we cannot or do not adequately understand the scenarios we develop, we risk building systems that do not address the actual practices and task-oriented needs of the people who will use those systems. There is no downstream correction for a major omission at this stage.

That having been said, it is useful to have "stopping" heuristics for scenario and claim generation. How many scenarios are enough? At what level of detail should scenarios be couched? How many claim trade-offs are an adequate analysis for a given scenario? Several heuristics were suggested in earlier sections. One could stop when every category of scenario in a given typology or theory (recall box 10.1) has been concretely instantiated; one might want to generate, say, two or three exemplars of each type. One could stop when every known goal and obstacle occurs in at least one scenario (Potts 1995; Kaindl 1997). An empirical heuristic is to stop when, say, half of the scenarios observed in a field study or suggested in participatory design have been identified before; to be more conservative, the proportion can be set higher.

For high-level design, often a very few scenarios is enough. Simpson (1992), writing from experience in strategic management, suggests that four scenarios are usually enough. He warns specifically against developing paradigmatic sets of scenarios, urging that each scenario should be fundamentally distinct ("archetypal" in Schoemaker's 1995 term). It can be a good idea to draw even a small set of scenarios from a variety of sources: ethnography, participatory design, typologies, theories, and so on.

Not all scenarios are equally significant. For example, system maintenance scenarios may occur rarely and be carried out by a professional system administrator, whereas routine editing scenarios may occur in every work session. In addition to stopping the generation of scenarios, it can be useful to rank or classify them with respect to their importance. In our experience, there are two principal dimensions of importance: typicality and criticality. Typical scenarios are the most frequent, most representative usage situations, including common confusions and mistakes. Critical scenarios are relatively rare episodes in which something surprisingly good or bad happens—a person draws an incisive generalization about the system, for example, or suffers a breakdown, confusion, or mistake (Carroll, Rosson, and Singley 1993; Flanagan 1954). Wack (1985a) suggests designing minimal scenario sets such that relevant issues are represented in proportion to their importance.

Because the number of scenarios considered in a design must be bounded, the individual scenarios cannot be infinitely detailed. It is useful to bear in mind that one of the central properties of scenarios is that they are both concrete and rough, tangible and vague, vivid and sketchy. It is not possible to write a complete scenario; it is not possible to specify completely a system design in any description. Scenarios are adequately detailed when they make significant design issues apparent—for example, enabling the identification of claims. In our experience, this can often be achieved with a fairly sketchy level of detail, as suggested by the examples throughout this book. Not surprisingly, more experienced designers can omit details in their scenarios that less experienced designers need to express explicitly (see also Wirfs-Brock 1995).

Although it is not necessarily problematic to generate mutually inconsistent scenarios initially, it is important at some point early in the process to identify inconsistencies and make decisions (Schoemaker 1995). Scenarios are seductively plausible, viewed one at a time, and people are notoriously bad at integrating probabilistic truth values (Tversky and Kahneman 1983). Claims analysis is an important tool for assessing the consistency of a set of scenarios. Splitting out the key causal relationships asserted and implied in scenarios allows them to be compared more objectively.

Pruning and refactoring the set of design scenarios also entrains reducing the scale of the claims analysis. However, it is still useful to consider stopping heuristics for claims; causality in the real world is not well bounded. A claims analysis has attained reasonable completeness when it provides some causal account for each critical and typical scenario. One can use boxes 10.3 and 10.4 to determine whether a particular analysis addresses every relevant stage of action in a scenario. One can similarly use analyses of relevant theories or design genres.

Just as one can rank or classify scenarios with respect to their design significance, one can evaluate claims within the scope of particular scenarios. A good scenario emphasizes key causal factors so as to evoke action on the part of designers. Consequences pertaining to the high-level goals in a scenario are often more significant than consequences pertaining to derived goals or side effects. However, derived goals and side effects are often the triggers for critical scenarios.

Not all claims are equally sound. Some are grounded in basic sciences such as psychology, anthropology, and sociology; others are grounded in folk science or common sense; still others are merely hypotheses or observed episodes without independent grounding. This suggests a value gradient for claims, but one must bear in mind that it is conservative: claims without independent grounding are potential sources of new knowledge, whereas claims grounded in well-credentialed science nonetheless may be misleading or incorrect.

What is the bottom line? Our experience is, of course, biased by the projects we have undertaken—for example, our projects tend to be relatively modest in scale and addressed to domains that are not already well understood. We have found that about a dozen scenarios provide a useful and manageable design representation. We know this is a heuristic. In projects for which many more than a dozen scenarios were developed, the additional scenarios were clearly useful (Chin 2000). In our experience, simple scenarios can often be adequately analyzed by a single claim; we rarely find it warranted to construct more than five or six claims as an explanation for a given scenario.

11

Getting Around the Task-Artifact Cycle

The task-artifact cycle (figures 3.2 and 6.1) is the background pattern in technology development: task outcomes and human experiences implicitly set the agenda for new technological artifacts, which alter subsequent task outcomes and experiences. Identifying and developing scenarios and claims is a straightforward approach to managing the task-artifact cycle. In this approach, the achievements and experiences of people using technology are deliberatively reconceived based on investigation and analysis of what people do and what they want to do. Possible courses of design and development are envisioned and evaluated in terms of their impacts on human activity—before they are pursued. Instead of technology's ultimately evolving to enhance human activities, it is directly engineered to do so.

Chapter 10 described a set of techniques for identifying and developing scenarios and claims, a potpourri of methods from which developers can select one, several, or all. This chapter complements this tool kit view with a more synthetic framework for the organization of the system development process. The goal of the chapter is to suggest how we can begin to integrate separate scenario-based activities into a system development methodology.

Scenario-Based System Development

Figure 11.1 is a starting point; it indicates various ways scenarios can be put to use in system development. The figure is laid out roughly as a task-artifact cycle, reading clockwise from System Vision, but the various development activities are not strictly ordered with respect to one another.

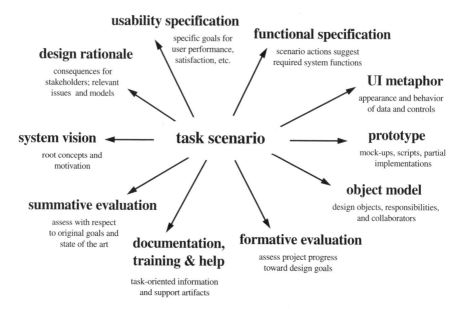

Figure 11.1
Roles of a scenario in system development

Descriptions of how work is carried out, and envisionments of how it could be carried out, given new tools and techniques, provide the root concepts and motivation for a development project, the system vision. Such a system vision can be articulated as specific trade-offs among consequences for people and their organizations and can be generalized in terms of issues and models for design domains—that is, for types of tasks, artifacts, and users. The design rationale serves initially as an analysis of the scenarios of the system vision, but is revisited and refined throughout the development process, serving as an account of the state of the design work.

Scenarios used to develop and codify the system vision and design rationale can be detailed as to specific human goals and actions, the learning experiences, performance time, and other social and behavioral concomitants that would constitute usability; we call this a usability specification (Carroll and Rosson 1985). The task scenarios can also be developed to determine what system functions would be required to allow the described actions and performance levels of a usability specification; this is called a functional specification. Usability specifications and functional specifications are mutually constraining and need to be developed together; contextualizing both in task scenarios facilitates that coordination.

Usability specifications and functional specifications are external views in the sense that they emphasize what people or systems should be able to do. User interface metaphors and software object models are relatively more internal views of scenarios. They describe how data and controls will appear and behave in the user interface and how the underlying software objects will interact in order to produce that appearance and behavior. Like all other scenario-based descriptions, these are open ended. In principle, a user interface metaphor describes specific cognitive consequences for every element of every interaction and information presentation; an object model enumerates all design objects, responsibilities, and collaborations. User interface metaphors and software object models are integrated in prototyping—a series of mock-ups, scripts, and partial implementations. From an evolutionary development perspective, like the task-artifact framework, the result of prototyping is the initial system implementation.

Formative and summative evaluation are also bound to task scenarios. Evaluation involves observing and measuring performance and experience with respect to tasks. The tasks of an evaluation suite must represent the typical and critical scenarios for the design. Training, help, and other documentation also must take into account the tasks people will want to undertake and try to undertake, since these tasks are the contexts from which the use of documentation arises. But they encompass as well the ensuing scenarios of using documentation resources (for example, the scenario of recovering from a given error using a reference manual). To some extent, the development of support information is directly driven by formative evaluation.

A key point of figure 11.1 is that scenarios identified or created for one purpose can be recruited to other purposes. Thus, developing an inspiring set of vision scenarios leverages formative evaluation by providing an starting set of test cases. The various roles of scenarios in figure 11.1 continue to be mutually leveraging throughout the design process. Developing a scenario with respect to any given role potentially improves its utility in other roles and at the same time improves the overall coherence

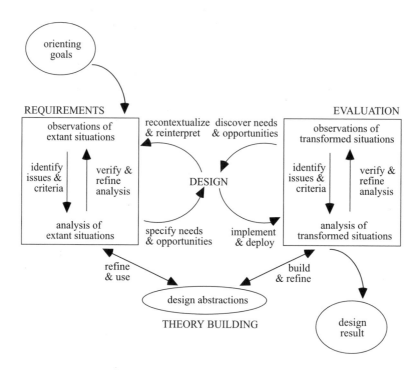

Figure 11.2
Information flow for scenario-based system development

of the design process. For example, all activities can alter the initial design rationale, but the design rationale also constrains each of the other views. Anticipated consequences for stakeholders help designers identify key usability goals, required functions, plausible metaphors and objects, evaluation tasks, and documentation support.

Figure 11.2 presents a simplified information flow for a scenario-based system development methodology, one that is more structured relative to figure 11.1 and perhaps is more useful as a management tool. The basic idea is that a set of scenario-based design representations is transformed from vision scenarios to an implemented design result. The method is not a waterfall. Like figure 11.1, it is intended to convey that many scenario-based design activities support system development, each potentially leveraging the others. Thus, in this method it is not exceptional for evaluation to trigger redesign and for redesign then to trigger requirements analysis. Such a convolution is required to address the emergence of new requirements throughout the development process (Brooks 1995; Carroll et al. 1998).

In figure 11.2, a set of orienting goals, embodied in vision scenarios, seed an iterative subprocess of requirements development in which issues and criteria are identified in situations of use and then successively verified and refined through further observations. Existing design knowledge can be brought to bear on the analysis of observed and hypothesized situations of use; reciprocally, the requirements analysis can be a means of refining currently understood design abstractions. Thus, this subprocess includes design rationale, usability specification, and functional specification, as depicted in figure 11.1. In the Raison d'Etre project, we used a variety of scenario-based techniques to generate and analyze requirements: analysis of the technology affordances of video information, our theory-based commitment to supporting reflection, interviews with the developers we sought to support, as well as scenario brainstorming and other scenario transformations. The main outcome of the requirements subprocess is the specification of needs and opportunities for design as a set of scenarios and claims analyses.

Design is at the center of the information flow. This subprocess incorporates the development of user interface metaphors, software object models, and prototypes, as depicted in figure 11.1. Requirements scenarios are transformed by substitutions of new objects and activities; their associated claims are also transformed as rationale for the new design. In some cases, the design transformations raise further requirements questions, recontextualizing and reinterpreting the original requirements analysis and possibly provoking new requirements. In other cases, designs are initially implemented and deployed to an extent sufficient to permit evaluation.

Like requirements development, evaluation is an iterative subprocess in which issues are identified, refined, and verified. In formative evaluation, emergent needs and opportunities provoke redesign work (and potentially, thereby, further requirements development). In summative evaluation, implemented designs are validated with respect to their usability specifications, functional specifications, and design rationale. Evaluation can also contribute to building and refining design abstractions by providing an empirical test of the principles underlying a design rationale. The process of prototyping and evaluating Raison d'Etre unfolded as an investigation of small group communication, in terms of social influence, but also—and more surprising—in terms of interpersonal responsiveness, learning on-demand, and day-to-day project management.

One of the distinctive characteristics of figure 11.2 is that theory building is incorporated as a routine activity of system development. Our methodological framework takes seriously the notion that design is inquiry—so salient in the writing of general design theorists like Rittel and Schön and so absent in most software development methods (DeGrace and Stahl 1990). Developing, maintaining, and generalizing design rationales is a hinge for the overall process. Design knowledge is systematically applied through principled emulation and activity modeling, and then assessed and refined through mediated evaluation.

MiTTS Again

The methodology schematized in figure 11.2 is more a framework than a proved formula, but it encompasses the examples discussed throughout this book. Thus, it integrates and summarizes the discussion of the book. For example, an orienting goal or vision might be that of creating a minimalist tutorial for Smalltalk programming and object-oriented design, or of building a video information system for design history. Every development project receives some sort of initial charter or mandate; this may come from a customer or from customer surrogates, such as market analysts. In a research project, it may come from leading-edge challenges in science and technology. The MiTTS project was oriented to the concrete problems of IBM programmers who were learning object-oriented software design. There was a widespread belief that developing these skills took too long and was more difficult than it needed to be. At the same time, my colleagues and I were looking for an instructional design domain that could present challenges beyond those we had addressed in our prior work with office systems.

Such orienting goals initialize the iterative subprocess of requirements analysis. We understand requirements to be statements about situations of use. Extant situations that implicitly describe human needs and opportunities for new tools support, as well as envisioned situations, enhanced, and perhaps otherwise transformed, design intervention. In the MiTTS project, we initially identified three driving requirements issues in our observations of and interviews with Smalltalk programmers: (1) the complexity of the Smalltalk code library and environment, (2) programmer motivation toward rapid prototyping and graphical user interfaces, and (3) the object-oriented software design paradigm (chapter 5). We developed this analysis by examining state-of-the-art tutorial materials and learning scenarios. For example, we critiqued trivial step-by-step exercises like the one schematized in box 5.1, and hypothesized what was going wrong in discovery learning scenarios like the one in box 6.1.

This requirements analysis was guided by our prior research on learning and problem solving in instructional contexts and by the minimalist design model that summarized our results. Thus, our investigation of the paradox of sensemaking helped us recognize that rote practice activities like that of box 5.1 would often frustrate and fail to engage learners, whereas discovery learning activities like that of box 6.1 could lead them into tangled errors. This design analysis described current user needs and opportunities to enhance activities, articulated in terms of scenarios and claims. The analysis process incorporated most of the methods enumerated in chapter 10, field studies of Smalltalk programming, specific prior analyses of learning situations, scenario typologies like box 10.1, theory-based minimalist scenarios, scenario brainstorming, and so forth.

Our analysis of a tutorial system for the Smalltalk programming language included the scenario in which a learner analyzes the design of a blackjack game using a simplified system debugger (box 5.2). In Scriven's (1967) term, this was an "intrinsic" evaluation of the scenario, in which we identified its key features. Our particular approach, claims analysis, involved identifying the leading positive *and* negative consequences for features in the scenario (boxes 6.4 and 6.12). These claims are often grounded explicitly in principles from sciences like psychology and sociology. One example is the claim that incompletely specifying instructions could encourage people to reason and improvise, thereby strengthening connections between goals and the actions needed to accomplish these goals, qualified by the potential downside that incomplete instructions could lead to people learning self-improvised procedures that are nonoptimal, as well as experiencing anxiety about generating their own course of action. This intrinsic evaluation guided our subsequent observations of extant learning situations ("mediated" evaluation, in Scriven's term). The analysis also contributed to the body of minimalist design abstractions by extending minimalism to a more complex instructional domain.

In using claims analysis to guide design, one cannot alter claims directly. Claims are causal relations between artifacts in use and the people who use them. One might want to improve the consequences of using the artifact, but one can do this only by altering features of the artifact itself. Claims guide attention to potentially relevant features by making explicit the underlying trade-offs that inhere in using the artifact. We reason backward, mitigating or denying a downside, maintaining or strengthening an upside, and then projecting a changed design that could bring those consequences about.

The scenarios and claims analyses described in chapters 5 and 6 were our design envisionment for MiTTS. In sum, we conjectured that the issues of complexity, motivation, and design could be addressed through a learning environment in which programmers debugged and enhanced small but intriguing interactive applications. One of our key design ideas in the View Matcher was the metaphor of a programming environment for learners—the idea of coordinating multiple views of an active application process. We initially prototyped the View Matcher along the lines of box 5.2 (see also Carroll 1990a). This design envisionment itself directly provoked and guided refinement of the original design analysis by recontextualizing that analysis, by triggering a reinterpretation of the original observed situations of use (this is the feedback arc from DESIGN to REQUIREMENTS in figure 11.2).

It is typical for problems and issues to become apparent as soon as a design is codified in a prototype, a point emphasized in discussions of rapid prototyping (Wasserman and Shewmake 1982). This consideration of an initial prototype can be more articulate, and therefore more effective, with an explicit usability rationale in hand to guide reinterpretation of the design prototype as well as further requirements development. Our first design for what ultimately became the View Matcher did not adequately address the complexity issue. We came to this conclusion by walking through the design and by implementing a prototype—in the context of constructing claims analyses for the scenarios we wanted to support. Our subsequent design work reemphasized complexity, incorporating the Bittitalk Browser into the View Matcher.

The idea for Bittitalk Browser arose through consideration of complexity management techniques. Specifically, we refined and reused the design abstractions of menu dimming and function blocking. These techniques were known to support incidental learning about functionality that is visible in the user interface but disabled. Our function-hiding technique deliberately subordinated the goal of teaching programmers *all* of Smalltalk; we wanted to eliminate more conclusively the potential distraction of functionality not relevant to the task at hand. More broadly, this process of reconsideration helped us to promote explicitly the notion of scaffolding realistic tasks in our MiTTS work (see also Rosson and Carroll 1996b), again contributing to refinement of a general design abstraction. We became more committed to the design principle of the View Matcher that the tools of the learning environment are the real system tools, which led, for example, to the decision to provide permanent access to the Smalltalk Inspector in subsequent versions of View Matcher.

When MiTTS was sufficiently complete, robust, and stable to be realistically useful, we began evaluation work. Evaluation, as shown in figure 11.2, is an iterative subprocess. As in the requirements subprocess, one thrust of evaluation is design analysis; the other is verification and refinement. In design analysis, issues and criteria are identified in the situations of use enabled by the design. This analysis is guided by and compared to the requirements analysis of usage situations that antedated the new system. As formative evaluation, this analysis can identify emergent needs and opportunities for redesign—factors that might become apparent only through actual use of the new system. As summative evaluation, this analysis can directly contrast different features and approaches in the two designs or assess performance of the new design against particular design objectives. Ultimately, the evaluation subprocess addresses the questions of how the new system is an improvement over predecessor systems and whether it meets its usability specifications. Evaluation results also can be generalized to build and refine the body of design abstractions, as discussed in chapter 8.

Evaluation in the MiTTS project employed a mediated approach: intrinsic evaluations of scenarios in terms of claims guided the conduct and interpretation of payoff evaluations of observed programmer performance. We energetically focused on formative evaluation goals—the discovery of needs and opportunities that could be direct redesign work. Through the several years of development, we studied about thirty learners as they worked through the tutorial while thinking aloud about their goals, expectations, successes, and problems. As is typical in such work, we attempted to identify critical incidents or breakdowns in the learner's activities. The usability rationale for MiTTS helped us to make sense of these observations, as well as to think about how to address them through redesign. An example is the sparse procedure for "dealing a hand," described in connection with box 8.4. Our explicit usability rationale for sparse procedures, attuned us to payoff phenomena that might pertain to this property (which we might otherwise have failed to notice at all), helped us interpret these phenomena (for example, we saw the "deal" episode as a case in which a sparse procedure successfully provoked user-initiated retrieval and generation of procedures, but did not adequately signal goal criteria), and guided our redesign (in this case of an even more sparse procedure with a clear goal: "Deal a new game").

Another example, discussed in chapter 5, is history mode. We had originally introduced the Stack View as a list of messages sent during the current application session—for example, during the current game of blackjack. But we found that this was subsequently an obstacle to understanding the halted stack. The animated stack view was technically a simpler approach that addressed this problem. Watching the stack grow and shrink as the application objects carry out their computations prepares learners for their subsequent exploration of the (halted) stack; a potential downside is that learners could also experience frustration, since they cannot halt the application's message passing. Of course, many other examples of formative evaluation pertain to the myriad details of implementation—saying enough but not too much about the rules of blackjack, providing the right hint at the right point for a given error recovery, and so forth. Several of these were described at the end of chapter 5.

Later in the project, we used intrinsic evaluations to mediate summative evaluations of MiTTS, in both lab and field settings. We directly contrasted instructional outcomes for the commercial tutorial with outcomes for MiTTS. We used our intrinsic evaluations of the two tutorials to design a suite of programming tasks such that that half of the test tasks addressed skills emphasized in the commercial tutorial (for example, writing code to invert a list), and half addressed skills emphasized by MiTTS (for example, functional design of a simple application). We had to do this because the two tutorials took quite different approaches to training, and hence we could not design a training-neutral test task. Our comparative analysis focused in detail on two programmers. The programmer working with the commercial tutorial studied hard for the entire twelve hours we allowed; he was able to carry out some of the code-centered tasks at the end of the tutorial but made little headway on the tasks requiring a basic understanding of design. He succeeded partially on two of six tasks. The MiTTS learner finished the tutorial in less than six hours and was generally successful on all six of the test tasks (Koenemann-Belliveau et al. 1994).

Even during the summative evaluation activities, we questioned, extended, and refined our underlying intrinsic analysis. For example, it was during our summative evaluation work that we developed the concept of thread-level claims, discussed in chapter 8. When we came to evaluate the *whole* tutorial structure and outcomes, we noticed larger patterns: misleading analogies for classes (like data container), unrepresentative "data structure" examples of classes, and so forth. These patterns explained difficulties programmers experienced, but they also illustrated a general design abstraction we expect to reuse in subsequent work.

Requirements Development in LiNC

The MiTTS project specially highlights the evaluation subprocess of figure 11.2 and the benefits of integrating evaluation and theory building in design. One of our ongoing projects, called LiNC (Learning in Networked Communities), has focused on the requirements subprocess of figure 11.2. Our starting point was Brooks's (1995) observation that significant requirements often emerge in later stages of system development. Ultimately, we would like to create a better articulated description of various requirements discovery activities, and how they can work together to contribute different kinds of information about needs and opportunities.

During the past five years, we have worked with a group of high school and middle school teachers to design a virtual physics laboratory. Our orienting goals reflected nationally articulated needs in public school (K-12) education, such as supporting collaborative, project-based classroom learning, increasing school-community involvement, improving access of rural schools to educational opportunities, enhancing gender equity in science and mathematics education, and controlling material costs (box 11.1; American Association for the Advancement of Science 1991; National Science Teachers Association 1990).

We also sought to develop and exploit the networking infrastructure of the Blacksburg Electronic Village, an advanced community network project (Carroll and Rosson 1996). As we began the project in 1994, T-1 Ethernet was being run to several county schools, enabling many new opportunities for school activities exploiting Internet and community resources. In the fall of 1994, we developed the scenario in box 10.2 as an expression of our orienting goals. The scenario describes a collaborative, project-based activity in which a mixed-gender group of students construct and analyze simulation experiments, despite being physically dispersed.

With this vision in mind, we initiated an ethnographic study of the classroom context. We needed to understand the classroom context and the teachers at work better; they needed to understand better our research and development interests and activities as they would manifest in the classroom setting. Most important, we all needed to work together to achieve these objectives. We documented many classroom scenarios and discovered many critical properties: teachers recruit and blend a variety of teaching styles; student-driven discovery, as in our initial scenario, may not be the right style for every situation. Classrooms are cluttered with tables, equipment, and other materials; there is no room for every student to have his or her own computer. Students already collaborate in classrooms; thus the remote collaborations we were envisioning might often

Box 11.1
Orienting goals for a virtual physics laboratory

- Support collaborative, project-based classroom learning
- Increase community involvement in public schools
- Improve access of rural schools to educational opportunities
- Enhance gender equity in science and mathematics education
- Reduce equipment costs and handling

---

be group-to-group, not person-to-person. Students collaborate in different ways; cooperation and consensus building is only one pattern. The classroom scenarios became the concrete touchstones for our analysis and also helped us to identify significant categories of classroom activity: didactic discussion, demonstration, experiment set-up and data collection, group poster presentation, and so forth.

We selected a subset of these scenarios for claims analysis. We tried to cover the main categories and distinctions we had identified in the classroom context. At a summer workshop, our entire design team of about a dozen people spent two days identifying features and consequences. One scenario we analyzed involved five high school students studying inelastic collisions among cars mounted on a rail. The students were using photogates to measure initial and final velocities; their goal was to obtain measurements within 3 percent of the theoretical values. The scenario continued as in box 11.2.

Two salient features of the inelastic collision scenario are the individual initiative taking displayed by Godfrey and the conflict resolution and consensus building displayed by Matilda. Our claims analysis of these features in box 11.3 was a more usefully articulated analysis of leadership and collaboration styles, a technical advance on our orienting goal regarding gender equity, and our earlier conflation of cooperation with collaboration. The two claims regarding collaborative styles are couched at a general level; they are potential design abstractions that could find application in other computer-supported cooperative work (CSCW) projects.

We also analyzed the role of physical activities, such as set-up, calibration, and measurement. We identified some of the downsides implicit in our orienting goals, such as the tedium and distraction of setting up rails

Box 11.2
Inelastic collision scenario

- After approximately a dozen runs of the experiment, the group has been unable to achieve the 3 percent threshold. At this point, Godfrey believes that the photogates are too far apart. He moves the two photogates closer together and positions the two cars for another run.
- Looking over the results of previous runs, Matilda suggests, "You know what? Maybe if we increase the distance . . . " Before Matilda completes her sentence, Dexter interjects with, "Yes, we should!" and grabs one of the photogates to slide it farther down along the ramp. Grabbing the same photogate, Godfrey objects, "No, I want to put them closer." Dexter argues, "No, we just put them closer and we got a 43 percent error." Pushing Dexter's hand away and resetting the photogates, Godfrey continues, "We didn't put them close enough."
- Matilda makes a suggestion and seeks group consensus: "We should go around in a circle and have our own theories, and we'll test them out and see who gets the lowest. You guys want to do that?" Both Esther and Hildegarde approve; Godfrey and Dexter grudgingly agree.

---

and photogates, but we also identified specific benefits, such as practice with mechanical skills, application of concepts to physical situations, and negotiation of roles and division of work. The constraint of limited classroom space, which would not allow one computer for each student, was tempered by the upside that sharing equipment set-ups encouraged collaboration among students. The claim that sharing resources can encourage collaboration also seems to be a general design abstraction for CSCW systems. Some of the other claim relations, such as those pertaining to managing space limitations and access to equipment and to practicing mechanical skills, seem somewhat more specific to the educational domain; they may be narrower as potential design abstractions. In this work, we encountered an interesting argument for the efficacy of participatory design: the four teachers contributed more upside and downside consequences than did the experienced system developers or user interface developers on our design team (Chin, Rosson, and Carroll 1997).

Concurrent with these analyses, we began to explore the technology space of computer-mediated communication mechanisms on which we

Box 11.3
Claims from classroom scenarios

Consensus-building
+ ensures that all ideas are considered
+ enhances group dynamics and the self-esteem of members
− requires a selfless and energetic leader
− may be inefficient and/or inconclusive.

Individual initiative-taking
+ is efficient, challenging
+ provides opportunities for group members to play leadership and supporting roles
− requires an assertive leader
− may fail to evoke or consider the group's best ideas
− can demotivate or annoy group members

Focus on physical equipment set up, calibration, measurement and error
+ conveys authentic scientific practice
+ teaches general mechanical skills
+ puts concepts in context
+ provides an opportunity to negotiate roles and work together
− can be tedious for students
− may require extensive preparation from the teacher
− may confuse or de-emphasize underlying concepts

Few equipment stations in the classroom
+ take up little classroom space
+ encourage cooperative learning interaction among students
− the teacher must manage access to equipment
− any given student may have limited access to equipment

---

wanted to base the virtual physics laboratory. These included shared whiteboards, videoconferencing, World Wide Web forums, multiuser domains, voice and text chat, and capabilities for collaborative writing and joint manipulation of simulation experiments that we were developing. These explorations consisted of group walk-throughs and exercises in which the entire design team modeled basic collaborative interactions. We asked ourselves how groups of students would select tasks and allocate roles, why they would be motivated to work together, how they would coordinate their activity and report on their results, and so forth. Our goal was to understand how various networking mechanisms could map into classroom activities and their trade-offs.

Students sometimes engage in activities for which the process and interim results, as well as the outcome, may be useful to maintain. For example, in developing experimental procedures, carrying out experiments, and developing interpretations and conclusions, it may be useful to be able to revisit the details of what was planned and what was done; it may be useful to be able to revisit ideas that were rejected in earlier discussions about results. Communication mechanisms that create a record are good for such activities: structured forums, shared documents, and perhaps e-mail provide appropriate support. Other activities that students engage in require real-time interaction and may actually be better served if a record is not maintained. For example, in forming groups, negotiating about roles, and brainstorming, it is important to have synchronous interaction but might stifle honesty and creativity to save contributions to the discussion. Communication mechanisms like videoconferencing, voice chat, and perhaps text chat provide appropriate support. Some activities students engage in involve sharing graphs and images: whiteboards and video support this, voice and text mechanisms do not.

Claims, as in box 11.3, specified needs we had recognized—consequences for students and teachers that should be preserved (upsides) or changed (downsides). Our explorations of computer-mediated communication specified opportunities for our design, new capabilities and affordances for classroom situations, entraining new consequences for students and teachers. This requirements analysis was embodied as a set of scenarios for new classroom activities. We designed these activities to meet the teachers' real pedagogical goals, address the upsides and downsides in our claims analyses of classroom scenarios, and appropriately exploit the affordances of various networking mechanisms. An example scenario is in box 11.4. A high school student is mentoring three middle school students on a force and motion activity, using a software simulation and other tools such as an electronic whiteboard, a video teleconferencing package, a spreadsheet, and a World Wide Web application for storing and viewing questions and answers.

The activity described in box 11.4 is not just a test of computer-mediated communication mechanisms; it is an integral part of the classroom curriculum. Indeed, mentoring activities powerfully support reciprocal learning: both the mentors and the mentored students benefit from the interaction (Cazden 1988). Mentoring exploits high-bandwidth, syn-

Box 11.4
Activity designed to include mentoring by high school students

- Terri, a high school student, has been assigned to mentor Merty, Ethel, and Sandy. Prior to the session, she familiarizes herself with the simulation and uses a World Wide Web forms-based question-and-answer application to prepare a set of questions to guide her interactions with the younger students.
- During the session, Terri meets and communicates with the three girls using a video teleconferencing package. She guides the students through the use of the simulation, running through the steps of the simulation on her computer and describing the process as she proceeds. She occasionally picks up the camera and aims it toward her screen to show the state of the simulation on her screen. Sometimes she copies a snapshot of her screen onto an electronic whiteboard and annotates interesting features.
- Next, Terri directs the group to the prepared questions. The group answers the questions by experimenting further with the simulation, entering their answers into the Web forms provided. Terri stays on-line to provide guidance as needed.
- When the students have finished Terri's questions, they discuss their answers with Terri over the videoconferencing channel. For incorrect answers, Terri sends the group back to the simulation with guidance on how to find the correct solutions. After Terri and the group are satisfied with the set of answers, the questions and answers remain on the Web page for later review by the two teachers.
- Subsequently Merty, Ethel, and Sandy work on a Matchbox car experiment, exploring many of the same concepts exemplified in the simulation, while other groups of middle school students have a chance to interact with the mentors. Each group develops a poster that describes its experiences, findings, and conclusions from the two activities.

chronous communication, like videoconferencing and shared simulation runs, tightly coupling feedback with student actions. Mentoring also effectively uses structured asynchronous mechanisms, like Web forums, in which mentors and mentored students jointly create a discourse object. Working with a mentor and a simulation experiment is also highly complementary to working only with peers on a physical experiment (as in the inelastic collision scenario of box 11.2): different materials are manipulated, different collaborative interactions occur, and so on.

Designing new classroom activity scenarios helped us to develop the requirements we had identified in our classroom ethnography, participatory claims analysis, and analysis of technology affordances. We addressed issues like the scarcity of computers and of space for computers by developing the concept that computer-based activities would complement existing noncomputer classroom activities, that the two sorts of activities would be carried out simultaneously by different student groups, and that the reports that students developed would integrate across the two sorts of activities. We developed the requirement that remote collaborations must manifestly enhance classroom activities by specifying categories of such collaborations: mentoring, pooling data, sharing special equipment or other resources, comparing and debating results and conclusions.

In the terminology of figure 11.2, this design work helped us recontextualize and reinterpret these issues as requirements for our virtual physics laboratory. In particular, it helped us to hypothesize that sharing resources is a key to intrinsically well-motivated collaboration. As a result, this particular design abstraction became far more critical to us as the project went forward.

In this project, we took a further step in actually implementing the scenarios (Carroll et al. 1998). Our approach was to employ shareware and off-the-shelf software to the greatest extent possible. Thus, the early prototypes we studied were in many ways hodgepodges of loosely integrated parts, not an implementation of the virtual physics laboratory. On the other hand, they were relatively easy to produce and allowed us to encounter requirements we might not otherwise have foreseen. For example, when we tried to schedule concurrent classes at different schools, we found that even within a single public school system, there is no single class schedule template. Moreover, because many factors are juggled in scheduling and rescheduling, the partial overlap between class meeting periods can erode or even disappear. This helped us develop requirements scenarios like box 11.4 as comprising a sequence of brief mentoring interactions, supplemented with e-mail—as opposed to a single, comprehensive session.

More generally, our work with off-the-shelf prototypes yielded many arguments and directions for integrating synchronous and asynchronous network mechanisms. Recall that the original Marissa scenario in box 10.2 envisioned a self-contained and purely synchronous interaction. However, we found that as students attained even beginning skill with various communication tools, they wanted to be able to share work context among the tools.

We found that the microphones and speakers bundled with personal computers perform poorly in environments with high levels of ambient noise, like classrooms. Students removed microphones from their mounts, held them up to their mouths, and passed them around to produce better sound; they bent and leaned into mounted speakers in order to hear better. Working with off-the-shelf prototypes helped us develop specific further requirements for local sound damping.

We also implemented prototypes as paper mock-ups and in Macromedia Director. These prototypes were better-integrated views of our own design ideas than were our shareware/off-the-shelf prototypes, but they were also less functional. We invited teachers and students to walk through interaction scenarios as if they were using these prototypes; we asked them to focus on how well various classroom activities were supported, as opposed to focusing on details of user interface look and feel. This work helped us to uncover many requirements pertaining to the virtual physics laboratory as an integrated environment (see also Ehn and Kyng 1991).

Although the teachers and students were enthusiastic about collaborative, project-oriented classroom work, when confronted with a mock-up of the environment that would support such activities, various issues of information access and coordination became problematic to them. This was very productive for identifying and addressing design issues. For example, the teachers discovered the issue of awareness (Dourish and Bellotti 1992), that is, the need to apprise remote collaborators of who is present in a work session and what they are doing.

Walking through specific scenarios with a concrete mock-up also elicited elaborations of features for the shared notebook. Students wanted to distinguish personal and group information spaces—to partition group projects into areas managed by individuals. This raises many questions—for example, what unit of data should be shared among group members: project notebooks, sections of notebooks, pages of sections, objects on pages? What should be visible to other groups or persons outside the virtual laboratory environment; for example, what should be visible to parents and other community members? Teachers wanted to be able to coordinate groups and review group progress. For example, they wanted ways to broadcast suggested project topics to all groups and to manage a process through which groups claim and develop those topics. They wanted support for group planning and outlining of project activities and for maintaining project bibliographies. And they wanted to be able to query and track the progress of groups. What sort of record should the virtual laboratory maintain of changes made to notebooks and other data? What should be attributed to individuals and what to groups?

Through this work we identified several critical session management issues that inhere in the classroom context. In the virtual school situation, groups of students initiate a session together, that is, from the same workstation; the session may also be shared with one or more other groups at remote locations. We still need the capability for ordinary single-user log-ons and sessions, since students may use virtual laboratory capabilities from home. But the shared sessions can be quite complex. For example, three students could log on together at one school in order to work with two other students who log on together at another school; during the session, a third student could ask to join the group of two. Groups need to be able to specify who is participating in a given group log-on and to add members to the group and to the session easily.

Through projects like the virtual laboratory, we are trying to characterize a requirements development process as sketched in figure 11.3 (Carroll et al. 1998). This figure shows how the five orienting goals of the project evolved through ethnographic observation of extant situations, were verified and refined through participatory claims analysis of identified scenarios, and were embodied in prototype activities and prototype technological support, enabling further observation and analysis. Through the course of this process, requirements were elaborated, discovered, dropped, or superseded. For example, our starting concern with facilitating participation by girls was elaborated into an analysis of collaboration possibilities and leadership styles. Our ethnography of the classroom helped us discover new requirements regarding teaching styles. Focusing on the classroom also led us to drop our original orienting concern with community involvement in education. Our initial goal of improving access to science for rural students through networking was superseded by the requirement that any remote collaboration be intrinsically motivated in the activity.

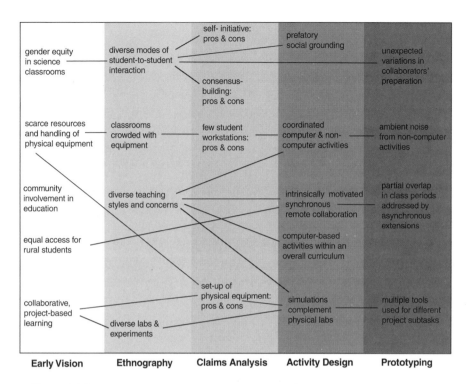

Figure 11.3
Linearized view of a scenario-based requirements development process

Although the process view in figure 11.3 is merely a summary of our case study, it has been a useful resource in maintaining the visibility of requirements. For example, when our software became robust enough to distribute, we "rediscovered" our orienting goal of supporting community involvement in public education. In the past two years, we have made versions of this system available to community members wishing to serve as mentors to student groups (Carroll and Neale 1998; Gibson et al. 1999). This description also suggests possibilities for future work. In particular, it would be useful to differentiate more formally types of steps in requirements development (elaborate, discover, drop, supersede), to model the knowledge underlying requirements at different stages, and to validate the resulting formalism with further cases. This would better define the information flow in figure 11.2—for example, by specifying terms like *reinterpret* and *refine*.

Figure 11.4
Collaboration tools in the virtual physics laboratory

The requirements development process employed in the LiNC project
defined a virtual laboratory system that was used extensively during the
1998–99 school year; some of the central tools are shown in figure 11.4.
The main window (in the upper left) displays members of the student
group, indicating who is currently logged on, a list of the group's project
notebooks, and a notice board summarizing recent activity. The list of
group members supports awareness of who is "in" the virtual lab at a
given time. The notice board helps collaborators coordinate their efforts,
particularly when work occurs asynchronously over a span of time. The
main window also provides single-keystroke initiation of chat and videoconferencing sessions, and of e-mail. We have found that students often
prefer text chat to videoconferencing, because the latter is more degraded
by ambient classroom noise and provides no reviewable history for late
joiners to a collaborative session.

The centered window shows a project notebook; the student is working on the Robot Pictures section, contributing to a resource that all members of the project can share. Indeed, the robot project is a good example of an activity that integrates use of the virtual laboratory with manipulations of physical equipment. The student is currently placing an annotation in that section, soliciting comments from other group members. One of the student's remote collaborators has locked the Introduction section.

Toward a Scenario-Based Methodology

The framework in figure 11.2 is roughly consistent with current thinking about the system development process. That is, it recognizes familiar subprocesses like requirements development and evaluation, and it incorporates feedback and iteration of steps and subprocesses (Boehm 1981, 1985; DeGrace and Stahl 1990). The framework is somewhat distinctive in its explicit emphasis on the development and reuse of design abstractions, eschewing a privileged emphasis on the creation and management of functional specifications, and countenancing rather sweeping and routine interaction among development subprocesses.

These characteristics derive from construing the system development process as one of developing and managing scenario descriptions of human activity. The scenario-based process allows all the activities of figure 11.1 to communicate and cumulate in a common vocabulary: orienting goals and visions, workplace needs analysis, design walkthroughs, envisionments, prototypes and rationales, evaluation of critical incidents and test cases, and potential generalizations and abstractions. The common vocabulary of scenarios, and of issues and trade-offs that inhere in them, makes it more feasible to integrate the insights and products of various system development activities in order to develop design abstractions of significant scope, like those discussed in chapters 7 and 8. The pervasive use of scenarios as a working design representation concomitantly makes traditional functional specifications somewhat less pivotal as a representation.

The system development methodology in figure 11.2 is an elaboration of what is widely called iterative development (Carroll and Rosson 1985;

see also Bennett 1984; Butler 1985; Gould and Lewis 1985). In its simplest form, iterative development is a methodology constituted by cycles of rapid prototyping and formative evaluation. A fundamental problem with the simplest version of this methodology is that it does not describe any systematic means of saving what is learned in one cycle for use in the next. Indeed, "iteration" can be a euphemism, since the term implies successive approximation. The simplest version of iterative development is really just optimistic thrashing: successive design moves are informed by the immediately prior design cycle. The information flow in figure 11.2 attempts to confront this through both the explicit and unifying design vocabulary of scenarios and claims and the central role of theory building to the overall process: successive design moves are informed by everything that has been learned to that point.

More specifically, the methodology schematized in figure 11.2 summarizes an effective approach to the five key issues for design methods and technology development discussed in chapter 3. One of these issues was the conflict between reflection and action—the tendency of developers to become captured by actions and the need to couple reflection and action more effectively in design and development. Scenarios are transparently the most natural language for envisioning impacts of future technology on the people who will use that technology. By making future situations of use tangible and vivid, they provoke discovery of hidden requirements, considerations that might otherwise become apparent only after the system was implemented and used. It is almost impossible to imagine designing an interactive system without developing scenarios, at least once one has encountered the idea.

Moreover, we have seen that the scenarios employed to envision and develop a system can also provide appropriate and effective framing for the identification and evaluation of specific advantages and disadvantages of candidate designs in given contexts of use. The vocabulary of claims and scenarios directly links that which designers can alter (artifact features) to that which matters most but which can be altered only indirectly (consequences for people). Scenario analysis can also provide appropriate framing for the development of models and generalizations about the implementation and use of technology. Perhaps the most significant advantage of a scenario-based system development methodology is that the effort directed at design action is ipso facto recruited to design reflection.

Another issue considered in chapter 3 was the fluidity of design situations and the somewhat paradoxical nature of scenarios with respect to this instability: that they are both concrete and rough. Scenarios are experienced as tangible and vivid because they stimulate human imagination. The mind is already adept at filling in the details of stories and recalling details that are accidentally omitted in a telling of a story. This makes scenarios excellent tools for brainstorming and excellent shorthand representations for temporarily maintaining interim results in design work. In this sense, they are to the designer of work activities and human-computer interactions what the sketch is to a graphic designer (Verplanck et al. 1993). Scenarios are compatible with provisional commitment, hypothetical move testing, and reiteration in design work—for example, in requirements development, design walk-throughs, and formative evaluation.

Scenarios allow designers to marry the subjunctive and the present tense. They support the development of a design space of possible approaches by supporting the development of specific candidate designs, by allowing designers to make clear commitments and to immediately investigate their consequences for people and their activities. Scenarios permit the articulation, analysis, and evaluation of a design to move forward in concert and without becoming bogged down in the specification and management of premature details. They permit designers to verify and validate a design more effectively at the earliest stages of system development and to integrate their consideration of functional requirements (that is, what activities the system can support) with quality requirements (that is, how well it supports these activities) when the design is still just stories about future situations.

A third issue was that any design move has myriad direct and derived consequences. Scenarios are contexts, triggers, and grist for multiple views of a designed situation. We have paid special attention to scenarios as contexts for developing design rationale, more specifically for analyzing trade-offs among consequences for people caused by particular features of a designed situation. Articulating these trade-offs allows each scenario to represent a family of possible variations in which different combinations of upside and downside consequences obtain. Individual scenarios can also be detailed to various different degrees, as required by the design task at hand. For designing the space of application tasks (such as "understanding the reply-to-interest group function"), just a name or a phrase may be sufficiently descriptive; for designing specific interaction details like the operation of menus and buttons, it may be necessary to specify scenarios at the level of primitive actions (pressing a particular key, moving the mouse). Scenarios can be developed from different points of view, including the viewpoints of task objects, to explore how the same course of events might affect different participants differently.

Scenarios can help to coordinate planning at many different levels of analysis. Thus, each application task is ultimately articulated as sets of particular user interface interactions, as well as sets of events in the system software and hardware. Each application task is also articulated as particular cognitive, affective, and performance consequences for the person or persons who carry out the task, as well as consequences for their immediate work organization and society in general. These various events and their consequences can be fathomed and integrated as views of scenarios. Scenarios are not a silver bullet for succinctly capturing and managing the unbounded web of consequences and side effects that inhere in design and technology development. But we have seen suggestive examples here, and in any case, the alternative, and still the official status quo, is that we will continue to develop technology pretty much in the dark.

A fourth issue was that the state of codified technical knowledge bearing on the design of new technology characteristically lags the leading edge of design and development work. Rather than merely being an arena for applying codified science and engineering practice, technological design is more typically a context in which new generalizations are first recognized and developed and in which new techniques are invented and refined. The Catgut Society's work on violin designs is an excellent example of how this can occur (Hutchins 1981). The approaches and results in chapters 6, 7, and 8 also show how a design science based on scenarios can be developed and applied. The central role of theory building as a system development activity differentiates figure 11.2 from many other methodological programs. Indeed, figure 11.2 can be seen as a research cycle with incidental system design by-products.

Scenarios also address the inherent shortfall of codified technical knowledge by allowing all stakeholders to have a view of a development project and a voice in directing the project. By being accessible to the full range of people who can contribute diverse kinds of expertise, scenarios permit all that is known and relevant to be brought to bear. This has the derived benefit that subsequent generalizations and abstractions captured in design work will be more likely to incorporate a broader and more useful body of knowledge and expertise, avoiding the narrowness and inapplicability that often characterize the codified science base (Barnard 1991).

A fifth issue was that design is highly sensitive to constraints residing in the larger (real-world) context beyond the technical issues. Design problems cannot be insulated from organizational conflict and inertia, from professional conventions and fashions, from considerations of cost and benefit, from what the designers are most familiar with, or even from personal ups and downs of design team members. Large and complex undertakings exceed the human span of attention; they exceed what can be accomplished in a single sitting or a single day. They usually exceed what can be accomplished by a single person. They are expensive; they involve managers. Having a concrete vision that is vividly grounded in the use situations that are being addressed and being created can help designers stay focused on use as the ultimate consideration. It is easy to lose this focus in the cacophony of voices lobbying for more glitz, less memory, a different layout, a more conservative look, lower cost, and so forth.

Ideally, external factors should be evaluated in terms of their impacts on use, but it is difficult to maintain a focus on consequences for use if the grounds for discussion shift—for example, to the cost of particular features. Many of the best-known approaches to design representation and rationale implicitly diminish the weight of consequences for people and their activities by analyzing designs as sets of decisions taken in the design process (where the decision context is other design decisions, not a description or analysis of use; Rittel and Webber 1970) or specific features in the design space (where the context of use is considered feature by feature; Jones 1970; MacLean et al. 1996).

It is sometimes said that the objective of building a methodology is that one does not have to think; the thought required is preempted just to the extent that the principles of the methodology actually do some work. This orientation can easily get out of hand. It is most appropriate for addressing relatively low-level tasks (Gilbreth 1911; Taylor 1911) or for addressing low-level aspects of more complex tasks (Card, Moran, and Newell 1983; Carroll and Campbell 1986). A methodology for the overall task of developing useful and usable interactive systems should save designers some effort and attention by providing a set of general techniques and a framework for engaging the techniques. But it must do much more. Scenario-based design seeks to use and enhance the designer's expertise, not through a mechanism but through inquiry—inquiry into extant human activities, and possibilities for new activities. The goal of scenario-based design is not to make it less necessary for designers to think about what they are doing; rather, it is to help designers think more.

12

The Scenario Dilemma

When I joined the staff of the IBM Thomas J. Watson Research Center in 1976, one of my first managers told me that the main characteristic that predicted success of scientists in that environment was tolerance for ambiguity. This remark caught my attention, I think largely because it made no sense to me whatsoever at the time he said it. The whole point of science and technology, after all, is to reduce, to eliminate ambiguity. Ambiguity indicates that we do not yet understand. Shouldn't we be *in*tolerant of ambiguity?

I believe I can make more sense of his remark today. For me, this took over a decade of lived experience, and began to gel only when I read Donald Schön's (1967) *Technology and Change.* In Schön's view, humans have a fundamental need for stability and an existential dread of uncertainty. To deal with this dread, we have created the myths that pervade our institutions and regulate our lives. In design and technology development, we created the myth of bounded and rational change, the myth of science-based technology, the myth of specification-driven design. Tolerance for ambiguity is not a measure of our failure in science and technology; it is a measure of our readiness to accept actual circumstances and complexities as they present themselves, to struggle against the tendency to simplify and idealize them too quickly, and to accept that we may never fully understand the phenomena we deal with *even if* we manage them effectively in our designs.

Scenario-based design is well suited for life on that razor's edge between creative intuition and grounded analysis. It embraces the ambiguities of technology, not merely with resignation, but with a constructive enthusiasm. The properties that make scenarios uniquely appropriate design objects all stem from their ambiguity. Scenarios ambiguously support both reflection and action; they are simultaneously concrete and incomplete; they are at once dreams, design arguments, scientific analyses, and software specifications; they are descriptions and interpretations of the past and the future, of the achievements, shortcomings, and trade-offs behind us and forever in front of us; they are all about us by being all about the contexts within which we experience and act.

But a fundamental dilemma lurks in the emergence of scenario-based design: though informality, subjectivity, and flexibility are central to the effectiveness of scenarios as tools to cope with the complexity and ambiguity of design and technology development, they also constitute methodological limitations to scenario-based design. A scenario must be structurally analyzed in order to be indexed for documentation and reuse; it must have defined parts and relations. And a scenario-based method must be systematically structured in order to be replicable, manageable, or teachable; it must have subprocesses, enabling objectives, sequences of steps, and so forth. Some of this structure is already there and has been discussed in the previous chapters. A major question for the future of scenario-based design is how much further structuring is necessary and desirable.

Some Status on Scenario-Based Design

This book has sought to motivate the need for a use-oriented approach to design for interactive systems and applications and to make an existence case that scenario-based design, as described here, could be that approach. At a general level, we showed that scenarios address key issues in design and technology development and offer fundamental advantages over rational decomposition into features and functions. More specifically, we showed how analysis of the causal relations constituted in scenarios (claims analysis) can support design envisionment driven by explicit rationale, development of reusable design abstractions, joint evaluation of particular design instances with the concepts they embody, and object-oriented software modeling.

Further evidence for the efficacy and potential of scenario-based design is developing rapidly throughout the information technology industry and the science and engineering disciplines that support it. For example, a recent study of fifteen technology companies in northern Europe revealed that all were using various scenario-based techniques (Weidenhaupt et al. 1998). Most of the projects studied used scenarios in the development and analysis of prototypes, typically in an iterative process of requirements development similar to that of figure 11.2. Scenarios were found particularly useful in helping development teams reach sufficient agreement to enable work to proceed and in ensuring partial consistency with predecessor systems. Two of the projects turned to scenario-based techniques after the formal modeling approaches they had been pursuing became too cumbersome.

The world no longer waits for research to lead practice. Some the most important work on scenario-based design can be found in the reflections and suggestions of consultants who have applied scenario-based techniques in various contexts. In chapter 9 we discussed the work of Wirfs-Brock, Wilkerson, and Wiener (1990) and of Jacobson et al. (1992) as influences on the Scenario Browser. Their work emerges from consulting case studies. More recently, McGraw and Harbison (1997) have described a "scenario-based engineering process" that integrates scenario-based design with traditional structured development methods, and therefore perhaps renders it more easily assimilated by organizations already practicing these traditional methods. Beyer and Holtzblatt (1998) described "contextual design" as a set of participatory analysis and design activities coordinated by vision scenarios. Constantine and Lockwood (1999) presented a comprehensive reworking of structured design hinging on the notion of task model, itself hinging on the notion of scenario. These books are strong on suggestions about techniques, but weaker on presenting evidence about how the techniques work. The area is developing so rapidly that these most recent practitioner-oriented discussions appear to have been developed independently of one another and of research-oriented work on scenario-based design. This is a good thing in the sense that a relatively diverse set of perspectives is developing.

Many research communities in information technology areas have incorporated scenario-based design methods and tools into their agendas. Indeed, one of the roles that scenarios are playing in research on software and systems is to integrate diverse disciplinary views originating, for example, in human-computer interaction, software engineering, and strategic management. It appears that scenarios may provide a common, minimally structured description that various approaches can specialize and elaborate for their distinct purposes. In 1998, an international Dagstuhl Seminar was convened to examine interdisciplinary issues in scenario management (Bui, Carroll, and Jarke 1999; Jarke, Bui, and Carroll 1998); this seminar led to special issues of two journals, *IEEE Transactions on Software Engineering* (vol. 24, no. 12) and *Requirements Engineering* (vol. 3, no. 3–4).

Human-computer interaction work seeks to describe and direct the appearance, operation, and application of technology and its consequences for people, organizations, and their practices. In this work, scenarios of people interacting with current and envisioned technology have become pervasive. They are used to elicit customer attitudes, perceptions, and expectations about new applications (Karat 1995); support design brainstorming and prototype development (Nielsen 1995); generate issues and trade-offs in a design (MacLean and McKerlie 1995); transfer ideas from advanced development groups to product development groups in large organizations (Erickson 1995; Wexelblat 1987); guide development of documentation and training materials (Karat 1995); and focus usability walk-throughs to ensure that system features are evaluated relative to a specified context of use (Nielsen 1995; Polson 1992).

Scenarios are particularly pervasive in participatory design approaches to human-computer interaction. Muller et al. (1995) developed the CARD (Collaborative Analysis of Requirements and Designs) technique to allow users and other development team stakeholders to participate directly in the analysis of how work processes are supported by information technology and to plan further design interventions. They developed the PICTIVE (Plastic Interface for Collaborative Technology Initiatives through Video Exploration) technique to support detailed design of user interfaces through user-enacted scenarios. In both techniques, physical materials are used to represent human actions, data transformations, and display objects. The physical materials are manipulated as groups walk through scenarios of interaction.

Some human-computer interaction work has described comprehensive design processes that involve creating and manipulating sets of scenarios.

For example, Kyng (1995) describes a substantial development case study that involved three separate scenario phases: *use scenarios*, to describe how computer support and entrained organizational changes may alter future work situations; *exploration/requirement scenarios*, more detailed descriptions used to assess whether designs will meet user needs; and *explanation scenarios*, to develop rationale for designs in terms of work situation descriptions and use scenarios.

Because interaction scenarios foreground the use of functionality, as opposed to underlying computations or system events, they provide a view of systems and applications and a vocabulary for working with them that is uniquely suited to the concerns of human-computer interaction (Carroll and Rosson 1990; Kuutti 1995). Scenarios emphasize qualitative descriptions of human activity, directly engaging the laws of the social and behavioral sciences—our knowledge of what people need to do and wish to do, what they are most likely to do, how they will go about doing it, what they are most likely to recall or forget, what sorts of performance errors they are most susceptible to make, and so forth. As we have seen, this can provide guidance to the design of tasks, functionality, and user interface metaphors.

To develop detailed designs for user interface displays and controls, it is also necessary to articulate parameters of human performance more finely, specifying how long it will take on average for someone to perform a task, the probability that a person will recall a given command name, and so forth. Scenarios provide a bridge between models of human performance, cognition, motivation, and so forth, and the individual parameters of designed artifacts in use (Young and Barnard 1987, 1991).

Where human-computer interaction envisions scenarios to analyze and evaluate human goals and activities, software engineering envisions the use of a system in order to articulate system requirements and software structures to implement those requirements. Software engineering builds models of functionality. Within software engineering, scenarios have had their greatest effect on requirements engineering. They have been used to generate requirements, detect ambiguities in requirements, uncover missing features and inconsistencies among specified features, to verify and validate requirements, and integrate analysis of functional and nonfunctional, or "quality," requirements, such as security, safety, reliability, portability, and cost (Holbrook 1990; Hooper and Hsia 1982; Kaindl 1997; Potts, Takahashi, and Antón 1994).

For example, Kaindl (1997) described an approach to requirements definition that involves building a scenario-based model of the problem domain. In this approach, scenarios describe the interactions that need to be supported (Kaindl calls them "behavioral requirements") and help analysts identify domain objects presupposed in the scenarios and the specific functions associated with each object that allow the scenarios to obtain (what Wirfs-Brock, Wilkerson, and Wiener 1990 call responsibilities). In several projects, Kaindl has found that explicit domain modeling helps to identify and understand requirements better, relative to capturing requirements only as natural language (see also Hsia, Davis, and Kung 1993). He urges the use of hypertext to link functional and quality requirements to relevant objects in the domain models and to link scenarios to the objects and functions they presuppose.

Kazman et al. (1996) developed a scenario-based method for analyzing software architectures with respect to various quality criteria. They argue that scenarios are especially suited for such analyses because quality attributes are inherently vague and often not amenable to quantitative measurement scales. Their method classifies each design object in terms of the scenarios it participates in and each scenario in terms of the redesign work required to implement it. This allows project managers to prioritize and direct redesign effort. Moreover, this approach appeared to encourage designers to carry out the analysis very early, to avoid costly redesign after implementation is already underway. They report that scenarios helped designers to focus on the question of how the architecture will accommodate change.

In chapter 9 we discussed the role of scenarios in objected-oriented analysis and design as minimal contexts for object modeling. Although the use case concept of scenario that is prevalent in object-oriented software engineering is relatively limited, it has created a broader receptiveness to scenario-based modeling and methods in software engineering. Work like that of Kaindl, Hsia, and Kazman illustrates the emergence of new roles for scenarios in software engineering.

Strategic planning is actually the deepest root of scenario-based design. Tanaka (1994) describes scenario-based work in the Rand Corporation from the late 1940s (see Go and Carroll, forthcoming, for additional historical and cross-disciplinary discussion of scenarios). Strategic management scenarios are employed to concretize the complex uncertainties that inhere in envisioning future opportunities and risks. They are used to expose hidden assumptions about the present and the future and to allow analysts to contrast entailments of alternate policies, each encompassing a constellation of assumptions and conjectures about the current situation and its likely course of evolution. They have been found to help with the enumeration prerequisite actions that would need to be taken in order for some envisioned future to occur.

An early example of this work is in Herman Kahn's *Thinking About the Unthinkable* (1962). Kahn considered the accidental war scenario: an incident of equipment malfunction or unauthorized behavior results in the launch of a single Soviet missile. The missile detonates in Western Europe, and this is immediately detected and the information disseminated throughout Western military and civilian installations. Although the incident is not interpretable as an attack, the level of anxiety throughout the Strategic Air Command results in one officer's misunderstanding or disobeying orders and firing the missiles under his command. The counter-attack is also not interpretable as an all-out first strike; however, it is an escalated military response to the original mistake and could provoke the Soviets to launch their own ready missiles and bombers. In response, the United States might well order the rest of its missiles to be fired, as well as launching its bombers to protect them from the Soviet assault and to position them for a subsequent response.

Kahn's planning scenario became a shared nightmare for much of the world for a quarter-century. But it was also a very useful design aid. It is still shocking to know that in early 1961, no one had considered planning to communicate with the USSR during the five to forty minutes it would take for accidentally launched missiles to reach their targets, and yet doing so could literally save the world. This possibility was identified by working through the accidental war scenario. Kahn also developed extensions of this scenario in which the United States and USSR negotiated a limited nuclear war (this was later explored in the 1960s movies *Fail-Safe* and *Dr. Strangelove*) and in which they unilaterally established a world government (after surveying the first 10 million casualties of Armageddon).

Kahn called scenarios "a strange aid to thought," because they seemed so different from the more formal approaches of decision theory. However, he argued that scenarios provide distinct advantages to strategic planners. Scenarios force analysts to confront contextual details and temporal dynamics in problems, which are often overlooked in decision trees. By concretely illustrating a complex space of possibilities, scenarios help analysts deal with several aspects of a problem situation simultaneously. They facilitate the comprehension and integration of many interacting elements: psychological, social, political, and military. Scenarios stimulate the imagination, helping analysts to consider contingencies they might otherwise overlook. Shell Oil's scenario analysis of the oil industry in the 1970s is a more recent example (Wack 1985a, 1985b).

As depicted in figure 12.1, human-computer interaction is concerned with scenarios of intermediate scope, relative to software engineering and strategic planning. Software engineering defines the functions, commands, and keystrokes that constitute a system. Strategic planning is concerned with possible futures of greater scope: the organizational and societal context for the system and the people using it. Human-computer interaction is concerned with the meaningful tasks and task sequences that people experience, understand, and carry out. Understanding and designing scenarios of human-computer interaction benefits from an interdisciplinary perspective that incorporates the other disciplines. The interdisciplinary development of scenario-based methods raises fundamental issues in a greater variety of contexts and levels, which should help to produce more widely applicable and more robust scenario-based concepts and techniques.

Challenges for the Future

The most important developments in scenario-based design lie in the future. They pertain to the challenge of establishing an effective engineering practice. A pivotal issue in this challenge is cost. The case material presented in this book was inordinately "expensive." The MiTTS project, for example, consisted of several related research efforts carried out over five years and involving a half-dozen people. Although it was never the full-time concern of anyone, this is still a substantial investment of one to

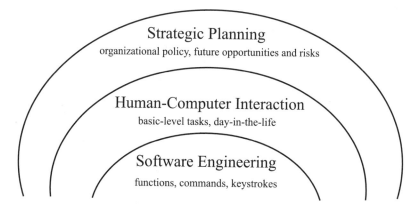

Figure 12.1
Scenarios of differing scope are employed in the different disciplines of human-computer interaction, software engineering, and strategic planning

two person-years. Of course, many of the concepts and techniques described in this book were initially created in the MiTTS project, and this framework can perhaps be regarded as a one-time cost. Also, some of the specific modeling and analysis effort was directed at potentially reusable design abstractions (for example, the usability rationale for example-based interactive environments); these costs could be amortized if the abstractions are in fact reused.

The other side of the outcome equation is benefit. There are many potential benefits to employing scenario-based design; they have been emphasized and illustrated throughout the book. Scenarios are an integrated and flexible, use-oriented design representation, easily developed, shared, and manipulated, and applicable to many system development activities. But these demonstrations are only existence arguments based on a small sample of design cases, developed by a single team and in a research laboratory environment. What benefit may be obtained when scenario-based methods are employed in various kinds of development projects, by various kinds of teams, in various kinds of environments? And more pointedly, just *who* will benefit, how will they benefit, and when? Innovative resources and activities often fail when their benefits are enjoyed chiefly by participants other than those actually creating the resource or performing the work activity (Grudin 1994).

Costs and benefits interact and trade off. The flexible applicability of scenario-based design is definitely a strength in affording a range of cost-benefit options. But we need to investigate the nature of favorable balance points. Thus, designers can sketch out one or two touchstone scenarios in an hour, develop them no further than that, and get some guidance. It may indeed be difficult to find contemporary development teams that do not make at least this minimal use of scenarios. At the other extreme, the entire development process could be anchored in scenarios. We have no example yet of a project that comprehensively implemented all of the scenario-based techniques described in this book. What are the cost-benefit entailments of such an approach compared to the already pervasive use of scenarios as design touchstones?

The effectiveness of scenario-based design will depend on training and support for designers, and perhaps on other characteristics of designers and their projects. Designers need to be motivated to adopt scenario-based techniques; they need to be trained and assisted in developing expertise. We have tried to address the constraint that working developers have little time for retraining by assuming piecemeal adoption: One or a couple of touchstone scenarios can be employed to supplement current design and development practices, but additional scenario-based techniques can be successively adopted: more comprehensive scenario analysis, causal claims analysis, analysis based on scenario and claim abstractions, scenarios spanning the development process from requirements analysis and envisionment through formative and summative evaluation. We see this adoption gradient as an advantage of scenario-based design, but we have not yet directly evaluated this adoption strategy or its consequences for new adopters (see Carey et al. 1991; Clarke 1991).

What kinds of training needs are there? What kinds of training resources need to be developed? We have taught professional seminars over the years and included scenario-based design in various undergraduate and graduate courses in human-computer interaction and software engineering, so we have reason to believe that the concepts and techniques can be conveyed. But no specific training resources, such as a tutorial or textbook for scenario-based design, have been developed and evaluated. We do not have a systematic understanding of the problems developers encounter as they learn and employ scenario-based techniques in the workplace. It is reasonable to suspect that scenario-based design might entail characteristic fallacies and misconceptions, just as traditional, structured-decomposition approaches are associated with particular problems. It is important to direct research to the characterization of these possible problems in order to develop a mature and balanced view of what scenario-based design is, so that it can be more effectively taught and practiced.

The effectiveness of scenario-based design will be shaped by the tools and resources available to designers. What sorts of tools might be useful for successively detailing scenarios and maintaining histories of scenario development? Our Scenario Browser tool, described in chapter 9, allows designers to interleave scenario development and software model development; it helps them coordinate and develop sets of scenarios. It does not maintain structured change histories or differentiate between essential and merely collateral information in scenarios. In their recent survey of scenario use, Weidenhaupt et al. (1998) found that scenarios are maintained and used in development organizations over significant spans of time. The development teams surveyed reported problems, identifying the right level of detailing and abstraction for given purposes and circumstances in system development, as well as difficulties managing different versions and representations of scenarios through the system life cycle. The interviewees expressed a need for tools and techniques to trace envisionment scenarios systematically through to final test cases. In current practice, the identity of given scenarios becomes obscure as they evolve through the development process. At the end of the process, the test case scenarios are so different from the envisionment scenarios that the customer may wonder whether the implemented system really embodies the initially agreed-on requirements.

Providing such support requires developing representation languages for scenarios. Such work is underway and runs from transparently conceptual representations (Kaindl 1997; Potts 1995; Sutcliffe and Carroll 1998) to the formal methods (Rolland, Souveyet, and Ben Achour 1998; van Lamsweerde and Willemet 1998). Some of this work has been directed to the development of computer-aided software engineering (CASE) tools for scenario-based software development (Leite et al,

1997). It is, however, still an open question just how much and what kind of structural detailing is useful, and for what.

Reusable design abstractions can deliver a savings in development effort only if they can be found and used when they are needed. This raises myriad information retrieval issues: How should scenarios be structured and indexed? What kinds of repositories can be created? What search and browsing support is required? In the foregoing chapters, we employed minimal schematic definitions for scenarios and claims; we are now investigating structural templates that could be used to organize repositories (Sutcliffe and Carroll 1998). These might also categorize relations *among* claims, for example, as suggested in figure 7.6 and elsewhere. But here again, the question is open of how much explicit structure is desirable. Monk and Wright (1991a 1991b) argued that a repository appropriate for designers would index specific observation descriptions linked to the specific design innovations they evoked, that is, it would consist of concrete usage instances and design features—usability rationale and other scenario structures remain implicit in this approach.

Another tool issue is support for creating and manipulating scenario presentations. Scenario narratives are not defined to be text, but they often are codified in text. Text is easy to create and manipulate. Nevertheless, some of the most effective design envisionment scenarios have been videos—for example, the Apple "Knowledge Navigator" (Dubberly and Mitsch 1992). But video was quite cumbersome in the early 1990s. Generic tools for producing and editing drawings, animations, and videos are now very good and widely accessible; multimedia development techniques are becoming routine. This is not to say that it is obvious that higher-fidelity media are better *tout court:* an animated Gantt chart may overspecify temporal relations in a scenario; a video may make a user interface envisionment too concrete. Such inadvertent detailing could entrain premature commitment to poorly motivated design ideas, undermining a key strength of scenarios. The day-in-the-life video produced for the multimedia project, discussed in chapter 1, may have encouraged the team to worry too little about how real users would react to their technology. The utilization and the consequences of various multimedia presentations of scenarios are important areas for research and development in scenario-based design.

Scenario-based design may be differentially effective for different kinds of development projects. The design cases described here did not involve safety-critical applications, embedded systems, or concurrency. How should scenario-based techniques be employed in these domains? For example, do scenario-based techniques make safety conditions more or less salient to various stakeholders (Johnson, Johnson, and Wilson 1995; Einbinder, Remz, and Cochran 1996)? Do scenarios entrain a bias for linearity that obscures opportunities and requirements for concurrency relative to other software engineering methodologies, or does the flexibility afforded by scenarios for thinking about temporal relations actually encourage and support exploring possibilities for concurrency? Addressing these questions will require a broader sample of design case studies.

As scenarios are employed more widely in system development, we need to investigate how they are and can be integrated with various extant methodologies. Development organizations often assimilate new techniques piecemeal; they do not merely shed current practices for new ones. In any case, it is far from clear that scenario-based design will provide a completely general and comprehensive system development methodology. Again, the way forward would appear to be analysis of actual case studies to follow up the initial results of recent surveys, like that of Weidenhaupt et al. (1998).

The emerging modal paradigm for system development work seems to be large, dispersed, and cross-organizational project teams developing distributed groupware systems. Such projects have greater coordination needs and different kinds of coordination needs than do small projects like MiTTS. Can scenario-based techniques help to alleviate development team coordination problems? Might they raise new kinds of coordination problems? We explored some of these issues in the Raison d'Etre project (chapter 4), but this was only a starting point for a very complex set of issues. We have argued that scenarios can serve as a common language for diverse stakeholder groups and examined some of these issues in the LiNC project (chapter 11). But for the most part, the application of scenarios to large, distributed systems, and the social-level analysis entailed, remain open questions for investigation (Mantovani 1996).

A final challenge for scenario-based design pertains to the internationalization of system development methods and products. For example, the ISO 9241–11 international usability standard requires an analysis of the context of use as part of the development process (International Standards Organization 1998). The standard provides a template of issues to address, but the context analysis can be carried out in a variety of ways. Dzida and Freitag (1998) describe a method in which the template of the standard is incorporated into context scenarios, developed cooperatively through an iterative interview process with domain experts. In an industrial case study, they used this approach to identify several critical incompatibilities between the context of use and the envisioned use of an information system. This encourages the possibility that scenario-base methods will be incorporated more centrally in future international usability standards.

No More Sorcerers

In their survey of scenario use, Weidenhaupt et al. (1998) consider it problematic that scenario development was regarded "as a craft instead of as an engineering task." They saw this as indicating an urgent need for greater formalization. On the other side, Wack (1985b), after describing how scenario-based planning had transformed Shell Oil's business in the 1970s, acknowledged that scenarios were effective only at precipitating and guiding organizational change when they raised uncomfortable questions and clearly challenged assumptions. This is what provoked constructive interest in planning and redesign.

We cannot resolve the scenario dilemma today. More development and more experience with scenario-based design approaches may help to do that. More likely, I think, we may find that the dynamic tension between specification and imagination is fundamental to why scenarios are a uniquely powerful and appropriate design representation. On this view, the overarching challenge of scenario-based design will remain that of balancing and integrating the rather closed and formal with the rather open-ended and ambiguous. Either way, it seems certain that research and practice in scenario-based design will continue to grow for the foreseeable future.

Like any other human activity, the task of designing interactive systems can capture the designer; perhaps it must if the designer is truly to engage the task creatively. The inherent risk is that it is easier to design a system conceived of as a list of functions than it is to design the human-computer interactions afforded by the system. Software and hardware are complex, and growing more complex all the time, but they will hold still to be analyzed; human-computer interaction will not hold still. Yet the simplification of seeing interactive systems as hardware and software, of seeing tools merely as objects, often leaves the designer holding only bathwater.

A system is a tool for people to do their work, to seek information and education, to relax and to be entertained. A system is what people can do with it and with what consequences. Representing system designs with a set of user interaction scenarios makes that use explicit, and in doing so orients design and analysis, and all the processes and activities of system development, toward a broader view of information technology. It can help designers to focus attention better on characteristics of people and their tasks that are facilitated—and obstructed—by systems. It can help designers isolate just what it is about people or about a design that allows a scenario to occur.

The challenge of creating a more appropriate set of attitudes toward design methods and information technology is significant. We must overcome the dread of uncertainty, the cognitive and cultural inertia of seeing technology design and development as systematic, rational, and predictable. We must come to see design and development as an opportunity to investigate and learn, to explore boundary conditions and master new problem domains. Scenario-based design embraces and deliberately nurtures what rationality there is and can be in technology evolution.

Designing acceptable and effective systems should not be a black art. It should not depend on sorcerers. We will always need to manage the technical design of efficient and reliable devices. If we see devices as artifacts of human activity, as enablers of designed situations, as participants in causal relations with human experiences, we will improve our chances for deliberately designing technology that stimulates and empowers people.

References

Ackerman, M. S. 1994. Augmenting the organizational memory: A field study of Answer Garden. In *Proceedings of CSCW'94: Conference on Computer-Supported Cooperative Work.* New York: ACM Press, pp. 243–252.

Ackoff, R. L. 1979. The future of operations research is past. *Journal of the Operations Research Society, 30*(2), 93–104.

Ackroyd, S., and Hughes, J. A. 1992. *Data collection in context.* London: Longmans.

Alexander, C. A. 1964. *Notes on the synthesis of form.* Cambridge, MA: Harvard University Press.

Alexander, C. A., Ishikawa, S., Silverstein, M., Jacobson, M., Fiksdahl-King, I., and Angel, S. 1977. *A pattern language: Towns, buildings, construction.* New York: Cambridge University Press.

Allport, F. H. 1920. The influence of the group upon association and thought. *Journal of Experimental Psychology, 3,* 159–182.

Alpert, S. R., Singley, M. K., and Carroll, J. M. 1995. Multiple mutimodal mentors: Delivering computer-based instruction via specialized anthropomorphic advisors. *Behaviour and Information Technology, 14,* 69–79.

Alpert, S. R., Singley, M. K., and Carroll, J. M. 1999. Multiple instructional agents in an intelligent tutoring system. In *Proceedings of the Workshop on Instructional Uses of Animated and Personified Agents.* LeMans, France: International Artificial Intelligence in Education Society.

American Association for the Advancement of Science. 1991. *Science assessment in the service of reform.* Washington, D. C.: AAAS.

Anderson, J. R., Boyle, C. F., Farrell, R., and Reiser, B. J. 1989. Cognitive principles in the design of computer tutors. In P. Morris (Ed.), *Modeling cognition.* New York: Wiley, pp. 93–134.

Anderson, J. R., and Jeffries, R. 1988. Novice LISP errors: Undetected losses of information from working memory. *Human-Computer Interaction, 1,* 107–131.

Asch, S. E. 1958. Effects of group pressure upon the modification and distortion of judgments. In E. E. Maccoby, T. M. Newcomb, and E. L. Hartley (Eds.),

Readings in social psychology (3rd ed.). New York: Holt, Rinehart and Winston, pp. 174–183.

Ausubel, D. R. 1960. The use of advance organizers in the learning and retention of meaningful verbal material. *Journal of Educational Psychology, 51,* 267–272.

Baecker, R. M. (Ed.). 1993. *Readings in groupware and computer-supported cooperative work.* San Mateo, CA: Morgan-Kaufmann.

Bandura, A., and Schunk, D. 1981. Cultivating competence, self-efficacy, and intrinsic interest through proximal stimulation. *Journal of Personality and Social Psychology, 41,* 586–598.

Barnard, P. 1991. Bridging between basic theories and the artifacts of human-computer interaction. In J. M. Carroll (Ed.), *Designing interaction: Psychology at the human-computer interface.* New York: Cambridge University Press, pp. 103–127.

Bartlett, F. C. 1932. *Remembering: An experimental and social study.* Cambridge: Cambridge University Press.

Bass, L., Kazman, R., and Little, R. 1992. Toward a software engineering model of human-computer interaction. In *Engineering for Human-Computer Interaction, Proceedings of the IFIP TC2/WG2.7 Working Conference.* Amsterdam: North-Holland, pp. 131–153.

Beck, K., and Cunningham, W. 1989. A laboratory for teaching object-oriented thinking. In *Proceedings OOPSLA'89: Conference on Object-Oriented Programming Systems, Languages, and Applications, SIGPLAN Notices,* 24(10), 1–6.

Bellamy, R. K. E., and Carroll, J. M. 1990. Redesign by design. In D. Diaper, D. Gilmore, G. Cockton, and B. Shackel (Eds.), *Proceedings of INTERACT'90: Third IFIP Conference on Human-Computer Interaction.* Amsterdam: North-Holland, pp. 199–205.

Bellamy, R. K. E., and Carroll, J. M. 1992. Structuring the programmer's task. *International Journal of Man-Machine Studies,* 37(4), 503–527.

Bennett, J. B. 1984. Managing to meet usability requirements: Establishing and meeting software development goals. In J. Bennett, D. Case, J. Sandelin, and M. Smith (Eds.), *Visual display terminals.* Englewood Cliffs, NJ: Prentice-Hall, pp. 161–184.

Bentley, R., Hughes, J. A., Randall, D., Rodden, T., Sawyer, P., Shapiro, D., and Sommerville, I. 1992. Ethnographically-informed systems design for air traffic control. In *Proceedings of CSCW'92: Conference on Computer-Supported Cooperative Work* New York: ACM Press, pp. 123–129.

Beyer, H., and Holtzblatt, K. 1998. *Contextual design: Defining customer-centered systems.* San Mateo, CA: Morgan Kaufmann.

Bhaskar, R. 1979. *A realist theory of science.* Sussex, United Kingdom: Harvester.

Bias, R. G., and Mayhew, D. J. (Eds.). 1994. *Cost-justifying usability.* Orlando, FL: Academic Press.

Blomberg, J. L. 1995. Ethnography: Aligning field studies of work and system design. In A. F. Monk, and N. Gilbert (Eds.), *Perspectives on HCI: Diverse approaches*. London: Academic Press, pp. 175–197.

Bloom, B. S. 1984. The 2 sigma problem: The search for methods of group instruction as effective as one-to-one tutoring. *Educational Researcher, 13,* 107–131.

Boehm, B. W. 1981. *Software engineering economics*. Englewood Cliffs, NJ: Prentice Hall.

Boehm, B. W. 1985. A spiral model of software development and enhancement. In J. C. Wileden and M. Downson (Eds.), *Proceedings of ACM SIGSOFT International Workshop on the Software Process and Software Environments*. New York: ACM Press.

Bonar, J. 1988. Intelligent tutoring with intermediate representations. In *Proceedings of ITS'88: Intelligent Tutoring Systems Conference*. New York: ACM Press, pp. 25–32.

Booch, G. 1986. Object-oriented development. *IEEE Transactions on Software Engineering, 12*(2), 211–221.

Booch, G., Rumbaugh, J., and Jacobson, I. 1998. *The Unified Modeling Language user guide*. Reading, MA: Addison-Wesley.

Bransford, J. D., and Johnson, M. K. 1973. Consideration of some problems of comprehension. In W. G. Chase (Ed.), *Visual information processing*. New York: Academic Press.

Brooks, F. 1995. *The mythical man-month: Essays on Software Engineering*. Reading, MA: Addison-Wesley (Anniversary edition; originally 1975).

Brown, J. S., Burton, R. R., and deKleer, J. 1982. Pedagogical, natural language, and knowledge engineering techniques in SOPHIE I, II, and III. In D. Sleeman and J. S. Brown (Eds.), *Intelligent tutoring systems*. New York: Academic Press.

Brown, R. 1973. *A first language: The early stages*. Cambridge, MA: Harvard University Press.

Bruner, J. S. 1966. *Toward a theory of instruction*. Cambridge, MA: Harvard University Press.

Bruner, J. S. 1973. *Beyond the information given*. New York: Norton.

Bui, X. T., Carroll, J. M., and Jarke, M. (Eds.) 1999. *Scenario management*. Wadern, Germany: Schloss Dagstuhl, Internationales Begegnungs—und Forschungszentrum für Informatik.

Butler, K. A. 1985. Connecting theory and practice: A case study of achieving usability goals. In *Proceedings of CHI'85: Human Factors in Computing Systems*. New York: Association for Computing Machinery, pp. 85–88.

Campbell, R. C. 1990. Developmental scenario analysis of Smalltalk programming. In *Proceedings of CHI'90: Human Factors in Computing Systems*. New York: Association for Computing Machinery, pp. 269–276.

Card, S. K., Moran, T. P., and Newell, A. 1983. *The psychology of human-computer interaction.* Hillsdale, NJ: Erlbaum.

Carey, T., McKerlie, D., Bubie, W., and Wilson, J. 1991. Communicating human factors expertise through design rationales and scenarios. In D. Diaper and N. Hammond (Eds.), *People and computers VI.* Cambridge: Cambridge University Press, pp. 117–130.

Carroll, J. M. 1990a. *The Nurnberg Funnel: Designing minimalist instruction for practical computer skill.* Cambridge, MA: MIT Press.

Carroll, J. M. 1990b. Infinite detail and emulation in an ontologically minimized HCI. In J. C. Chew and J. Whiteside (Eds.), *Proceedings of CHI'90: Human Factors in Computing Systems.* New York: ACM, pp. 321–327.

Carroll, J. M. 1991. History and hysteresis in theories and frameworks for HCI. In D. Diaper, D. and N. V. Hammond (Eds.), *People and computers VI.* Cambridge: Cambridge University Press.

Carroll, J. M. 1994. Making *use* a design representation. *Communications of the ACM, 37/12,* 29–35.

Carroll, J. M. (Ed.). 1995. *Scenario-based design: Envisioning work and technology in system development.* New York: Wiley.

Carroll, J. M. 1996. Becoming social: Expanding scenario-based approaches in HCI. *Behaviour and Information Technology, 15*(4), 266–275.

Carroll, J. M. (Ed.). 1998. *Minimalism beyond "The Nurnberg Funnel."* Cambridge, MA: MIT Press.

Carroll, J. M. 1999. Five reasons for scenario-based design. In *Proceedings of the 32rd Annual Hawaii International Conference on Systems Sciences* Los Alamitos, CA: IEEE Computer Society Press.

Carroll, J. M., and Aaronson, A. P. 1988. Learning by doing with simulated intelligent help. *Communications of the Association for Computing Machinery, 31,* 1064–1079.

Carroll, J. M., Alpert, S. R., Karat, J., Van Deusen, M. D., and Rosson, M. B. 1994. Capturing design history and rationale in multimedia narratives. In *Proceedings of CHI'94: Human Factors in Computing Systems.* New York: ACM Press/Addison-Wesley, pp. 192–197.

Carroll, J. M., and Campbell, R. L. 1986. Softening up hard science: Reply to Newell and Card. *Human-Computer Interaction, 2,* 227–249.

Carroll, J. M., and Campbell, R. L. 1989. Artifacts as psychological theories: The case of human-computer interaction. *Behaviour and Information Technology, 8,* 247–256.

Carroll, J. M., and Carrithers, C. 1984. Training wheels in a user interface. *Communications of the Association for Computing Machinery, 27,* 800–806.

Carroll, J. M., and Isenhour, P. 1999. *Mediated formative evaluation of an activity-oriented on-line tutorial.* Technical Report. Center for Human-Computer Interaction, Virginia Tech, Blacksburg, VA.

Carroll, J. M., and Kellogg, W. A. 1989. Artifact as theory nexus: Hermeneutics meets theory-based design. In T. Bice and C. H. Lewis (Eds.), *Proceedings of CHI'89: Human Factors in Computing Systems.* New York: ACM, pp. 7–14.

Carroll, J. M., Kellogg, W. A., and Rosson, M. B. 1991. The task-artifact cycle. In J. M. Carroll (Ed.), *Designing interaction: Psychology at the human-computer interface.* New York: Cambridge University Press, pp. 74–102.

Carroll, J. M., Koenemann-Belliveau, J., Rosson, M. B., and Singley, M. K. 1993. Critical incidents and critical threads in empirical usability evaluation. In J. Alty, D. Diaper, and S. Guest (Eds.), *People and computers VIII: Proceedings of HCI'93.* Cambridge: Cambridge University Press, pp. 279–292.

Carroll, J. M., and Mack, R. L. 1985. Metaphor, computing systems, and active learning. *International Journal of Man-Machine Studies, 22,* 39–58.

Carroll, J. M., Mack, R. L., Robertson, S. P., and Rosson, M. B. 1994. Binding objects to scenarios of use. *International Journal of Human-Computer Studies, 40,* 243–276.

Carroll, J. M., and Mazur, S. A. 1986. LisaLearning. *IEEE Computer, 19/11,* 35–49.

Carroll, J. M., and Neale, D. C. 1998. Community mentoring relationships in middle school science. In A. S. Bruckman, M. Guzdial, J. L. Kolodner, and A. Ram (Eds.), *Proceedings of ICLS'98: International Conference of the Learning Sciences.* Charlottesville, VA: Association for the Advancement of Computing in Education, pp. 302–303.

Carroll, J. M., and Rosson, M. B. 1985. Usability specifications as a tool in iterative development. In H. R. Hartson (Ed.), *Advances in human-computer interaction.* Norwood, NJ: Ablex.

Carroll, J. M., and Rosson, M. B. 1987. The paradox of the active user. In J. M. Carroll (Ed.), *Interfacing thought: Cognitive aspects of human-computer interaction.* Cambridge: MIT Press/Bradford Books, pp. 80–111.

Carroll, J. M., and Rosson, M. B. 1990. Human-computer interaction scenarios as a design representation. In *Proceedings of the 23rd Annual Hawaii International Conference on Systems Sciences.* Los Alamitos, CA: IEEE Computer Society Press, pp. 555–561.

Carroll, J. M., and Rosson, M. B. 1991. Deliberated evolution: Stalking the View Matcher in design space. *Human-Computer Interaction, 6,* 281–318.

Carroll, J. M., and Rosson, M. B. 1992. Getting around the task-artifact cycle: How to make claims and design by scenario. *ACM Transactions on Information Systems, 10,* 181–212.

Carroll, J. M., and Rosson, M. B. 1994. Putting metaphors to work. In *Proceedings of GI'94: Graphics Interface,* pp. 112–119.

Carroll, J. M., and Rosson, M. B. 1995. Managing evaluation goals for training. *Communications of the ACM, 38*(7), 40–48.

Carroll, J. M., and Rosson, M. B. 1996. Developing the Blacksburg Electronic Village. *Communications of the ACM, 39*(12), 69–74.

Carroll, J. M., Rosson, M. B., Chin, G., and Koenemann, J. 1998. Requirements development in scenario-based design. *IEEE Transactions on Software Engineering, 24* (12), 1156–1170.

Carroll, J. M., Rosson, M. B., Cohill, A. M., and Schorger, J. 1995. Building a history of the Blacksburg Electronic Village. In *Proceedings of DIS'95: First ACM Symposium on Designing Interactive Systems.* New York: ACM Press, pp. 1–6.

Carroll, J. M., Rosson, M. B., and Singley, M. K. 1993. The collaboration thread: A formative evaluation of object-oriented education. In C. R. Cook, J. C. Scholtz, and J. C. Spohrer (Eds.), *Empirical studies of programmers, Fifth Workshop.* Norwood, NJ: Ablex, 26–41.

Carroll, J. M., Singer, J. A., Bellamy, R. K. E., and Alpert, S. R. 1990. A view matcher for learning Smalltalk. In J. C. Chew and J. Whiteside (Eds.), *Proceedings of CHI'90: Conference on Human Factors in Computing Systems.* New York: ACM, pp. 431–437.

Carroll, J. M., Singley, M. K., and Rosson, M. B. 1991. Toward an architecture for instructional evaluation. In L. Birnbaum (Ed.), *Proceedings of the International Conference on the Learning Sciences.* Charlottesville, VA: Association for the Advancement of Computing in Education, pp. 85–90.

Carroll, J. M., Singley, M. K., and Rosson, M. B. 1992. Integrating theory development with design evaluation. *Behaviour and Information Technology, 11,* 247–255.

Carroll, J. M., and Thomas, J. C. 1982. Metaphor and the cognitive representation of computing systems. *IEEE Transactions on Systems, Man, and Cybernetics, 12,* 107–115.

Carroll, J. M., Thomas, J. C., and Malhotra, A. 1979. A clinical-experimental analysis of design problem solving. *Design Studies, 1,* 84–92.

Cartwright, D. 1968. The nature of a group's cohesiveness. In D. Cartwright and A. Zander (Eds.), *Group dynamics: Research and theory* (3rd ed.). New York: Harper, and Row.

Cazden, C. 1988. *Classroom discourse: The language of teaching and learning.* Portsmouth, NH: Heinemann.

Chin, G. 2000. *Students and teachers turn software designers: A case study in the implementation, deployment, and assessment of participatory design in the science classroom.* Ph. D. Dissertation, Virginia Tech, Blacksburg, VA.

Chin, G., Rosson, M. B., and Carroll, J. M. 1997. Participatory analysis: Shared development of requirements from scenarios. In S. Pemberton (Ed.), *Proceedings of CHI'97: Human Factors in Computing Systems.* New York: ACM Press/ Addison-Wesley, pp. 162–169.

Churchman, W. 1970. Operations research as a profession. *Management Science, 17*(2), 37–53.

Clarke, L. 1991. The use of scenarios by user interface designers. In D. Diaper and N. Hammond (eds.), *People and computers VI*. Cambridge: Cambridge University Press, pp. 103–115.

Clausen, H. 1993. Narratives as tools for the system designer. *Design Studies,* 14, 283–298.

Clemons, E. K. 1995. Using scenario analysis to manage the strategic risks of reengineering. *Sloan Management Review,* Summer, 61–71.

Constantine, L. L., and Lockwood, L. A. D. 1999. *Software for use: A practical guide to the models and methods of usage-centered design.* Reading, MA: Addison-Wesley.

Craig, R. C. 1965. Discovery, task completion, and the assignment of factors in motivation. *American Educational Research Journal, 2,* 217–234.

Crowder, R. G. 1976. *Principles of learning and memory.* Hillsdale, NJ: Erlbaum.

Curtis, B, Krasner, H., and Iscoe, N. 1988. A field study of the software design process for large systems. *Communications of the ACM, 31,* 1268–1287.

DeBono, E. 1990. *Lateral thinking: Creativity step-by-step.* New York: Harper-Collins (originally published in 1970).

DeGrace, P., and Stahl, L. H. 1990. *Wicked problems, righteous solutions: A catalogue of modern software engineering paradigms.* Englewood Cliffs, NJ: Prentice Hall.

Dewey, J. 1966. *Democracy and education.* New York: Free Press (originally published 1916).

Digitalk. 1990. *Smalltalk/V: Object-Oriented Programming System.* Los Angeles, CA: Digitalk.

Dixon, P. 1987. The processing of organizational and step information in written directions. *Journal of Memory and Language, 26,* 24–35.

Dourish, P., and Bellotti, V. 1992. Awareness and coordination in shared workspaces. In *Proceedings of CSCW '92: Conference on Computer-Supported Cooperative Work.* New York: Association for Computing Machinery, pp. 107–114.

Dreyfus, H. L., and Dreyfus, S. E. 1988. *Mind over machine: The power of human intuition and expertise in the era of the computer.* New York: Free Press.

Dreyfuss, H. 1955. *Designing for people.* New York: Simon & Schuster.

Dubberly, H., and Mitsch, D. 1992. Knowledge navigator. In B. A. Myers (Ed.), *CHI'92 Special Video Program: Conference on Human Factors in Computing Systems.* New York: ACM SIGCHI.

Dzida, W., and Freitag, R. 1998. Making use of scenarios for validating analysis and design. *IEEE Transactions on Software Engineering, 24*(12), 1182–1196.

Ebbinghaus, H. 1885. *Memory, a contribution to experimental psychology,* (H. A. Ruger and C. E. Bussenius (trans.) New York: Dover.

Ehn, P., and Kyng, M. 1991. Cardboard computers: Mocking-it-up or hands on the future? In J. Greenbaum and M. Kyng (Eds.), *Design at work: Cooperative design of computer systems*. Hillsdale, NJ: Erlbaum, pp. 169–196.

Einbinder, L. H., Remz, J. B., and Cochran, D. 1996. Mapping clinical scenarios to functional requirements: A tool for evaluating clinical information systems. In J. J. Cimino (Ed.), *Proceedings of 1996 American Medical Informatics Association Annual Fall Symposium*. Philadelphia: Hanley, and Belfus, pp. 747–751.

Erickson, T. 1995. Notes on design practice: Stories and prototypes as catalysts for communication. In J. M. Carroll (Ed.), *Scenario-based design: Envisioning work and technology in system development*. New York: Wiley, pp. 37–58.

Erikson, E. H. 1980. *Identity and the life cycle*. New York: Norton.

Erskine, L., Carter-Todd, D., and Burton, J. 1997. Dialogical techniques for the design of Web sites. *International Journal of Human-Computer Studies, 47*, 169–195.

Festinger, L. 1957. *A theory of cognitive dissonance*. New York: Harper, and Row.

Festinger, L., Riecken, H. W., and Schachter, S. 1956. *When prophecy fails*. Minneapolis: University of Minnesota Press.

Fetterman, D. 1989. *Ethnography: Step by step*. Newbury Park, CA: Sage.

Fischer, G., Grudin, J., Lemke, A. C., McCall, R., Ostwald, J., Reeves, B., and Shipman, F. 1992. Supporting indirect collaborative design with integrated knowledge-based design environments. *Human-Computer Interaction, 7*, 281–314.

Fisher, G. 1987. Cognitive view of reuse and redesign. *IEEE Software 4*, 60–72.

Fischer, G., Grudin, J., Lemke, A. C., McCall, R., Ostwald, J., and Shipman, F. 1992. Supporting indirect, collaborative design with integrated knowledge-based design environments. *Human-Computer Interaction, 7*, 281–314.

Fischer, G., Lemke, A. C., Mastaglio, T., and Morch, A. I. 1990. Using critics to empower users. In *Proceedings of CHI'90: Conference on Human Factors in Computing Systems*. New York: ACM, pp. 337–347.

Flanagan, J. C. 1954. The critical incident technique. *Psychological Bulletin, 51*(28), 28–35.

Fowler, M. 1998. *Analysis patterns: Reusable object models*. Reading, MA: Addison-Wesley.

Freud, S. 1900. *The interpretation of dreams*. Standard Edition, Vol. IV. London: Hogarth.

Frishberg, N., Laff, M. R., Desrosiers, M. R., Koons, W. R. and Kelley, J. F. 1991. John Cocke: A retrospective by friends. In *Proceedings CHI'91: Conference on Human Factors in Computing Systems*. New York: ACM Press, pp. 423–424.

Furnas. 1986. Generalized fisheye views. In *Proceedings of CHI'83: Human Factors in Computing Systems*. New York: ACM Press, pp. 13–23.

Gagné, R. M., and Briggs, L. J. 1979. *Principles of instructional design.* New York: Holt, Rinehart and Winston.

Gagné, R. M., Briggs, L. J., and Wagner, W. (1988). *Principles of instructional design* (3rd Ed.). New York: Holt, Rinehart and Winston.

Gibson, S., Neale, D. C., Van Metre, C. A., and Carroll, J. M. 1999. Mentoring in a school environment. In *Proceedings of CSCL'99: Conference on Computer-Supported Cooperative Learning.* Hillsdale, NJ: Erlbaum, pp. 182–188.

Gilbreth, F. B. 1911. *Motion study: A method for increasing the efficiency of the workman.* New York: Van Nostrand.

Go, K., and Carroll, J. M. Forthcoming. Blind men and an elephant: Views of scenario-based system design.

Gold, E. 1967. Language identification in the limit. *Information and Control, 16,* 447–474.

Gold, E., and Rosson, M. B. 1991. Portia: An instance-based environment for Smalltalk. In *Proceedings of OOPSLA'91: Conference on Object-Oriented Programming Systems, Languages, and Applications.* New York: ACM Press, pp. 62–74.

Goldberg, A. 1984. *Smalltalk-80: The interactive programming environment.* Reading, MA: Addison-Wesley.

Goldberg, A. 1990, Information models, views, and controllers. *Dr. Dobb's Journal,* July, no. 166, 54–61.

Goldberg, A., and Robson, D. 1983. *Smalltalk-80: The language and its implementation.* Reading, MA: Addison-Wesley.

Goldstein, I. L. 1987. The relationship of training goals and training systems. In G. Salvendy (Ed.), *Handbook of human factors.* New York: Wiley, pp. 963–975.

Gould, J. D., and Lewis, C. H. 1985. Designing for usability: Key principles and what designers think. *Communications of the ACM, 26,* 295–308.

Graesser, A. C., and Clark, L. F. 1985. *Structures and procedures of implicit knowledge.* Norwood, NJ: Ablex.

Greenbaum, J., and Kyng, M. (Eds.). 1991. *Design at work: Cooperative design of computer systems.* Hillsdale, NJ: Erlbaum.

Grudin, J. 1994. Groupware and social dynamics: Eight challenges for developers. *Communications of the ACM, 37*(1), 92–105.

Grudin, J. 1996. Evaluating opportunities for design capture. In T. P. Moran and J. M. Carroll (Eds.), *Design rationale: Concepts, techniques, and use.* Hillsdale, NJ: Erlbaum, pp. 453–470.

Guindon, R. 1990. Designing the design process: Exploiting opportunistic thoughts. *Human-Computer Interaction, 5,* 305–344.

Harrison, M. D., Roast, C. R., and Wright, P. C. 1989. Complementary methods for the iterative design of interactive systems. In G. Salvendy and M. J. Smith (Eds.), *Designing and using human-computer interfaces and knowledge-based systems.* Amsterdam: Elsevier, pp. 651–658.

Hayes-Roth, B., and Hayes-Roth, F. A. 1979. A cognitive model of planning. *Cognitive Psychology, 3*, 275–310.

Holbrook, H. 1990. A scenario-based methodology for conducting requirements elicitation. *ACM SIGSOFT Software Engineering Notes, 15–1*, pp. 95–103.

Holland, J. H., Holyoak, K. J., Nisbett, R. E., and Thagard, P. R. 1987. *Induction: Processes of inference, learning, and discovery.* Cambridge, MA: MIT Press.

Hollnagel, E. 1993. *Human reliability analysis context and control.* Orlando, FL: Academic Press.

Hooper, J. W., and Hsia, P. 1982. Scenario-based prototyping for requirements identification. *ACM SIGSOFT Software Engineering Notes, 7–5*, pp. 88–93.

Hsia, P., Davis, A., and Kung, D. 1993. Status report: Requirements engineering. *IEEE Software, 10/6*, 75–79.

Hsia, P., Samuel, J., Gao, J., Kung, D., Toyoshima, Y., and Chen, C. 1994. Formal approach to scenario analysis. *IEEE Software*, March, pp. 33–41.

Hughes, J., King, V., Rodden, T., and Andersen, H. 1994. Moving out of the control room: Ethnography in system design. In *Proceedings CSCW'94: Conference on Computer-Supported Cooperative Work.* New York: ACM, pp. 429–239.

Hutchins, C. M. 1981. The acoustics of violin plates. *Scientific American, 245*(4), 170–186.

Hutchins, E. 1995. *Cognition in the wild.* Cambridge, MA: MIT Press.

International Standards Organization. 1998. *ISO 9241–11, Ergonomic Requirements for Office Work with Visual Display Terminals (VDTs)—Guidance on Usability.* Geneva, Switzerland: ISO.

Jacobson, I. 1987. Object-oriented development in an industrial environment. In *Proceedings of OOPSLA'87: Conference on Object-Oriented Systems, Languages and Applications. SIGPLAN Notices, 21*(11).

Jacobson, I. 1995. The use-case construct in object-oriented software engineering. In J. M. Carroll (Ed.), *Scenario-based design: Envisioning work and technology in system development.* New York: Wiley, pp. 309–336.

Jacobson, I., Booch, G., and Rumbaugh, J. 1998. *The unified software development process.* Reading, MA: Addison-Wesley.

Jacobson, I. Christersson, M. Jonsson, P., and Övergaard, G. 1992. *Object-oriented software engineering—A use-case driven approach.* Reading, MA: Addison-Wesley.

Jarke, M., Bui, X. T., and Carroll, J. M. 1998. Scenario management: An interdisciplinary approach. *Requirements Engineering, 3*(3–4).

Johnson, P., Johnson, H., and Wilson, S. 1995. Rapid prototyping of user interfaces driven by task models. In J. M. Carroll (Ed.), *Scenario-based design: Envisioning work and technology in system development.* New York: Wiley, pp. 209–246.

Johnson, W. L. 1985. *Intention-based diagnosis of errors in novice programs.* Ph. D. dissertation, Yale University, New Haven, CT.

Johnson, W. L., and Benner, K. M. 1993. Developing formal specifications from informal requirements. *IEEE Expert,* August, 82–90.

Jones, J. C. 1970. *Design methods: Seeds of human futures.* New York: Wiley.

Kahn, H. 1962. *Thinking about the unthinkable.* New York: Horizon Press.

Kahneman, D. 1973. *Attention and effort.* Englewood Cliffs, NJ: Prentice-Hall.

Kaindl, H. 1997. A practical approach to combining requirements definition and object-oriented analysis. *Annals of Software Engineering, 3,* 319–343.

Karat, J. 1995. Scenario use in the design of a speech recognition system. In J. M. Carroll (Ed.), *Scenario-based design: Envisioning work and technology in system development.* New York: Wiley, pp. 109–133.

Karat, J., and Bennett, J. B. 1991. Using scenarios in design meetings—A case study example. In J. Karat (Ed.), *Taking design seriously: Practical techniques for human-computer interaction design.* Orlando, FL: Academic Press, pp. 63–94.

Karat, J., Carroll, J. M., Alpert, S. R., and Rosson, M. B. 1995. Evaluating a multimedia history system as support for collaborative design. In K. Nordby, P. Helmersen, D. Gilmore, and S. Arnesen (Eds.), *Proceedings of INTERACT'95: Fifth IFIP Conference on Human-Computer Interaction.* London: Chapman, and Hall, pp. 346–353.

Kazman, R., Abowd, G., Bass, L., and Clements, P. 1996. Scenario-based analysis of software architecture. *IEEE Software,* November, pp. 47–55.

Kellogg, W. A. 1990. Qualitative artifact analysis. In D. Diaper, D. Gilmore, G. Cockton, and B. Shackel (Eds.), *Proceedings of INTERACT'90: Third IFIP Conference on Human-Computer Interaction.* Amsterdam: North-Holland, pp. 193–198.

Koenemann-Belliveau, J., Carroll, J. M., Rosson, M. B., and Singley, M. K. 1994. Comparative usability evaluation: Critical incidents and critical threads. In *Proceedings of CHI'94: Human Factors in Computing Systems.* New York: ACM Press/Addison-Wesley, pp. 245–251.

Koenemann, J., Carroll, J. M., Shaffer, C. A., Rosson, M. B., and Abrams, M. 1999. Designing collaborative applications for classroom use: The LiNC Project. In A. Druin (Ed.), *The design of children's technology.* San Mateo, CA: Morgan-Kaufmann, pp. 99–123.

Kuhn, S., and Muller, M. J. (Eds.) 1993. Special section on participatory design. *Communications of the ACM, 36*(4), 24–103.

Kuutti, K. 1995. Work processes: Scenarios as a preliminary vocabulary. In J. M. Carroll (Ed.), *Scenario-based design: Envisioning work and technology in system development.* New York: Wiley, pp. 19–36.

Kyng, M. 1995. Creating contexts for design. In J. M. Carroll (Ed.), *Scenario-based design: Envisioning work and technology in system development.* New York: Wiley, pp. 85–107.

Lange, B. M., and Moher, T. G. 1989. Some strategies of reuse in an object-oriented programming environment. In K. Bice and C. Lewis (Eds.), *CHI'89: Human Factors in Computing Systems.* New York: ACM, pp. 69–73.

Latane, B. 1981. Psychology of social impact. *American Psychologist, 36,* 343–356.

Laughton, S. 1996. *The design and use of Internet-mediated communication applications in education: An ethnographic study.* Ph. D. dissertation, Virginia Tech, Blacksburg, VA.

Lave, J. 1988. *Cognition in practice: Mind, mathematics, and culture.* New York: Cambridge University Press.

Leite, J. C., Rossi, G., Balaguer, F., Maiorana, V., Kaplan, G., Hadad, G., and Oliveros, A. 1997. Enhancing a requirements baseline with scenarios. In *Proceedings of RE'97: Third International Symposium on Requirements Engineering.* Los Alamitos, CA: IEEE Computer Society Press, pp. 44–53.

Lévi-Strauss, C. 1967. *Structural anthropology.* Garden City, NY: Anchor Books.

Lewin, K. 1953. Studies in group decision. In D. Cartwright and A. Zander (Eds.), *Group dynamics: Research and theory.* Evanston, IL: Row, Peterson.

Lewis, M. L., and Anderson, J. R. 1985. Discrimination of operator schemata in problem solving: Learning from examples. *Cognitive Psychology, 17,* 26–65.

Mack, R. L., Lewis, C. H., and Carroll, J. M. 1983. Learning to use office systems: Problems and prospects. *ACM Transactions on Office Information Systems, 1,* 254–271.

Mack, R. L., and Nielsen, J. April, 1987. *Software integration in the professional work environment: Observations on requirements, usage, and interface issues.* IBM Research Report-RC 12677. Yorktown Heights, NY: IBM T. J. Watson Research Center.

Malhotra, A., Thomas, J. C., Carroll, J. M., and Miller, L. A. 1980. Cognitive processes in design. *International Journal of Man-Machine Studies, 12,* 119–140.

Malone, T. W., and Lepper, M. R. 1987. Making learning fun: Intrinsic motivation for learning. In R. E. Snow and M. J. Farr (Eds.), *Aptitude, learning and instruction: III. Conative and affective process analysis.* Hillsdale, NJ: Erlbaum.

Mantovani, G. 1996. Social context in HCI: A new framework for mental models, cooperation and communication. *Cognitive Science, 20,* 237–269.

MacLean, A., and McKerlie, D. 1995. Design space analysis and use representations. In J. M. Carroll (Ed.), *Scenario-based design: Envisioning work and technology in system development.* New York: Wiley, pp. 183–207.

MacLean, A., Young, R., Bellottii, V., and Moran, T. P. 1996. Questions, options and criteria: Elements of a design rationale for user interfaces. In T. P. Moran and J. M. Carroll (Eds.), *Design rationale: Concepts, methods and techniques.* Hillsdale, NJ: Erlbaum, pp. 53–105.

McGraw, K., and Harbison, K. 1997. *User-centered requirements: The scenario-based engineering process.* Hillsdale, NJ: Erlbaum.

McKendree, J. 1990. Effective feedback content for tutoring complex skills. *Human-Computer Interaction, 5,* 381–413.

Mesthene, E. G. 1970. *Technological change: Its impact on man and society.* Cambridge, MA: Harvard University Press.

Milgram, S. 1968. Some conditions of obedience and disobedience to authority. *International Journal of Psychiatry, 6,* 259–276.

Mills, C. W. 1959. *The sociological imagination.* New York: Oxford University Press.

Monk, A. F., and Wright, P. C. 1991a. Claims, observations and inventions: Analyzing the artifact. *SIGCHI Bulletin, 23*(1), 52–54.

Monk, A. F., and Wright, P. C. 1991b. Observations and inventions: New approaches to the study of human-computer interaction. *Interacting with Computers, 3*(2), 204–216.

Monk, A., Wright, P., Haber, J., and Davenport, L. 1993. *Improving your human-computer interface: A practical technique.* Englewood Cliffs, NJ: Prentice-Hall.

Moran, T. P., and Carroll, J. M. (Eds.) 1996. *Design rationale: Concepts, methods and techniques.* Hillsdale, NJ: Erlbaum.

Muller, M. J., Tudor, L. G., Wildman, D. M., White, E. A., Root, R. A., Dayton, T., Carr, R., Diekmann, B., and Dystra-Erickson, E. 1995. Bifocal tools for scenarios and representations in participatory activities with users. In J. M. Carroll (Ed.), *Scenario-based design: Envisioning work and technology in system development.* New York: Wiley, pp. 135–163.

National Science Teachers Association. 1990. *Scope, Sequence, and Coordination of Secondary School Science.* Washington, D. C.: NSTA.

Neale, D., and Carroll, J. M. 1997. The role of metaphors in user interface design. In M. Helander, T. K. Landauer, and P. V. Prabhu (Eds.), *Handbook of human-computer interaction,* (2nd ed.). Amsterdam: North-Holland, pp. 441–462.

Newell, A., and Card, S. K. 1985. The prospects for psychological science in human-computer interaction. *Human-Computer Interaction, 1,* 209–242.

Newman, W. M. 1988. The representation of user interface style. In D. M. Jones and R. Winder (Eds.), *People and computers IV.* Cambridge: Cambridge University Press, pp. 123–143.

Nielsen, J. 1995. Scenarios in discount usability engineering. In J. M. Carroll (Ed.), *Scenario-based design: Envisioning work and technology in system development.* New York: Wiley, pp. 59–83.

Nielsen, J., and Mack, R. L. (Eds.). 1994. *Usability inspection methods.* New York: Wiley.

Nielsen, J., and Richards, J. T. 1989. The experience of learning and using Smalltalk. *IEEE Software, 6*(3), 73–77.

Nisbett, R. E., and Wilson, T. D. 1977. Telling more than we can know: Verbal reports on mental processes. *Psychological Review, 84,* 231–259.

Norman, D. A. 1986. Cognitive engineering. In D. A. Norman and S. Draper (Eds.), *User centered system design: New perspectives on human-computer interaction.* Hillsdale, N. J.: Erlbaum.

Norman, D. A. 1988. *The psychology of everyday things.* New York: Basic Books.

Norman, D. A. 1991. Cognitive artifacts. In J. M. Carroll (Ed.), *Designing interaction: Psychology at the human-computer interface.* New York: Cambridge University Press, pp. 17–38.

O'Shea, T., Beck, K., Halbert, D., and Schmucker, K. 1986. Panel: The learnability of object-oriented programming systems. In N. Meyrowitz (Ed.), *Proceedings of OOPSLA'86: Conference on Object-Oriented Programming Systems, Languages, and Applications.* New York: ACM, pp. 502–503.

Orr, J. E. 1986. Narratives at work. *Proceedings of CSCW'86: Conference on Computer-Supported Cooperative Work.* New York: ACM, pp. 62–72.

Papert, S. 1980. *Mindstorms: Children, computers, and powerful ideas.* New York: Basic Books.

Piaget, J. 1985. *The equilibration of cognitive structures: The central problem of intellectual development.* Chicago: University of Chicago Press.

Poltrock, S. E., and Grudin, J. 1994. Organizational obstacles to interface design and development: Two participant observer studies. *ACM Transactions on Computer-Human Interaction, 1*(1), 52–80.

Polson, P. G., Lewis, C. H., Rieman, J., and Wharton, C. 1992. Cognitive walkthroughs: A method for theory-based evaluation of user interface. *International Journal of Man-Machine Studies, 36,* 741–773.

Potts, C. 1995. Using schematic scenarios to understand user needs. In *Proceedings of DIS'95: First ACM Symposium on Designing Interactive Systems.* New York: ACM, pp. 247–256.

Potts, C., Takahashi, K., and Antón, A. I. 1994. Inquiry-based requirements analysis. *IEEE Software,* March, pp. 21–32.

Propp, V. 1958. *Morphology of the folktale.* The Hague: Mouton. (original edition 1928)

Raj, R. K., and Levy, H. M. 1989. A composition model for software reuse. In S. Cook (Ed.), *Proceedings of ECOOP'89: Third European Conference on Object-Oriented Programming.* London: Cambridge University Press, pp. 3–24.

Reason, J. 1990. *Human error.* New York: Cambridge University Press.

Reitman, W. R. 1965. *Cognition and thought: An information processing approach.* New York: Wiley.

Resnick, L. B. 1987. Learning in school and out. *Educational Researcher, 16(9),* 13–20.

Rittel, H., and Weber, M. 1973. Dilemmas in a general theory of planning. *Policy Science, 4,* 155–169.

Roberts, T. L., and Moran, T. P. 1983. The evaluation of text editors: Methodology and empirical results. *Communications of the ACM, 26,* 265–283.

Robertson, S. P. 1995. Generating object-oriented design representation via scenario queries. In J. M. Carroll (Ed.), *Scenario-based design: Envisioning work and technology in system development.* New York: Wiley, pp. 279–308.

Robertson, S. P., Carroll, J. M., Mack, R. L. Rosson, M. B., Alpert, S. R., and Koenemann-Belliveau, J. 1994. ODE: A self-guided, scenario-based learning environment for object-oriented design principles. In *Proceedings of OOPSLA'94: Conference on Object-Oriented Programming Systems, Languages and Applications. ACM SIGPLAN Notices,* Vol. 29, No. 10. New York: ACM Press, pp. 51–64.

Rolland, C., Souveyet, C., and Ben Achour, C. 1998. Guiding goal modeling using scenarios. *IEEE Transactions on Software Engineering, 24(12),* 1055–1071.

Rosch, E., Mervis, C. B., Gray, W., Johnson, D., and Boyes-Braem, P. 1976. Basic objects in natural categories. *Cognitive Psychology, 7,* 573–605.

Ross, B. H., and Moran, T. P. 1983. Remindings and their effects on learning a text editor. In *Proceedings of CHI'83: Conference on Human Factors of Computing Systems.* New York: ACM, pp. 222–225.

Rosson, M. B., and Alpert, S. R. 1990. Cognitive consequences of object-oriented design. *Human-Computer Interaction, 5,* 345–379.

Rosson, M. B., and Carroll, J. M. 1990. Climbing the Smalltalk mountain. *SIGCHI Bulletin, 21(3),* 76–79.

Rosson, M. B., and Carroll, J. M. 1992. Extending the task-artifact framework. In H. R. Hartson, and D. Hix (Eds.), *Advances in Human-Computer Interaction, 4.* Norwood, NJ: Ablex, pp. 31–57.

Rosson, M. B., and Carroll, J. M. 1993. Active programming strategies in reuse. In O. Nierstrasz (Ed.), *Proceedings of ECOOP'93: Seventh European Conference on Object-Oriented Programming.* Amsterdam: Springer-Verlag, pp. 4–20.

Rosson, M. B., and Carroll, J. M. 1995a. Narrowing the specification-implementation gap in scenario-based design. In J. M. Carroll (Ed.), *Scenario-based design: Envisioning work and technology in system development.* New York: Wiley, pp. 247–278.

Rosson, M. B., and Carroll, J. M. 1995b. Integrating task and software development for object-oriented applications. In *Proceedings of CHI'95: Conference on Human Factors in Computing Systems.* New York: ACM, pp. 377–384.

Rosson, M. B., and Carroll, J. M. 1996a. The reuse of uses in Smalltalk programming. *ACM Transactions on Computer-Human Interaction,* 3(3), 219–253.

Rosson, M. B., and Carroll, J. M. 1996b. Scaffolded examples for learning object-oriented design. *Communications of the ACM, 39*(4), 46–47.

Rosson, M. B., and Carroll, J. M. 1996c. Introduction to object-oriented design tutorial. CHI'96 Conference on Human Factors in Computing Systems, Vancouver, Canada, April 14.

Rosson, M. B., Carroll, J. M., and Bellamy, R. K. E. 1990. Smalltalk scaffolding: A case study in minimalist instruction. In J. C. Chew and J. Whiteside (Eds.), *Proceedings of CHI'90: Conference on Human Factors in Computing Systems.* New York: ACM, pp. 423–429.

Rosson, M. B., and Gold, E. 1989. Problem-solution mapping in object-oriented design. In *Proceedings of OOPSLA'87: Conference on Object-Oriented Systems, Languages and Applications, SIGPLAN Notices, 21*(11), 7–10.

Rumbaugh, J., Jacobson, I., and Booch, G. 1998. *The Unified Modeling Language reference manual.* Reading, MA: Addison-Wesley.

Schein, E. H., Schneier, T., and Barker, G. H. (1961). *Coercive persuasion: A socio-psychological analysis of the "brainwashing" of American prisoners by the Chinese communists.* New York: Norton.

Schoemaker, P. J. H. 1995. Scenario planning: A tool for stragic thinking. *Sloan Management Review,* Winter, 25–40.

Schön, D. A. 1967. *Technology and change: The new Heraclitus.* New York: Pergamon Press.

Schön, D. A. 1983. *The reflective practitioner: How professionals think in action.* New York: Basic Books.

Schön, D. A. 1987. *Educating the reflective practitioner.* San Francisco: Jossey-Bass.

Schriver, K. 1997. *Dynamics in document design.* New York: Wiley.

Schuler, D. and Namioka, A. (Eds.). 1993. *Participatory design: Principles and practices.* Hillsdale, NJ: Erlbaum.

Schwartz, P. 1992. Composing a plot for your scenario. *Planning Review,* May–June, 4–8, 46.

Scriven, M. 1967. The methodology of evaluation. In R. Tyler, R. Gagne, and M. Scriven (Eds.), *Perspectives of curriculum evaluation.* Chicago: Rand McNally, pp. 39–83.

Sharrock, W., and Anderson, B. 1996. Organizational innovation and the articulation of the design space. In T. P. Moran, and J. M. Carroll (Eds.), *Design rationale: Concepts, techniques, and use.* Hillsdale, NJ: Erlbaum, pp. 429–451.

Shulman, L. S., and Keislar, E. R. (Eds.). 1966. *Learning by discovery: A critical appraisal.* Chicago: Rand McNally.

Simon, H. A. (1973). The structure of ill-structured problems. *Artificial Intelligence, 4,* 181–201.

Simpson, D. G. 1992. Key lessons for adopting scenario planning in diversified companies. *Planning Review,* May–June, 10–17, 47–48.

Singley, M. K. 1990. The reification of goal structures in a calculus tutor: Effects on problem solving performance. *Interactive Learning Environments, 1,* 102–123.

Singley, M. K., and Anderson, J. R. 1989. *The transfer of cognitive skill.* Cambridge, MA: Harvard University Press.

Singley, M. K., and Carroll, J. M. 1990. Minimalist planning tools in an instructional system for Smalltalk. In D. Diaper, D. Gilmore, G. Cockton, and B. Shackel (Eds.), *Proceedings of INTERACT'90: Third IFIP Conference on Human-Computer Interaction.* Amsterdam: North-Holland, pp. 937–944.

Singley, M. K., and Carroll, J. M. 1996. Synthesis by analysis: Five modes of reasoning that guide design. In T. P. Moran, and J. M. Carroll (Eds.), *Design rationale: Concepts, techniques, and use.* Hillsdale, NJ: Erlbaum, pp. 241–265.

Singley, M. K., Carroll, J. M., and Alpert, S. A. 1991. Psychological design rationale for an intelligent tutoring system for Smalltalk. In J. Koenemann-Belliveau, T. G. Moher and S. R. Robertson (Eds.), *Empirical studies of programmers, IV.* Norwood, NJ: Ablex, pp. 196–209.

Smith, D. C., Irby, C., Kimball, R., Verplank, B., and Harslem, E. 1982. Designing the Star user interface. *Byte, 7*(4).

Smith, R. B. 1987. Experiences with the Alternate Reality Kit: An example of the tension between literalism and magic. In *Proceedings of the CHI+GI'87: Conference on Human Factors in Computing Systems and Graphics Interface.* New York: ACM, pp. 61–67.

Stokke, P. R., Boyce, T. A., Ralston, W. K., and Wilson, I. H. 1991. Visioning (and preparing for) the future: The introduction of scenario-based planning into Statoil. *Technological Forecasting and Social Change, 40,* 73–86.

Suchman, L. A. 1987. *Plans and situated actions: The problem of human-machine communication.* New York: Cambridge University Press.

Sutcliffe, A. G., and Carroll, J. M. 1999. Designing claims for reuse in interactive systems. *International Journal of Human-Computer Studies, 50*(3), 213–241.

Takeuchi, T., and Nonaka, I. 1986. The new new product development game. *Harvard Business Review,* January–February.

Tanaka, Y. 1994. *Designing scenarios for the near future: To enhance planning and development skills.* Tokyo: Design Research Institute, Tanioka Education Foundation.

Taylor, F. W. 1911. *The principles of scientific management.* New York: Harper and Row.

Terveen, L. G., Selfridge, P. G., and Long, M. D. 1995. Living design memory: Framework, implementation, lessons learned. *Human-Computer Interaction, 10,* 1–37.

Tversky, A., and Kahneman, D. 1983. Extensional vs. intuitive reasoning: The conjunctive fallacy in probability judgments. *Psychological Review, 90,* 293–315.

Van der Meij, H. 1994. Catching the user in the act. In M. Steehouder, C. Jansen, P. van der Poort, and R. Verheijen (Eds.), *Quality of technical documentation.* Amsterdam: Rodopi, pp. 201–210.

Van Lamsweerde, A., and Willemet, L. 1998. Inferring declarative requirement specifications from operational scenarios. *IEEE Transactions on Software Engineering, 24*(12), 1089–1114.

VanLehn, K. 1988. Toward a theory of impasse-driven learning. In H. Mandl and A. Lesgold (Eds.), *Learning issues for intelligent tutoring systems.* New York: Springer-Verlag.

Verplanck, W., Fulton, J., Black, A., and Moggridge, B. 1993. *Observation and invention: The use of scenarios in interaction design.* Tutorial at INTERCHI'93 Conference, Amsterdam, April 24–29.

Vlissides, J. M. 1998. *Pattern hatching: Design patterns applied.* Reading, MA: Addison-Wesley.

Voss, J. F., Wiley, J., and Carretero, M. 1995. Acquiring intellectual skills. *Annual Review of Psychology, 46,* 155–181.

Wack, P. 1985a. Scenarios: Uncharted waters ahead. *Harvard Business Review, 63*(5), 72–89.

Wack, P. 1985b. Scenarios: Shooting the rapids. *Harvard Business Review, 63*(6), 139–150.

Wasserman, A. I., and Shewmake, D. T. 1982. Rapid prototyping of interactive information systems. *ACM Software Engineering Notes, 7,* 171–180.

Wasserman, E. A., and Miller, R. R. 1997. What's elementary about associative learning? *Annual Review of Psychology, 48,* 573–607.

Weidenhaupt, K., Pohl, K., Jarke, M., and Haumer, P. 1998. Scenarios in system development: Current practice. *IEEE Software, 15*(2), 34–45.

Weiner, B. 1980. *Human motivation.* New York: Holt, Rinehart, and Winston.

Wexelblat, A. 1987, May. *Report on scenario technology.* Technical Report STP-139-87. Austin, TX: MCC.

Whiteside, J., Bennett, J., and Holtzblatt, K. 1988. Usability engineering: Our experience and evolution. In M. Helander (Ed.), *Handbook of human-computer interaction.* Amsterdam: North-Holland, pp. 791–817.

Winner, L. 1986. Do artifacts have politics? In L. Winner (Ed.), *The whale and the reactor: A search for limits in an age of high technology.* Chicago: University of Chicago Press.

Winograd, T., and Flores, F. 1986. *Understanding computers and cognition: A new foundation for design.* Norwood, NJ: Ablex.

Wirfs-Brock, R. 1993. Designing scenarios: Making the case for a use case framework. *Smalltalk Report,* November–December.

Wirfs-Brock, R. 1995. Designing objects and their interactions: A brief look at responsibility-driven design. In J. M. Carroll (Ed.), *Scenario-based design: Envisioning work and technology in system development.* New York: Wiley, pp. 337–360.

Wirfs-Brock, R., and Wilkerson, B. 1989. Object-oriented design: A responsibility-driven approach. In *Proceedings of OOPSLA'89: Conference on Object-Oriented Programming Systems, Languages, and Applications. SIGPLAN Notices,* 24(10), 71–76.

Wirfs-Brock, R., Wilkerson, B., and Wiener, L. 1990. *Designing object-oriented software.* Englewood Cliffs, NJ: Prentice Hall.

Young, R. M., and Barnard, P. B. 1987. The use of scenarios in human-computer interaction research: Turbocharging the tortoise of cumulative science. In *Proceedings of CHI+GI'87: Conference on Human Factors in Computing Systems and Graphics Interface.* New York: ACM, pp. 291–296.

Young, R. M., and Barnard, P. B. 1991. Signature tasks and paradigm tasks: New wrinkles on the scenarios methodology. In D. Diaper and N. Hammond (Eds.), *People and computers VI.* Cambridge: Cambridge University Press, pp. 91–101.

Zimmerman, B., and Selvin, A. M. 1997. A framework for assessing group memory approaches for software design projects. *Proceedings of DIS'97: Second ACM Symposium on Designing Interactive Systems.* New York: ACM Press, pp. 417–426.

Index